# Social Exchange

# Social Exchange

## Barter as Economic and Cultural Activism in Medellín, Colombia

BRIAN J. BURKE

**Rutgers University Press**

New Brunswick, Camden, and Newark, New Jersey, and London

Library of Congress Cataloging-in-Publication Data

Names: Burke, Brian J., author.
Title: Social exchange : barter as economic and cultural activism in Medellín, Colombia / Brian J. Burke.
Description: New Brunswick, NJ : Rutgers University Press, [2022] | Includes bibliographical references and index.
Identifiers: LCCN 2021055686 | ISBN 9781978829626 (paperback) | ISBN 9781978829633 (hardback) | ISBN 9781978829640 (epub) | ISBN 9781978829657 (pdf)
Subjects: LCSH: Barter—Economic aspects—Colombia. | Barter—Social Aspects—Colombia. | Social exchange.
Classification: LCC HF1019 .B87 2022 | DDC 332/.540986126—dc23/eng/20220210
LC record available at https://lccn.loc.gov/2021055686

A British Cataloging-in-Publication record for this book is available from the British Library.

References to internet websites (URLs) were accurate at the time of writing. Neither the author nor Rutgers University Press is responsible for URLs that may have expired or changed since the manuscript was prepared.

♾ The paper used in this publication meets the requirements of the American National Standard for Information Sciences—Permanence of Paper for Printed Library Materials, ANSI Z39.48-1992.

www.rutgersuniversitypress.org

Manufactured in the United States of America

For Nico and his *compas*, and for all of us. May something in these pages nurture our struggle for other, better worlds.

# Contents

# Preface

This project was bookended by two economic crises. In September 2009, during the worst global economic downturn since the Great Depression, I began studying grassroots alternatives to capitalism amid a bustle of conversations and inspirations—and equally notable silences—about the possibilities for change. In the United States, hundreds of thousands of people were suddenly more vulnerable than ever, having lost houses, businesses, jobs, and retirement funds. The economies of Ireland and Iceland had collapsed, and Greece was in shambles. Less than two years into the Great Recession, it was already clear that its economic and cultural effects would linger for decades. With the conventional economy in disarray, one would have thought that there could not have been a better time to explore economic alternatives.

I am now concluding this book amid the global economic disruptions sparked by the COVID-19 pandemic. If the Great Recession illustrated to many residents of the United States that risks, rewards, and government protections are far from equitable, the COVID Economy is underscoring the moral calculus that lies behind that inequity. The most vulnerable and exploited members of our society—immigrant farmworkers and meat plant workers, minimum-wage service workers, and grocery store clerks—are celebrated as essential yet treated as expendable. And as politicians, pundits, and neighbors debate when and how we should "reopen the economy," we are all engaged in thinly veiled conversations about how many deaths are justifiable, and whose deaths, in order to improve conventional economic indicators.

Remarkably, it seems that these two disruptions may have unleashed a real shift in what people in the United States take for granted when speaking of "the economy" and political possibilities. In 2009, public discussions of the recession offered virtually nothing in the way of radical rethinking (Harvey 2010a). Explanations of the crisis tended to emphasize a fundamentally sound system that suffered from lack of administrative oversight to rein in greedy and unethical behavior. Absent from the debate was a vast literature explaining crises as a predictable result of the workings of capitalism exacerbated by neoliberal policies of deregulation and the elimination of public safety nets. Even more troubling, until Occupy Wall Street briefly catalyzed people's imaginations, both apologists for and critics of capitalism seemed to agree that there was no viable alternative to the economic status quo. The debate had been narrowed to a question of degrees of government regulation.

Today, however, people are responding differently. This is due, I think, to a confluence of factors. Over the past decade, proposals for universal health care, a Green New Deal, and universal basic income have loosened previously rigid ideas of what government might do in the economic realm and nudged people to consider the possibility of economic human rights. At the same time, the challenge to consider how the United States would look if it were organized around Black lives mattering has drawn attention to systems and structures. This has been amplified by people's intuitive sense of who gained and lost during these economic crises and by populist movements on the right and left. Finally, the pandemic itself has shaped our economic imaginaries. People across the political spectrum have begun to advocate for localization and autonomy amid anxieties over the vulnerability inherent to globally distributed production, spurred on by pictures of rotting produce and euthanized livestock because our food system is designed to produce profits rather than avoid hunger, or graphs charting shortages of face masks and medical equipment manufactured in quarantined Chinese factories. Furthermore, the disruption of things we typically think of as "the economy" has led people to mobilize in remarkable ways around grassroots economies: sharing, bartering, mutual aid, ethical purchasing and loans, and other activities to maintain our lives and the businesses that enrich our communities. Looking out from their quarantine windows, people across this country are asking "what economy should we reopen?"

This is a critical moment when scholars might help rethink social and economic organization. But are we up to the task? Nearly forty years ago Foucault complained of "the absence of a socialist art of government," and in the 1990s J. K. Gibson-Graham lamented the inability of leftists to imagine a politics that we can practice in the here and now, rather than one that must wait for total social transformation or the conquest of state power. One reason for this imaginative poverty, it seems, is a fixation on that which we're against. This "capitalocentric" worldview, in which everything is related back to capitalism as the prime mover of history (Gibson-Graham [1996] 2006a), leaves us incapable of thinking about *non*capitalism and locks us into a "politics of the 'anti's'" (Ferguson 2010). Furthermore, it seems to be supported by a perverse joy in our cynical certainties. As Andy Merrifield puts it, the academics and activists who write "long, detailed articles and analyses of crises and disasters, of capitalist catastrophes . . . all appear to be happy in their alienation, or at least happy in their assessment of capitalist alienation, reveling in the one-way streets they've consecrated, in the dead-ends and no exits their portrayals have built" (2011, xiii). But the result is both political stasis and intellectual myopia, for how many of us are truly inspired by "Marxism's serial pessimism"? Who wants to rally around the "antis" when our theories of capitalist power and elite co-optation tell us that alternatives are doomed to fail? And why should we analyze those alternatives if we "know," prior to any investigation, that they can be only feeble localisms or false-conscious subsidies for capitalism? Like other critical scholars, I believe that academics' tendency to privilege critical commentary on large-scale problems—and to ignore imaginative exploration of small-scale or nascent alternatives—has supported a "poverty of the political imagination" that limits our "ability to conceive of real political alternatives" (Ferguson 2015, xiii). Contrary to Gramsci's advice, then, it seems we have allowed "cynicism of the intellect" to overtake "optimism of the will."

This book—and my work more broadly—is an effort to reinvigorate our political imaginations by exploring alternative ways of ordering our everyday lives, societies, economies, and politics. To do so, I draw from pools of knowledge beyond academia and formal politics, where people who lack the luxury of cynical entrapment are engaged in imaginative struggles to survive and thrive through economies and politics otherwise (Escobar 2020). I thus build on the work of scholars like Ferguson, who treats new public welfare policies as a "rich ethnographic archive" that may signal the emergence of "new ways of understanding the present and of envisioning possible futures" (2015, xiii, 27); and of Gibson-Graham and the Community Economies Collective's efforts to catalogue and describe the many faces of postcapitalism; and of Merrifield, who adds a dose of grounded mysticism to this literature by rebranding this ethnographic archive as a world of "mischief-makers" who seek not to smash the structures of oppression and alienation but rather to escape them, to tunnel out of our prison into a freer world, "the realm of the really lived," where we can create new forms of production and new ways of living in communality. These authors believe that revitalizing progressive politics requires bursting through the stale terms of debate to explore the unthinkable. Importantly, none of them expects vanguard intellectuals to chart the path to freedom and justice. The lessons are to be found in the experiments and innovations of people who are confronting injustice in the everyday—the people whose stories and aspirations fill these pages. And yet we must approach these experiments analytically, interrogating, among other things, the conditions that make them politically feasible and socially transformative, their transferability to other contexts, and the scales at which they function.

As I moved between the United States and Colombia during these moments of intense economic scrutiny, with images of mischief-makers and experimenters dancing in my head, I was struck by how much the two nations' views seemed to contrast. If the Great Recession was shocking to people in the United States, it was far less surprising to Colombians, and the problems inherent to capitalism less hidden. People across Latin America have generations of firsthand experience suffering at the (not so invisible) hands of capitalism. They have seen booms and busts related to capital flight and market speculation, extraction of raw materials to feed foreign empires and multinational industry, debt crises initiated by overaccumulation, the tendency of international trade regimes to undermine local development, and the privatization of vital natural resources. And they have benefited from public intellectuals, journalists, artists, and politicians who regularly reveal how the global economy "opens the veins of Latin America" (Galeano 1971). This is not to say that most Latin Americans do not appreciate consumer goods made available by capitalist production and international markets. However, I think many people in the United States would be shocked by how critical their Latin American peers are. Even everyday, working-class people and rural peasants often represent capitalism as an imperial project enacted against them by national elites who stand to benefit from U.S. power. And many of these people *can* envision alternatives. Activists in the United States and around the world have sought to build alternatives to neoliberal capitalism, but Latin America has given rise to a particularly large number of political economic experiments, including import-substitution industrialization, Zapatista autonomy, twenty-first-century socialism and regional economic blocs, and grassroots mobilizations against privatization and for democratic, communal resource management. That's why Goodale and Postero describe the region as a "global laboratory" for "new forms of governance, economic structuring, and social mobilization," even as it is home to renewed neoliberalizations (2013, 1).

Despite thirty years of scholarship on Latin America's "new social movements" for autonomy and solidarity, popular attention remains focused on the loud clamor of state-centered movements and the self-celebratory spin of leftist-populist presidents (Stahler-Sholk et al. 2008). Beyond these most visible manifestations of resistance, however, many communities are devising their own economies, alternatives to capitalism that do not depend on states that command little respect or revolutions that seem never to bring the new, just society that they promise. These alternatives defend society against the unfeeling calculus of the market (Polanyi 1944) and cultivate new senses of time, resourcefulness, relationality, and ourselves that may defy the logic of scarcity on which capitalism depends.

Medellín's barter projects are one example of such alternatives. They are small-scale experiments that help us understand what new radical imaginations look like and what obstacles people confront when trying to bring them to life. The barter projects are founded on the simple idea that money and the economy are nothing more than social constructs—albeit social constructs with significant material force—that can be reconstructed to achieve different economic, social, and environmental goals. These projects—this ethnographic archive of mischief-makers who are creatively experimenting with diverse economies in the realm of the really lived—represent the radical rethinking that has been seeded by the Great Recession and fertilized by COVID-19. They offer us a chance to examine how economies might be reconstructed and with what results. I hope their stories will offer inspiration and concrete lessons for those activists and scholars who are trying to understand and confront the social, economic, political, and ecological crises of our time, releasing what William Connolly (1999) calls "fugitive energies" for a more radical political practice.

# Social Exchange

# Introduction

It was early Saturday morning, and the countryside was still quiet. The people, the birds, even the clouds seemed to be lingering, waiting to see how much the sun would warm the mountains before venturing out of bed. We watched the fog tumble over a patchwork of fields and forests, and Diego let out a long breath.[1] "Look," he said, "this is why we're here. To see this. To be free."

We sat across from one another on the patio of his cabin. He looked like a magazine ad in some hipster lifestyle blog: an attractive, unshaven, thirtysomething sitting at a reclaimed wooden table in a room of mismatched furniture and metalwork. Below his well-worn hat, Diego wore dark-rimmed glasses. His eyes focused on the cups in front of him and the bottle of wine made from homegrown passion fruits. As Diego poured the wine, he explained that he and his brother moved to Santa Elena a few years earlier to get away from the hubbub of the city and live in a cleaner, more peaceful environment. "And look at this," he said, turning toward the interior of the house. "This is what we made. Let me show you."

This was one of two tourist cabins they had built. As we walked from room to room, he detailed the construction process. The old wooden beams, metal supports, stairs, doors, windows, appliances, nearly everything in the cabin had been acquired through barter. Most of these trades were made informally, exchanging his labor as a self-taught handyman with the owners of junkyards, but some was also through Medellín's monthly barter markets either as direct trade or using one of the city's alternative currencies.

"And it's not just for the business," he explained. "I haven't bought clothes in eight years. All of my clothes come from barter, and my books, and my music.

It's all reused. And of course the things for the cabin. See these plates, the silverware, this lamp—all of that was from the barter market. This is an interesting thing that starts to happen, is that you go to the fair and you see things that you didn't think about before and you say, 'Oh yeah, I could use that.' And it's good for you, but it's also good for the person you're trading with. And this blanket, that's from a family who wanted to stay for a few days, and I told them they could pay a little bit with money and they could trade a little bit." Diego's pride was clear, not just pride that he had built this himself, but also pride that he had done it *differently*.

We brought our wine back to the porch, and Diego explained how he became a barterer. Although he joined the Santa Elena barter fair only two years earlier, he had been bartering for much longer. When he and his brothers owned a restaurant in the city, they, like many businesspeople, would regularly engage in *vencambio*, combining sales and trades to find the best deal for both parties, but he never gave this much thought. There was a problem, though: the more successful the restaurant became, the more it dominated their lives. "I was totally inserted into the system," he complained. "We were working day and night, really hard, and there just came a moment when it became unbearable to continue."

It was then that Diego started to barter more. After feeling "enslaved" to his own restaurant, he was looking for work that would leave him in charge and guarantee his freedom. He didn't want a boss, another schedule, deadlines, or a bank loan to stress about, so he set out to sell juice on the streets. That's where he really learned what barter was and what it could do for you. "When I was on the streets," he explained, "it was really important to build social relationships, to have people who would look out for you and help you out, and one of the ways we would do that was to barter things. On a hot day I'd trade a cup of juice for an ice cream cone, or maybe I'd give someone a gallon of juice to take home in exchange for a new hat. And that's how we went about building relationships."

Seeing the possibilities in barter, he began to change his interests. Suddenly, new opportunities opened up, and he started trading with junkyards for building materials. He began to imagine the urban landscape differently. Behind every corner might lie something he could reuse, or within every home might be just the thing he needed to build and decorate the cabins. What he loved most about this new type of exchange was that it wasn't just about the materials. As he returned to the same junkyards or bartered with the same vendors, he "also exchanged trust, stories, and confidence." He started to create friendships.

Diego learned about Santa Elena's monthly barter markets by chance when he was still living in Medellín. One weekend he decided to bring his juices up the mountain to try it out. The Santa Elena market was more organized, more formal than the trades he had been making. This looked like your typical farmers' market or artists' fair, with fifty to sixty traders from across the city arranged in booths in the town's central plaza, except that their preference was to trade rather than sell. "They had their rules and their own currency," noted Diego. "You couldn't just do whatever you wanted, however you wanted to." But he liked it. He liked that it was consistent, that it offered a time and place where you knew people would gather just to barter. And he especially liked that it gave him a chance to be with "people who live differently, people who were looking for other types of possibilities."

Being with these people and dedicating himself to the sometimes-difficult task of operating as much as possible outside of the cash economy, Diego found that he himself began to change. He developed different desires, different expectations, a different sense of what it meant to be well—what scholars would call a new *subjectivity*. These changes weren't always easy. In fact, he lost important relationships because this new outlook steered him away from the hustle of urban consumerism that had framed his family's view of success. But in the end it was worth it. "Look at this," he said, gesturing again to the cabin and the now visible landscape around us. "The whole time I was asking myself, 'what other way is there to live without being a slave?' I was looking for whatever options I could find, and in barter I've found a solution. That's the great thing about barter," he concluded, "it's a way to go ahead and create a way of life without enslaving yourself."

Diego is, in many ways, a stereotypical barterer: a disaffected, slightly bohemian, middle-class Medellinense who uses alternative economies to forge a different relationship to other people and to his own daily existence.[2] Barterers extend far beyond this stereotype, however. In barter markets, he is joined by the urban poor and working class, *campesinos*, and a handful of wealthy traders. Their personal histories, ideologies, and motivations for engaging in alternative economies vary significantly, defying expectations about socioeconomic class, politics, or lifestyle. Some are drawn to barter by anticapitalist ideals, some by a desire to rebuild community in the face of violent social fragmentation, some as a basic economic strategy, and some simply for the pursuit of fun and personal well-being. They are certainly not all like Diego, but his story illustrates the broad social, cultural, and economic impacts of alternative exchange.

To understand the emergence and trajectory of alternative economies, we must examine how local economic dynamics and social histories generate site-specific opportunities and challenges. For example, the particular ways that capitalism, violence, precarity, and development have unfolded in Medellín have created not only widespread dissatisfaction but also a culture marked by what I call "pragmatic pluralism." The commonsense economic strategy in Medellín involves interweaving diverse capitalist and noncapitalist strategies in a pragmatic, nondoctrinaire way. As we saw in Diego's story, this mix of pragmatism and dissatisfaction drives economic experimentation both within and against capitalism. Barter is the principal form of *collective* experimentation emerging at the grassroots, allowing traders to realize benefits in new ways beyond the formal, peso-based economy.

In this book, I examine what happens when we take noncapitalist economic practices like barter—which are ever present but largely invisible—and we self-consciously and strategically organize around them. As Diego and other traders show, barter markets help build and sustain alternative modes of production, which then set in motion new relations to ownership, new conceptualizations of resources, and different types of social relations. Importantly, these material and social relations are based on different regimes of value than barterers find in the conventional economy. By detailing the experiences of Medellín's barterers and barter organizers, I illustrate when and how these alternative economies are liberating—enabling people to take control of the means of production and the experience of producing, establishing communities even in the most atomized contexts, and fostering new orientations toward well-being and consumption—and when and why their impacts are constrained.

Admittedly, I come to these questions not out of neutral intellectual curiosity, but out of a personal commitment to imagining and creating a better world, which I believe must include economies and societies guided by the pursuit of collective well-being rather than the exploitation of people and nature for private profit. Thus, beyond the specific case of alternative economies in Medellín, this book is also a sustained reflection on two contemporary modes of political-economic contestation that also seek to advance that goal. The first is a loose network of struggles to reject a single, unregulated global market and to create instead a solidarity economy comprising ethical markets such as solidarity purchasing networks, fair trade, federations of cooperatives, community-supported agriculture, and the like (Leyshon et al. 2003; Satgar 2014). The second is a range of movements that pursue social change not through reform or revolution, but by constructing autonomous spaces and community-managed social, political, and economic institutions (Day 2005; Juris and Khasnabish 2013). By examining the experience of alternative economies activists in Medellín, I hope to cut through some of the more polemical celebrations and condemnations of these political currents. Critics routinely highlight their limited scale, asking whether a politics of exchange can affect the "real" economy, whether small household producers can have a broader impact, and whether a politics beyond the state can be transformative and not merely escapist. On the other hand, defenders point to their depth, highlighting their ability to affect worldviews and spark change across many spheres of life. I argue that profound social transformations require both scale and depth, as well as persistence through time and breadth across individuals' lives. Rather than asking if these movements are good or bad, productive or unproductive, I therefore illuminate what kinds of differences they make, how they achieve those results, and how this does and does not support progressive social change.

## Barter in Medellín

Contrary to my expectations, Medellín's first barter experiments began in 1994 not as an alternative *economy* but as a social project. A small group of artists imagined trade as a way of reestablishing social connections in one of Latin America's most violent and unpredictable cities. "In those early days," many barterers told me, "it was just an excuse." An excuse to reclaim public spaces overtaken by drug violence, to rebuild community connections severed by fear, and to once again share time, space, and the fruits of one another's labor and creativity. It didn't take long, however, for these artists to consider the economic and political potential of barter in a city with extremely high unemployment, widespread poverty, and little civic participation. Over the past twenty-five years, they and others have spread the idea of barter across the city. As a result, dozens of grassroots organizers, community groups, solidarity economy institutions, and even government agencies have used some type of barter or local currency.

Lumped together under the label *trueque* or *trueke* (barter), these intentional economies are meant to spark the ethical reevaluation and reconstruction of production, consumption, ownership, and distribution, so the economy can more effectively serve Medellín's middle-class professionals, rural peasants, urban workers, students, and the chronically underemployed. Barter is meant to enhance livelihoods and decrease vulnerability by supporting the flow of goods through diverse economies, creating entrepreneurial opportunities unavailable within formal economies, providing alternative means of provisioning where money and jobs are lacking, and supporting local autonomy (Humphrey and Hugh-Jones 1992). A further benefit is that community currencies make our crisis-prone economic system more resilient by increasing economic diversity and slowing the destabilizing flows of finance capital (Hornborg 2016; Lietaer 2001; Goerner et al. 2009; North 2010). And of course barter is still about much more than economics: markets are designed to create the trust and reciprocity necessary to repair a social fabric rent by decades of violence, isolation, and the commodification of everyday life.

Today's barter projects assume three primary forms. The first mirrors the LETS (local exchange trading systems) common in so-called developed countries, in which there is more or less permanent trade managed by a centralized accounting system of credits and debits. The world's most popular form of grassroots exchange, LETS function like community IOUs. If I want three pounds of apples from a local orchard, I can acquire these (worth five LETS-dollars) even if I have no actual LETS-dollars to spend. I simply visit the orchard, receive the product, and the grower and I record our transaction. She gets a five LETS-dollar credit that she can redeem from any other member of the system, and I receive a debit that I can pay off by providing goods or services to any member. Products thus flow through the local economy quickly, without relying on

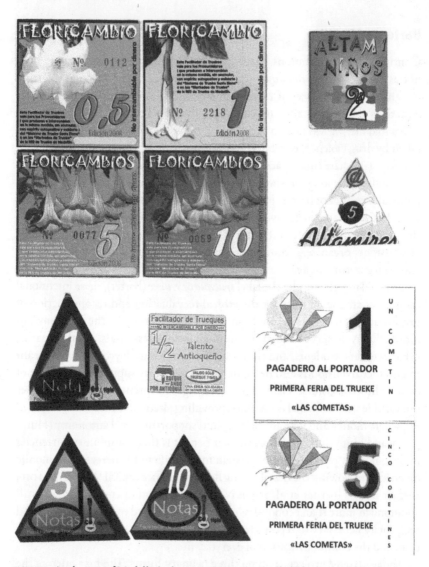

FIGURE 1  A selection of Medellín's alternative currencies, called "facilitators" because they make trading easier and faster. (Photo by the author.)

scarce money, but the system requires significant trust and a greater willingness to experiment.

The second type of barter in Medellín is the monthly or quarterly barter fair, such as the Santa Elena market that Diego joined. Similar to handicraft and *campesino* markets, these are often organized in parks or plazas and permit direct trade and trade using local currencies called facilitators (Figure 1). These community currencies all have rules designed to promote particular ethical outcomes. For example, some become void at the end of each market to prevent long-term accumulation, inequality, and speculation; others are usable only when bringing products to trade, ensuring that nobody comes "just to shop."

The third type is onetime or annual events sponsored by interested institutions. Through twenty-five years of activism, organizers have placed barter on the menu of solidarity economy possibilities; it has found its way into schools and universities, theater groups, walking clubs, environmental NGOs, agro-ecology training programs, multiple government agencies, some of the city's largest cooperatives and microcredit organizations, and the charitable foundation of the Éxito grocery stores (a Medellín-based multinational that has become the largest South American retail company). Many of these groups hold annual barter markets or incorporate barter into other activities, helping to spread the idea that other economies are possible and desirable.

Medellín is far from the only city with alternative exchange systems. Experiments with barter and alternative currencies date back centuries and span the globe. There are now thousands of alternative exchange systems globally (Blanc 2010; Lietaer 2001), with a total turnover of goods and services optimistically estimated at over $10 billion (Greco 2009, 160). Medellín's barter projects are also not the largest in the world. For many activists, the most inspiring examples are the *redes de trueque* (barter networks) in Argentina. When the 2000 economic crisis suddenly left millions of Argentines without money, they turned en masse to preexisting alternative currency experiments. Barter networks sprang up across the country, helping four million people survive one of history's most severe banking crises. They operated on such a large scale that they even affected industrial production (North 2007, 157). The Argentine experience offered a glimpse of a postcapitalist world, with worker-owned factories, extensive household production, and a network of community currencies and barter markets to facilitate exchange.

Medellín's barter projects yield unique insights, however, because more than two decades of barter experimentation provides a wealth of lessons about other ways of organizing social and economic relations. Medellín's experience is also novel because, unlike barter economies in Argentina, Russia, or Greece, the proliferation of barter there has not been significantly shaped by crisis. Or, to be more accurate, barter has developed in the normalized, chronic crisis of structural and physical violence and occasional livelihood crises, but not in an acute, countrywide economic crisis. We know people can make amazing changes when their backs are up against the wall, but Medellín allows us to examine socioeconomic innovation and transformation motivated more by *conviction* than bare necessity, when there is a different balance between the exigencies of survival and the luxury of cultural activism. Furthermore, unlike many of Latin America's most radical movements (Zibechi 2012), barter markets don't exist in semiautonomous territories, so they reveal the challenges people confront when establishing alternative economies within "functioning" state-capitalist economies. This is especially valuable because all of today's movements—from feminism and antiracism to economic justice and environmental movements—must achieve motivated action. Consider climate change: despite efforts to frame it as urgent and intimate, the individuals, communities, and states most responsible for destroying the global commons will need to act long before they feel the crisis. Medellín's barter movements provide lessons about how difficult such change is, but also how it can be initiated through strategies that foster a transformation of conventional values through experimentation on both the material and cultural fronts.

## A Slow Revolution . . .

The barter philosophy is simple: money and markets are mere tools. They are usually designed as antidemocratic tools of commodification and dehumanization, but they can be reengineered as democratic tools infused with community ethics.[3] However, real-world barter systems and alternative currencies have had highly variable political, economic, and social effects (North 2005). In the United States, the challenges of frontier living and the Depression spawned a plethora of alternative currencies, some built on utopian visions but others, like company scrip, designed simply to lubricate capitalist development and increase corporate profits and worker dependency. These less beneficent alternative economies remain common today, as corporations use points systems and frequent flyer miles to incentivize ecologically unsustainable levels of consumption, amoral libertarians promote cryptocurrencies such as Bitcoin or "dark web" markets as the ultimate versions of laissez-faire economics, and neoliberal governments hope self-help initiatives like community currencies will compensate for the destruction of public services (North 2005). We therefore cannot presume that the label "alternative" makes these economies more just, egalitarian, or sustainable; nor can we presume that they are necessarily co-opted by capitalist logics or neoliberal states. The true consequences of barter and alternative economies—which have as much to do with social relations and cultural values as economic flows—are an open, empirical question that is best addressed ethnographically.

Many barter activists, however, already know their answer to this question. For them, barter is revolutionary, and this book is about revolution. It is not about large-scale, made-for-TV revolutions. There are no Great Men in this story and no mass uprisings, no statues toppled, and constitutions rewritten. The ordinary and everyday activists whose stories I tell do not even seek political power. Most are far too cynical about Colombian politics to ever set such a goal and they have seen how bloody the path of opposition can be (Carroll 2011;

Gill 2016; Gómez-Suárez 2014; Roldán 2002). Rather, barterers' goal is at once simpler and more profound: it is to gain control over the ways they make a living, the ways they build a life, and the community structures that support those goals. They take to the streets not with placards and stones, but with sacks of used clothing, bottles of homemade wine, baked goods, and handicrafts. Through the simple act of exchange, they seek to create connection, trust, and dignity, to establish moments and spaces that are not defined by violence, inequality, exploitation, and ruthlessness. As one group of organizers put it: "Barter is a collective construction in which we reclaim, reuse, reconstruct our context; it is the possibility of another world, a different way of inhabiting it; an alternative, solidarity economy that proposes solutions in the face of fear, uncertainty, solitude, dispossession . . . ; a meeting place, the generation of a just market for our products, services, and knowledge" (Manual del Trueke [Bello] 2008, 23). The title of this book—derived from the barter slogan *para que cambiemos*—suggests just how profound organizers imagine their politics to be. This phrase carries a double meaning. They barter *para que intercambien* (so they can exchange goods and services) and *para que se cambien* (so they can change as people and as a society). This twofold goal is central to barterers' theory of change and must remain central in our analysis of barter's transformative effects.

That activists theorize economic activism as inseparable from sociocultural change is an intriguing parallel to anthropological holism. Economic anthropologists have repeatedly shown that economies are never merely systems for allocating scarce resources or organizing production and exchange and that they do not follow natural laws (such as the "law" of supply and demand). Rather, they are always deeply embedded in cultural systems and therefore fundamentally shaped by worldviews, values, and dispositions (Bourdieu 1977; Graeber 2001; Gudeman 2001; Hornborg 2016; Polanyi 1944; Taussig 1980). This is true even of the most apparently culture-free, "rational" economies, such as investment banking (Ho 2009), stock market trading (Zaloom 2006), and real estate (Bourdieu 2005). When barter organizers insist that economic activism must unfold through sociocultural change, they thus appear to be working from these anthropological insights that society, economy, and culture are co-constituting.

Medellín's experiments with barter markets and local currencies, with new economic subjectivities and new social relations, are therefore a different facet of revolution. Organizers are trying to change the co-constitution of society, economy, and culture. Their efforts to reconstruct their context, to find different ways of inhabiting another world, and to challenge the "fear, uncertainty, solitude, and dispossession" that reproduce grassroots powerlessness are all part of the slow churning that makes historical change possible. These experiments, however, often lack the cohesion and clarity of purpose of formal activism. They are disorderly and sometimes-floundering efforts to liberate imaginations, explore other possibilities, and loosen norms. They are also, of course, economic projects, attempts to live with more dignity in an economy that makes jobs and pesos hard to come by.

Many scholars would use a softer word, reserving "revolution" for military struggles over state power, but I believe this mistheorizes what it takes to truly revolutionize a society. While militancy is often part of social transformation, history clearly shows that cultural change is a necessary precondition for militant action, and that post-"revolutionary" societies are incompletely transformed without deep and enduring cultural change. I find it useful, therefore, to work with barterers' theorizations of economic and social change, including their claim that barter systems are revolutionary. "Working with" activist theories involves treating the intellectual work of organic intellectuals as legitimate claims to knowledge with which I engage in cothinking. It implies taking them seriously without fully accepting them, just as we do not blindly accept any theory. This stance is not mine alone; it builds on one of anthropology's most noble, unique, and underrecognized decolonial intellectual acts.[4]

I use ethnography to tease out these organic theories of social change and interrogate how they play out in practice. Examining how barterers like Diego actually experience change, I argue that deepening barter's transformative potential requires that activists successfully interweave cultural and economic impacts so they become, in Harvey's words, "co-revolutionary." "The trick," he writes, "is to keep the political momentum moving from one sphere of activity to another in mutually reinforcing ways" so that, for example, initial changes in the culture and economics of household production, market exchange, and ways of valuing products spill over into relations to nature, commonly shared features of language, the technologies that people apply in labor, or ways of perceiving Others (Harvey 2010b). My analysis of barter's impacts examines this co-revolutionary contagion.

## . . . Pero Sistemas No Hay

But can we honestly describe these solidarity-based exchange systems as revolutionary, even if they help individuals control the means of production, or repair social relations, or make visible other ways of conceptualizing well-being and economic organization? Even the most committed barter organizers aren't certain. They swing in bipolar fashion from celebrating the transformative nature of alternative economies to condemning their own limitations. My first weeks in Medellín, following every lead I could find, mirrored this bipolarity. Amazingly, every couple of days I learned of another barter experience in a different part of the city. A nun in one of the poorest and most violent neighborhoods was organizing barter fairs at her parish. A municipality to the north had run a barter fair for years and might still. An environmental organization started a barter system and local currency a couple of years ago. But each of these had lost steam, the organizers had moved on to other things, or they were never intended to be more than onetime events. Barter seemed to be everywhere, but nowhere.

Still, much of my hope was riding on a meeting with Luis Alberto, the man whom everyone immediately mentioned when I asked about barter in Medellín. He had promoted barter from the first experiments in Bello in 1994, through its expansion across the state of Antioquia, and up to the present day. For many people, the man is an embodiment of barter. On the night we finally met, I showed up in the bohemian neighborhood of Carlos E full of anticipation, but my excitement was far overshadowed by Luis Alberto's broad smile, gleaming eyes, and the exuberant two-handed handshake that nearly knocked me over. We stepped from the bustling pedestrian walkway into a candlelit bar, and Luis Alberto asked how I ended up in Medellín. I described how my previous experiences in Colombian ecovillages had led me to research barter systems, and he replied simply, "You're going to find surprises." He looked me squarely in the eyes as I waited uncomfortably, finally asking what he meant. "Well, there are no barter systems here. What we have are demonstrative experiences, *pero sistemas no hay.*" These words haunted me throughout my research and framed some of my central questions.

The monthly barter markets, demonstrative barter events, institutionalized barter programming, and onetime thematic events do not constitute a single integrated economic system, but they do offer tremendous potential for somebody who wants to include barter as a central element of their livelihood. A number of barterers, like Diego, also regularly negotiate informal barter with everyone from dentists to junkyard owners, magazine advertisers, and condominium associations. A savvy barterer could combine these strategies to virtually eliminate expenses for school, clothing, a portion of their food (or more if they took the initiative to increase *campesino* participation), some medical needs, legal assistance, English classes at the best school in the city, and raw materials and knowledge for operating a small business. In truth, though, only a handful of people significantly attempt to combine several of these options. And, as Luis Alberto noted, these different opportunities remain disjointed. They have not been integrated into a well-diversified system. Hence organizers' perilous seesawing between the optimistic appraisal that barter is revolutionizing cultural values and economic processes and the "*pero . . .*" ("but . . .") that rings incessantly in their fears.

It is tempting to interpret Medellín's lack of alternative economic *systems* as evidence of barter's failure or the impossibility of scaling up amid capitalist hegemony. However, I think it is more productive to interrogate this space between "revolution" and "pero" as a window onto the tensions that necessarily arise as people pursue their imagined barterworlds in a society deeply structured by poverty, inequality, and distrust. Some, of course, are basic economic challenges, like lack of access to significant means of production or transportation for alternative economies. The more intransigent challenges, however, are often cultural: competition among organizers for limited resources and prestige, the difficulty of shifting pragmatic pluralism to dedicated alternativity, and even activists' own belief in the self-reproducing power of capitalism. The challenges activists confront as they attempt to inspire utopian thinking and action serve as a "diagnostic of power" (Abu-Lughod 1990) that can guide counterhegemonic or nonhegemonic action (Blume 2018; Satgar 2014; Wright 2010). As an activist or analyst, it is easy to see whether the commanding heights of political and economic power have been conquered, but it takes a much more nuanced analysis to discern whether the cultural foundations of the status quo have been sufficiently eroded and the basis of a new worldview cemented in place, or to identify which spheres of society have begun to shift and how those shifts might translate to synergistic shifts elsewhere. Throughout this book I use the emotionally and analytically jarring tension of "revolution . . . pero" to move us away from simple notions of success or failure and to reveal barter's more subtle impacts, its transformative possibility, and the paradoxes of activist (dis)empowerment.

This raises a key strategic dilemma. All of Medellín's barter promoters share Luis Alberto's concern with the lack of alternative economic *systems*—in fact, this is one of the few things they all agree on! They are tired of running educational workshops and demonstrative activities that simply introduce people to barter; instead, they want to dedicate their time to weaving the city's diverse barter projects into a more systematic and intensive barter economy for everyday use. To use Harvey's (2010b) language, they want to shift from the sphere of consciousness and ideology to the sphere of everyday economic practices, in order to build a more cohesive anticapitalist transition. With broad support that has included funding from city and state governments, inclusion in official development plans, and widespread interest in local economic circuits, there is a solid foundation for strengthening Medellín's alternative economies. Yet organizers continue to dedicate much of their work to demonstrative activities. Exploring this paradox of barter activism allows us to examine barter's revolutionary potential without prematurely dismissing it as naïve romanticism or celebrating it as a panacea. I do this in two ways. First, I reveal the material, social, and subjective effects barter has, even in its nonsystematized form, among frequent barterers like Diego and more intermittent participants. Then I examine the forces that nudge organizers toward self-limiting forms of activism despite their wishes to the contrary. These include a range of common impediments such as the challenges of maintaining participation amid the stresses and uncertainties of everyday life, but they also include some surprising, locally specific challenges. Perhaps most important is the broader ethos of pragmatic pluralism that defines economic success in Medellín. While pragmatic pluralism makes people extremely open to barter and local currencies, it also makes them reluctant to commit to them in a deeper way. Activists struggle to create barter economies that are sufficiently connected to the mainstream economy that they dovetail with pragmatic pluralism, but sufficiently separate that they provoke anticapitalist effects. Detailing these political economic and sociocultural challenges allows us to consider how barterers might strengthen their activism and what impacts we might expect if they succeed in doing so.

## Theorizing Social Change: When Is "Alternative" Transformative?

Because our political energy is limited and the task of transformation both urgent and formidable, there is a real danger in throwing ourselves into work that is seductively "alternative" but offers little prospect of supporting deep and lasting change. Much social movement theory, however, provides too narrow a view of social change to help us tease out activism's true potential. Movements do not create change only by mobilizing people, building institutions, affecting policy, or installing new governments. They also generate "new political languages, new powers, new social groups, new desires and fears, new subjectivities" (Asad 1991, 322–323). This is particularly true of "new social movements" guided by autonomist, nonhegemonic, anarchist, and Indigenous values (Alvarez et al. 1998; Day 2005; Dixon 2014; Escobar 2008, 2020; Powell and Curley 2008; Whyte 2017; Zibechi 2012). Many of these movements pursue change not through direct confrontation with existing forms of power, but rather through the construction of parallel institutions that model the coexistence of alternative modernities, alternative glocalizations, and localizations (Appadurai 2001; Della Porta et al. 2006; Routledge 2003; Swyngedouw 1997). As Juris and Khasnabish (2013) argue, these other ways of doing politics demand different ways of evaluating change.

Here I focus on the changes generated as barter organizers and participants experiment with new ideas, values, relationships, and material practices in the context of their everyday lives. This approach is quite distinct from the dominant tradition of social movement research, which analyzes how movements mobilize resources, frame issues, and construct political identities and alliances in order to influence modern institutions and power relations (the state and its citizens, political parties and their followers, the national economy and workers). Traditional research would illuminate how barterers can use alternative markets to influence government agencies and other power players. However, as Juris and Khasnabish note, this perspective "often obscure[s] movements that aim to radically unsettle [rather than influence] existing power structures," and it fails to interrogate their success at creating "new sociopolitical relationships, subjectivities, and imaginations" (Juris and Khasnabish 2013, 6; Razsa and Kurnik 2012).[5] Capturing these more subtle impacts requires a shift from a sociological focus on institutions and populations to an ethnographic analysis of everyday life, for it is through the intentional restructuring of everyday social and material practices that these movements seek to create societies that are different from and resistant to the status quo (Burke and Arjona 2013; Escobar 2008; Juris 2008; Razsa 2015).

Evaluating these movements also requires that we train our lens not on analysts' predefined institutions and power structures, but rather on the specific alternatives the movements seek to build and the forms of exploitation they seek to challenge. For barter, that means focusing on four of the phenomena that most powerfully shape socioecological well-being in Medellín: capitalism, neoliberalism, development, and violence. Close attention to material and cultural dynamics reveals how barterers' work to move "beyond" capitalism, neoliberalism, development, and violence can also directly work "against" those forces (Dixon 2014).

*As an alternative to capitalism,* barter promises to counter the material forces of primitive accumulation and the cultural dynamics of exchange-value thinking and the logic of scarcity. Primitive accumulation is among the most powerful material foundations of capitalism—it is the processes of dispossession that create a class of people with so few options for survival that they must sell the only resource that is truly theirs, their labor. Though often described as "the bloody prehistory of capitalism," it is a continuous precondition for capital accumulation that occurs every time people's ability to produce for themselves is diminished and every time nonwage work (e.g., gardening, doing laundry, cooking, caring for the elderly) is marketized (Mies and Bennholdt-Thomsen 1999, 10; Perelman 2000; Harvey 2003). For alternative economies to actually challenge capitalism, they must therefore strengthen workers' and communities' control over the means of their own subsistence and the means of production. As we saw in Diego's case, barter enables people to make the most of the means of production that they already have in their possession, and to develop these into even more advantageous and liberating production systems. However, as Marxist and feminist scholars have argued, noncapitalist work can backfire: if nonwage labor becomes a side project rather than actually decreasing dependence on wage labor, it can pose a double labor burden that is especially likely to fall on women; and if partial self-sufficiency allows workers to survive on lower wages, it can inadvertently subsidize capitalist firms. This is one reason that barter *systems* matter; they enable more people to pursue noncapitalism as the focus of their labor rather than as a stopgap measure.

Barter's effects on capitalist culture—which derive from its recentering of use-value—are inextricable from reclaiming the means of production. Marx described the historical shift from use-value thinking to exchange-value thinking as an epochal change that marked the origins of capitalism. "The possessor of money becomes a capitalist," he wrote, only when the "passionate chase after exchange-value" becomes "the sole motive of [their] operations" (Marx [1867] 1999, vol. 1, chap. 4). When money becomes an end in itself because "the expansion of value" is seen as more important than "the satisfaction of wants," then economics becomes a realm of quantitative calculation rather than qualitative and ethical evaluation.[6] Workers are transformed from complex human beings to quantifiable bundles of "brains, nerves, and muscles." Nature is transformed from a realm of dynamic processes and diverse beings that inspire our actions, beliefs, and sense of place to a terrain of discrete resources to be capitalized upon. And as exchange-value is increasingly perceived as the *true* measure of value, market prices hide fundamental inequalities (Hornborg 2016). Through their ideologies, market rules, and incentives, Medellín's barter markets force traders to refocus on use-value rather than exchange-value.

Diego's alienated feelings toward "the system" and the transformations barter provoked illustrate these cultural impacts of noncapitalism. As a businessperson, Diego was deeply inserted into exchange-value thinking. The banks that financed his home and business viewed him not as a whole person but as a series of calculated risks that, when aggregated with others, would generate a profitable exchange. Accepting these loans allowed Diego to launch his business and explore new avenues for well-being, but it also compelled him to conceptualize his own business in the same manner: as a vehicle for chasing after ever more exchange-value rather than satisfying desires or promoting the general welfare. And what bothered him most viscerally was how this affected his life. To passionately chase after exchange-value, he began to treat himself as "brains, nerves, and muscles" rather than a human with complex concerns. Diego's embrace of exchange-value thinking also illustrates how capitalism generates scarcity as a cultural condition.[7] In the restaurant, Diego's wants and their satisfaction were no longer two sides of the same coin. His acts of production no longer immediately and directly addressed his own desires, or even his customers' desires. Instead, they addressed the economics of the restaurant.

Barter helped focus trade on use-value rather than profit maximization, and it combated the feeling and logic of scarcity: as Diego began to recognize other forms of local wealth, he felt less poor; and as he committed to local barter economies, he discovered a logic of production/consumption and needs/fulfillment that defied scarcity. He describes a change from seeing desires and their fulfillment as temporally and spatially separate—"I recognize that I have a need and then I seek out its fulfillment, making whatever sacrifices are necessary"—to seeing them as simultaneous and inseparable—"I see what's around me and that inspires thought and action about needs, wants, and possibilities." Esteva argues that this worldview is critical for noncapitalist, commons-based lifeways:

> The basic logic of human interactions inside the new commons *prevents scarcity from appearing* in them. People do not assume unlimited ends, since their ends are no more than the other side of their means, their direct expression. If their means are limited, as they are, their ends cannot be unlimited. Within the new commons, needs are defined with verbs that describe activities embodying wants, skills and interactions with others and with the environment. Needs are not separated into different "spheres" of reality: lacks or expectations on one side, and satisfiers on the other. . . . ([1992] 2010, 18–19, emphasis added)[8]

We will see, particularly in chapter 3, how Medellín's barterers are beginning to develop a new sense that needs and their satisfaction cannot be conceptualized or felt separately, that production and consumption are linked in the form and logic of the "prosumer" (producer-consumer), and that scarcity may be not a fact of life but rather a deeply engrained way of seeing life. Participation in barter markets has also led traders to develop new regimes of ethical and economic value centered around sociality and putting goods to the best possible use.

Barter systems, like the LETS that Aldridge and Patterson analyzed, do not "provide members with the opportunity to step completely outside the capitalist economy—rather they provide some complementary opportunities to those who already have access to economic resources and social networks" (2002, 379). However, barter markets do help traders use these resources and networks in ways that counter capitalism's material and cultural underpinnings. As we will see in chapters 3–5, barter markets have increased self-sufficiency and nurtured household businesses in which people control the means of production and their own profits. These markets have also established a collective mechanism for sharing among producers, and they have helped inspire people to recognize and expand their own capacities as producers. Like Diego, the most committed barterers are using these markets to escape more exploitative or alienating forms of work, and as a result they begin to see the economic landscape differently. In addition, by politicizing exchange and consumption and creating new norms promoting anticonsumerist values of simplicity and reuse, barter markets combat some of the cultural dynamics that lead people to accept growth, accumulation, scarcity, and dispossession as natural or necessary aspects of economies.

*As an alternative to neoliberalism*, barter markets and bartering logics root wealth, production, and consumption in specific places and frustrate the calculative rationality of accumulation and speculation. Neoliberal policies reorganize people, capital, commodities, ideas, places, and nature in order to make economic processes more mobile and context-independent than classical political economists ever imagined. Capitalists can then "envision taking apart and reassembling production processes in increasingly global ways rather than being dependent on ... inherited ... production systems" and the places and people of which they are composed (Greenberg and Heyman 2012, 247). Barter, at least as it is organized in Medellín, does exactly the opposite. Rather than accelerating and expanding flows so resources become more uniform, flexible, and context-free, it slows them. Barterers intentionally hold part of their wealth in currencies that are purely local, that are not accepted everywhere and for anything, and that are highly social. The informal policies that govern barter markets create boundaries and frictions so resources are more likely to support local communities and promote production in place. Barter thus interrupts the geography, temporality, and decision-making calculus of neoliberal capital, forcing a place-based social re-embedding of at least some economic action.

These slow and emplaced barter economies also challenge neoliberal culture. As Wainwright (2012) notes, people around the world increasingly apply the mentality of financial accounting to everyday life. Thus, creativity and skills are viewed as "human capital" that can be leveraged or squandered, retirees and welfare recipients are defined as liabilities or drains on society because they do not contribute to the national bottom line, and higher education is imagined as an investment, "as if everyone determined their future in terms of a personal rate of return rather than a contribution to society" (Wainwright 2012). This financialized culture entails greater acceptance of the logic of individualism and privatization, the reduction of ethical choice to a singular measure of efficiency, and the unproblematized celebration of growth. Barter disrupts this. Because all trades depend on the negotiation of value at the time of exchange, costs and benefits are unpredictable, impeding the speculative calculation that steers global capital and, increasingly, individual decision making. Furthermore, the barter ethic that all trades must yield mutual satisfaction forces constant negotiation of values based on a specific and holistic consideration of people, places, commodities, and ideas.

This finding, however, is paradoxical: barter's inefficiencies and inconveniences are part of its power but a constraint on its spread. Chapter 5 shows how these market inefficiencies create counterhegemonic subjects who increasingly resist neoliberal materialities, temporalities, and logics. By using less efficient grassroots markets and currencies, barterers sacrifice elements of individual freedom to create mutuality and establish a new community and new public goods over which they have some control. However, a key challenge for any alternative economies activist is to strategize around these inefficiencies, analyzing which support counterhegemonic material and cultural systems and which merely exhaust participants and discourage newcomers. This challenge is particularly acute in the context of pragmatic pluralism and in lower-income communities, where tolerance for inefficiencies is likely to be lower.

*As an alternative to development,* barter illustrates one way grassroots actors might establish economies, not just one-off projects, of their own design and for their own benefit. Development has long been criticized for reinforcing inequality, creating underdevelopment, extending state control over vulnerable communities, and even fomenting violence (Boserup 1970; Little and Painter 1995; Patterson 2001; Scott 1998; Simon 1997; Uvin 1998). Poststructuralists add that the spread of development allows global elites to extend their cultural power by introducing new regimes of knowledge and discipline and cultivating subjects who are driven by faith in modern "progress," a belief in their own poverty, and a desire for capitalism (Escobar 1995; Li 2007; Rahnema 1997). Although defenders of development are right that it is not monolithic, and although grassroots actors also creatively appropriate development for their own ends (Asher 2009; Gow 2008), this history has left many Third World intellectuals yearning for alternatives to development (Escobar 1995; Rahnema 1997; Esteva [1992] 2010). These truly decolonial initiatives, says Esteva, would allow people "to walk with [their] own feet, on [their] own path, in order to dream [their] own dreams. Not the borrowed ones of development" ([1992] 2010, 21). Postdevelopment critics thus place a great deal of hope in grassroots economies that enhance well-being, equity, and justice through locally derived practices of solidarity and sufficiency rather than logics of materialism, competition, and growth.

Barter may be one such alternative. Through barter projects, residents of Medellín demonstrated that they need not accept economic orthodoxy and official development plans focused on wage labor, industrialization, and capitalist entrepreneurialism. They exercised their power to create alternative economies based on cultural models that promote different forms of decision-making. Barterers' vision for well-being draws from sources as diverse as Marxism, ecological economics, the solidarity and popular economies, twenty-first-century socialism, and Latin American views on "holistic development." If it is to be a successful alternative to development, however, it must adequately support livelihoods and provide a desirable quality of life. Some people, after experimenting with barter, have decided that it does not meet these criteria. Many of the *campesinos* who once participated in the Santa Elena market, for example, left after concluding that barter offered too many handicrafts and not enough goods to satisfy basic needs. However, those who continue to participate actively receive substantial livelihood benefits, including reduced dependence on consumer credit, access to goods that might otherwise not be available, and support for family-based businesses. These benefits are large enough to suggest that more diverse, developed, and regular barter markets could support more just economies structured around worker-controlled businesses. In addition, the sociality of barter is an especially important component of its contributions to well-being. This brings us to barter's most important potential role, at least from the perspective of many people in Medellín.

For barter to provide *an alternative to violence*, it will need to establish economic processes, social relations, and worldviews that bind people together in ways that incentivize "peacefare" rather than warfare (Wolf 1987). Clearly this is no easy task in Colombia, where the liquidation and violent displacement of rural people have long been integral to Colombian development, household livelihood strategies, and social norms and expectations (Reyes Posadas 2009; Richani 2002; Roldán 2002; Ross 2003). Waves of violence in the 1920s and 1930s, during the period after 1948 known as La Violencia, and again since the 1980s due to the narco-economy have made death and displacement a transgenerational experience. The protracted war between the Colombian state, leftist guerrillas, and paramilitary groups has been so thoroughly intertwined with licit and illicit economies and the political elite that Richani (2002) describes it as a comprehensive and mutually beneficial "war system." In short, Colombia is a society deeply permeated not only by blood but also by fear, distrust, and uprooting, with perverse incentives to perpetuate multiple forms of violence.

In Medellín, people frequently refer to a torn social fabric, alienation and atomization, and distrust that have become the new normal. Salazar's (1990) oral histories of child assassins powerfully convey the nearly suffocating sense of futurelessness that presses down upon them, and their desperation to become protagonists in their own lives. These are people so powerfully subjected to forces beyond their control that the only way they can establish their own humanity is through death. And the onlookers, the neighbors and family members who watched throughout the 1980s and 1990s as more and more children enrolled in the war, were also left feeling powerless. This is one of the most pernicious effects of violence, that it becomes a basis for everyday practice, "patterns of sociality," and new "norms and normality" (Das and Kleinman 2000, 5, 15; Goldstein 2003; Green 1999).

In this context, surrounded by hopelessness and frustration, with fear eroding trust and even the most intimate social connections, where being different marks you as dangerously subversive, how do you go about making change? How do you begin to establish control and order in your life in a place where armed teenagers rule over neighborhoods, where "freedom fighters" kill and kidnap people, where the army can't be trusted, and where "self-defense" forces systematically disappear anybody whose lifestyle violates their sense of morality? How do you create order when a flood of drug money has meant that anything—and anyone—can be bought or sold? In 1994, just north of Medellín, one group of friends decided to start small, countering the disruptions of violence through the simple act of coming together to exchange friendship, to exchange time with one another, and to exchange the fruits born of their passions—their art, poetry, and music. The barter fairs that grew out of these gatherings were their attempt to rescale change, to counter displacement and disruption in a safe way, without entering politics and without taking up arms. Barter clearly will not rid Medellín of violence, but it does help heal some of the social disruption that violence creates, and it gives people a chance to be protagonists. Chapters 3 and 4 demonstrate how barter exchange promotes mutual recognition of each trader's humanity and establishes bonds of trust. Barter reduces the economy to the circle of traders you can see, to the person across the table from you whose product you're interested in. In barter markets, the traders decide; they are not subjected to the decisions of others. Barter offers them a chance to sit together with a group of people and imagine how to be ethical, how to be human, in a chaotic and amoral universe. It offers a space for other "patterns of sociality" to create different "norms and normality."

In sum, barter can disrupt and provide an alternative to capitalism, neoliberalism, development, and violence. To fully evaluate its transformative potential, however, it is necessary to examine how these seeds of change spread across four dimensions: depth within each individual, shifting from conscious or forced changes to the cultivation of new subjectivities characterized by new habits "of perception, affect, thought, desire, and fear" (Ortner 2006, 107); breadth within each individual, developing a co-revolutionary movement from the economic realm of one's life to other realms (Harvey 2010b); scale across society, spreading from individual production systems and subjectivities to economic modes of production and cultures; and perseverance across time. I argue that the revolutionary potential of all activism depends on proliferating change across all four of these dimensions.

## Ethnography of and for Alternative Economies

When I arrived in Medellín in September 2009, my goal was to conduct community-based participatory action research (CBPAR) that leveraged my experience with semistructured interviews and participatory methodologies, and to conduct a qualitative-quantitative survey of barter livelihoods, household vulnerability, and the links between barter and nonbarter economies. It quickly became apparent, however, that barter did not lend itself to that approach. While new markets continued to pop up, established projects faced challenges. Two key organizers had recently left Medellín to create regional barter systems for Venezuela's Ministerio de Economía Popular and one of the city's most established LETS systems had been abandoned due to threats from armed groups. In Santa Elena, the number of *campesino* participants had shrunk after government subsidies for transportation tapered off. With the number of truly dedicated barterers declining, a livelihoods survey made little sense, and with organizers scattered across the city and working more or less independently, the entire CBPAR approach had to be rethought.[9] I thus reduced my participatory ambitions and increased my attention to the ways barter is theorized and experienced at the grassroots, how organizers promote this economy, and the obstacles they face. My process of "working with" activist knowledge mirrors Casas-Cortés et al.'s description of ethnography as translation and weaving, with "the goal of spreading, sharing, and building connections among transnational nodes of engaged knowledge producers" (2013, 221). One question that has guided me throughout is how the threads of experience and knowledge that I add can make meaningful contributions to the dense tapestry of activist wisdom.

My fieldwork—conducted between September 2009 and September 2010 and during summer 2012—consisted primarily of semistructured interviews, active participation in alternative economy study groups and seminars, and much more participant observation than I initially expected. All told, sixty-seven people shared their perspectives on barter during fifty-one formal, semistructured interviews and numerous informal ones. These conversations provided some of the most explicit and intentional statements about barter, but participant observation was equally important for capturing the practices and impromptu observations of barterers. I attended thirty-three barter fairs in twelve different locations, almost always participating as a trader and/or organizer. Twelve of these were at the monthly market in Santa Elena, the city's "most successful remaining barter showcase," which I describe in chapter 3.

Some of the most valuable lessons came from routine collaboration with organizers. I worked with five of Medellín's most active barter organizers to formulate a common mission and vision, plan and manage projects, design trainings, and develop our organizing skills. My research was deeply informed by our efforts to expand barter across the city by building relationships with NGOs and government agencies and by designing and executing contracts for barter fairs and trainings as part of the city-funded Solidarity Economy School. It was also informed by the challenges of balancing research, activism, and the negotiation of intragroup conflicts. Medellín's barter projects have been plagued by conflict, distrust, and misunderstandings among leaders whose strong ideals and aspirations often lead to competition rather than collaboration. I was typically seen as a neutral outsider and ally interested in alternative economies in general rather than any particular local faction. Nonetheless, I found myself immersed in the dynamics of distrust that hamper grassroots collaboration in Medellín. These reached a crescendo toward the end of my research, in a nasty feud over who should receive credit, blame, and funding from a government contract. The irony of this battle over pesos was lost on none of us, and it was a sobering lesson on how difficult it is to nurture solidarity amid contemporary cultural norms and economic stressors.

Beyond interviews and participant observation, a third key source of information included seminars on the solidarity economy, capitalism, and barter, some of which I describe in chapters 5 and 6. Medellín offers a remarkably rich cultural environment: it is the home of an international poetry festival that won the "alternative Nobel prize," countless music and film festivals, Latin America's first network of public libraries, and a vibrant literary movement dating to the early twentieth century. Public and private institutions routinely try to harness "culture" to reduce violence and improve the quality of life, leading to a proliferation of seminars and study groups. I quickly became accustomed to research participants using Kafka's plays as parables for their activism or stating, "It's been a long time since I read Marx's *Critique of Political Economy*, but as I recall. . . ." Two city-funded programs—the Solidarity Economy School, which introduced low-income micro-entrepreneurs to the solidarity economy, and the Seminar in Solidarity Thought, which deepened the philosophical background of more experienced solidarity economy advocates—helped me appreciate how people from various social classes and solidarity economy organizations conceptualize their work and the socioeconomic challenges unique to Colombia.

Finally, this work is based on fourteen months of immersion in Medellín. It is difficult to describe in adequate detail the data that support an ethnography. Anthropologists can tally surveys and interviews and describe focus groups and other structured activities, but a central feature of ethnographic fieldwork is active immersion—not just "being there," but laboring to know a place. Reading newspapers, attending literature groups, peppering taxi drivers with questions, observing how people interact across a whole range of contexts, watching, hearing, absorbing: all of these activities inform my analysis. They help us understand what Malinowski called "the imponderabilia of actual life" (1922, 18). Even in a focused ethnography like mine, these contextual details help make sense of research questions because they are precisely what Medellinenses draw on to make sense of barter.

## Outline of This Book

This book makes four main interventions in scholarly and activist debates. First, it *makes alternative economies more visible* by describing the diverse, already-existing economies that provide resources for the construction of just and sustainable societies. This increases readers' awareness of their own noncapitalist practices and provides a sense of what it would mean to intentionally engage with these as a form of political work. Second, it *supports activist strategy* by analyzing how barter activists try to stimulate change, with what effects, and why they choose these particular strategies. We see how site-specific subjectivities centered on pragmatic pluralism, which are a legacy of violence and capitalism, shape and constrain activism. Third, it *models a way of analyzing sociocultural change* that is particularly well suited to contemporary autonomist strategies and assessments of movement potential. This model foregrounds the dialectical interplay of material and cultural changes in the realms activists choose to target, rather than via predetermined impacts on policies or states, and across the four dimensions of individual depth and breadth, societal scale, and temporal endurance. Finally, it details the cultural dynamics of barter by *enhancing the theorization of subjectivities*, revealing how conventional subjectivities shape economic politics and how people engage in politics to reshape subjectivities. These themes are thoroughly intertwined. For example, people's experiences in the diverse conventional economy generate an economic subjectivity that is strongly oriented toward "pragmatic pluralism," which then affects how activist strategies are received, who remains in the barter movement, and how they decide to use barter.

In chapter 1, I draw on Gibson-Graham's diverse economies framework to reveal the wide variety of capitalisms and noncapitalisms in Medellín. However, because economies and activism are always embedded within other social processes that are geographically and historically contingent, I argue that the diverse economies framework offers only a partial window onto economic realities and possibilities. To round out the picture for Medellín, we have to examine these diverse economies in the context of "the war system" (Richani 2002). Through a historical analysis of economies, violence, and subjectivities in Medellín and the broader region of Antioquia, I demonstrate that violence and capitalist exploitation are not the deep-rooted historical structures that many people assume; rather, they have been produced surprisingly recently, as interlinked processes. As importantly, I reveal that they exist alongside noncapitalist and nonviolent socioeconomic relations that, though hidden, might be mobilized and amplified. This deeply contextualized understanding of diverse economies is, I argue, essential for effective economic activism; and this argument is itself an important counterpoint to more essentialist theories of capitalism, Marxism, and economic change.[10]

Chapter 2 describes the emergence of barter first as a community-building response to violence in Medellín and later as a form of economic and political activism. I chart the rise and fall of the city's first three barter experiments and detail how the decisions, theorizations, and practices of early barter organizers framed later activism. The earliest barter projects generated a surprising amount of interest, which organizers leveraged to garner public and private support for spreading barter across the region and even to other parts of the country. This put barter on the map as a recognized possibility for social development and solidarity economy but raised key dilemmas about the appropriate scale of an alternative economy, the speed at which it should grow, and the trade-offs organizers should accept in order to proliferate their idea. We'll see how Medellín's barter expansionists were forced to "thin" their vision in order to make barter more legible for people still committed to mainstream economic values, while committed localists maintained a "purer," more radical vision of alternative economies, but at the cost of seeming isolated, parochial, or unrealistic. This tension is central to the contradictions of "revolution . . . pero" and important for activists beyond barter as well.

I then turn, in chapter 3, from barter's early days to the monthly market in Santa Elena, an idyllic, bohemian mountain town on the edge of Medellín. This market operated from 2005 to 2016, despite changes in leadership, membership, funding, and market rules, and was the most important barter showcase in the city. Although its limited diversity of goods was a constraint, the Santa Elena market offered a fun, fulfilling, and materially rewarding experience to a couple dozen traders each month. I describe the lived, sensual, and social experience of the market and the ways that *artesanos*, *campesinos*, small business owners, and others integrated barter into their household economies. Importantly, their negotiations in the marketplace were not only economic but also phenomenological and ethical. As barterers debated the rules of the market, formally and informally sanctioned one another, and decided what types of trades are fair and desirable, they were developing a barter ethics around values of satisfaction, egalitarianism, and solidarity. Barterers' experience in Santa Elena demonstrates how noncapitalism and alternative regimes of value are co-constructed through a dialectic of practice and theory.

Chapter 4 addresses the most common question about alternative economies: "do they really work?" Medellín's barter projects have faced many of the same challenges as alternative economy projects elsewhere, most notably the difficulty of overcoming the psychological and sociocultural power of the conventional economy among enough people that they can become diversified and dynamic economic systems. Nonetheless, they have generated significant economic and social benefits. In addition to evaluating barter, however, this chapter also aims to move past these "impact" questions, which are often deployed against radical social projects. To conclude, I therefore argue for other ways of seeing impacts that are more appropriate for incipient, counterhegemonic projects whose goal is transformation.

I argue that one key impact that we should look for in radical projects is sociocultural change manifested in alternative subjectivities. Because barter organizers believe that values, consciousness, and subjectivity are critical targets of political intervention, they have devoted tremendous energy to demonstrative activities and barter trainings. In chapter 5, I examine their efforts to attract and transform new barterers, as well as the intended and unintended subjective changes experienced by long-term barterers. This is a key facet of barter's revolutionary potential: barter can create a deep shift in how people see the economy, its purpose, and its place in their lives. Drawing heavily on barterers' own reflections, I show that barter alone does not revolutionize unwilling subjects, but it does provide a powerful "technology of the self," offering linguistic, cultural, social, and economic tools for people who aspire to nonnormative subjectivities. Interestingly, the inefficiencies of the barter markets—generally considered to be imperfections or shortcomings—structure economic practice in a way that encourages some of these changes, forcing traders to shift their orientation toward desire, expectations, and the temporality of economic life. The fact that these productive inefficiencies are so important for sociocultural change raises critical questions not only for barter organizers, but also for other activists: what are the productive inefficiencies that can be built into feminist, antiracist, and environmental activism, for example, and will they work the same way in these movements?

Having traveled from the initial inspiration for barter, through its germination and spread, and into the everyday experiences and impacts of barter, we return in chapter 6 to the question of strategy. What have organizers done to generate these impacts, and why do they continue to organize demonstrative activities rather than building diversified economic systems? While there are many practical obstacles to effectively developing barter systems, I argue that this paradox has deeper roots in organizers' "capitalocentric" imaginaries, the ways they understand capitalism, power, and their own agency. Because activists see the Capitalist Economic System as powerfully monolithic, they direct their efforts toward changing culture, consciousness, and morality and toward establishing "pure" barter systems. However, these strategies often backfire. They divert energy from the construction of diverse barter *economies*, create bounded barter markets that violate local commonsense notions of how to get by and get ahead in a diverse economy, and therefore reinforce some people's belief that capitalism is the only serious, useful game in town. Achieving transformations that are deep, broad, widespread, and enduring likely requires carefully designed strategies of articulation with capitalism.

To close this book, I reflect on how we might strengthen the counterhegemonic potential of barter as noncapitalist activism and on broader efforts to promote change via grassroots experimentation and market politics. People commonly ask if barter or alternative exchange systems are "real" alternatives. Their skepticism is reasonable: conventional political economic institutions seem incontestably strong and the cultural norms supporting capitalism are so entrenched that they are often mislabeled "human nature." However, to confront the grave social and ecological challenges of this century we must build a new imaginary that sees radical change as feasible and thus motivates the constant examination of how genuine alternatives might help us contest exploitation and construct a different world. Four aspects of barter seem particularly important for provoking counterhegemonic change: its focus on use-value and social-value; the productive inconveniences that it forces on traders through localization and community rootedness; its amplification of the local common sense of pragmatic pluralism, while infusing that common sense with ethical challenges; and its ability to shift barterers' sense of their productive capacity and their desires. These characteristics have the biggest impact when they are pursued via cultural and material changes that actually force barterers to change even beyond their initial intent, and when they are enforced via social pressures and mutual governance. However, impacts never flow seamlessly from strategy. Barter activists are engaged in a deeply contradictory struggle to live a dream for the future right now, in a conflicted present, and building upon a troubled past. All activists face this same struggle, and though our dreams and conflicts and troubles may be somewhat different from theirs, I think you'll find their story thought-provoking and insightful.

# 1

# Diverse Economies in the War System

Colombia is an infamous country and Medellín its most ill-reputed city. Best known for its drug traffickers, the city is also central to the military and economic activities of left-wing guerrillas and right-wing paramilitaries, street-level gangs, and the *milicias de limpieza* (death squads) that emerged in the late 1980s to "cleanse" the streets of undesirable elements. For two decades, homicide was the leading cause of death in the city, peaking at 18 murders per day and more than 320 per 100,000 residents. More than 55,000 people were killed in just thirteen years; most of them were poor, young men who died at the hands of other poor, young men (Cardona et al. 2005).

I was one of a small number of foreign social scientists to visit Colombia with the express goal of *not* studying violence. So many people have crisscrossed this country to expose the perpetrators of violence, the root causes, the psychology of the violated, the special effects of war on women, and social memory. The titles of scholarly literature on Colombia reflect this: *Blood and Fire* (Roldán 2002); *Counting the Dead* (Tate 2007); *Fragmented Land, Divided Society* (Safford and Palacios 2002); *A Study in Terror and Healing* (Taussig 1987); *A Nation in Spite of Itself* (Bushnell 1993); and *Between Legitimacy and Violence* (Palacios 2006). I wanted to show a different face of Colombia, to provide a glimpse of the thousands of hopeful experiments that have cropped up amid these battlefields.

But the violence, perhaps not surprisingly, was inescapable. Behind the staggering statistics about deaths and displacements hides a darker horror, a secret so painful that many people simply ignore it: those of us who live in the city all support this war. Throughout my fieldwork, nearly every day, I supported the gangs and death squads that tear families apart, turn children into assassins, and create "invisible borders" between communities. And I was not alone. In our phone calls and bus rides, in our lottery tickets and the fruits we buy in the market, in the protection money we paid to armed groups to keep our corner stores safe, in so many little, everyday acts, the residents of Medellín purchased the guns, bullets, and bombs that tore the city apart. We bought the still hearts of the victims, the dehumanized souls of the killers, and the regime of fear that weighed so heavily on the city.[1]

This is the genius of the war: that it has entwined itself so thoroughly into the economy of this town that it sustains itself through everyday practices. It permeates people's lives to such a degree that one of my informants can honestly say, "Oh yes, things are good [where I live] now. We hear bullets only two or three times a week." This is how the war is reproduced, not automatically but parasitically, growing as people go about their lives, meet their needs, pursue their desires, and spend their pesos, and sheltered by the fear and silences it creates (Green 1999; Penglase 2014).

The centrality of violence is also clear in activists' complaints that the war undermines collective action and in more hopeful analyses of how it mobilizes people. During a goal-setting workshop, Olga, the leader of the Santa Elena barter fair, explained that barter is largely a response to violence:

> The most important reason [for barter to exist] is that, well, when you create ties or promote values, when people start to recognize the capacities of everybody else, to recognize the humanity of their neighbors, this creates security. It's unbelievably important to create real security in communities so that we don't need this "democratic security" [a reference to then-President Uribe's policies of militarization]. The truth is that it's not the market. The market is a means to achieve this more important goal. The goal is to get to know each other, to begin to recognize each other, and to create true trust.

Barter exemplifies human creativity in the face of violence. If the most enduring effects of violence are "the destruction of home and humanity, of hope and future, of values and traditions and the integrity of the community" (Nordstrom 1997, 123), then simply reestablishing normal community life can be a "monumental" act (Lutz and Nonini 1999, 103; Green 1999). The barter project confronts not only material economies, economic politics, and economic subjectivities (Gibson-Graham 2006b) but also the economic and cultural politics of "the war system" (Richani 2002). Just as I could not escape violence as a research topic, activists cannot escape it as a key factor in their mobilization.

In this chapter, I present "the economies of violence and the violence of economies" in Medellín (Lutz and Nonini 1999), describing how political economies and systems of violence interact at the macro level and how they shape people's everyday experience. I analyze the material economies and economic imaginaries that barter activists confront and illuminate the different processes of ownership, exploitation, and empowerment within them. It is not sufficient to simply map economic diversity, however. To understand what these diverse economies mean to people in Medellín we must place them in local cultural and historical context. This means turning to regional history, violence, and fear, which shape the political imaginaries and subjectivities that barter activists are trying to change and the alternatives they hope to create. The instabilities generated by violence and economic diversity create subjects adept at negotiating pluralism, uncertainty, risk, and open-endedness. In Medellín, it is these subjects—whom I call "pragmatic pluralists"—who barter activists need to convince. As we will see in later chapters, this significantly shapes activist strategies and impacts.

## Diverse Economies: Reframing the Economy for Ethical-Political Reflection

Economic anthropologists have long argued that economies assume diverse forms and represent radically different logics and values. They have also provided rich analyses of the ways that noncapitalist and capitalist economies interact, or "articulate."[2] With increasing concern about globalization and the spread of capitalism, however, there has been less attention to noncapitalist economies. I argue that the spread of capitalism makes the analysis of economic diversity more important than ever. Analyzing the economy as a more-than-capitalist sphere helps us identify forms of exploitation we would otherwise miss, while also offering a glimpse of new possibilities for social change that might complement old strategies of working-class solidarity and struggles for systemic change.

As Gibson-Graham and the Community Economies Collective argue, because economic policy and activism are generally oriented just toward the tip of the economic iceberg—wage labor for a capitalist firm producing for sale on the cash market—they often neglect other crucial sectors (Community Economies Collective 2001; Gibson-Graham 2002; Gibson-Graham et al. 2013; Roelvink et al. 2015). However, below the water line are a vast range of economic practices that mobilize labor, property, finance, and nature in different ways, through different systems of production, management, and exchange (Table 1). These practices differ significantly in terms of who makes decisions, based on what values, and with what impacts. And their articulations produce diverse

## Table 1
## The diverse economy

| Transactions | Labor | Surplus Distribution |
| --- | --- | --- |
| *Goods and services flow through the economy in many ways* | *Labor is managed and rewarded through different systems* | *Profits are produced and controlled by businesses with diverse interests and powers* |
| **Market** | **Wage** | **Capitalist** |
| "Free" trade | Salaried | Multinational |
| Monopolized | Unionized | Public company |
| Regulated | Nonunionized | Private firm |
| Protected | Temporary | Family firm |
| Subsidized | Seasonal | |
| | Formal | |
| | Informal | |
| **Alternative market** | **Alternative paid** | **Alternative capitalist** |
| Fair trade | Cooperatives | Environmental ethic |
| Informal markets | Self-employed | Social ethic |
| Underground markets | Sharecropping | Solidarity economy |
| Alternative currencies | Labor exchanges (*mano* | Worker-owned |
| Local trading systems | *cambiada*) | Cooperative management |
| Black markets | Bartered | Narco-economy |
| Barter or hybrid barter-sale | "Workfare" | Nonprofit |
| (*vencambios, permutas,* | Protection rackets | |
| *trueque, cambalache*) | Votes for favors | |
| **Nonmarket** | **Unpaid** | **Noncapitalist** |
| Household flows | Volunteer | Communal |
| State allocations | Housework | Independent |
| Barter within business | Family care | Feudal |
| consortia | Neighborhood work | Domestic |
| Self-provisioning | Self-provisioning | Slave |
| Patronage obligations | Slave labor | |
| Sharing | Shared labor (*minga*) | |
| Gifts | | |
| Theft | | |

SOURCE: Adapted from Community Economies Collective (2001).

relationships of power and exploitation that offer a much broader field of politics than is conventionally recognized. Representing economic diversity "helps one resist the tendency to see all forms of economic activity as becoming capitalist merely because they interact with capitalism" (Escobar 2008, 101) and helps us explore different pathways toward equity, justice, and radical environmental sustainability.

In this chapter, I describe how economic diversity works in the life of a single barterer, Santiago, and at the scale of Medellín as a whole. First, however, I want to underscore a critical point. Critics of the diverse economies framework often argue that Gibson-Graham's efforts to inspire a sense of openness and possibility lead to a naïve blindness to power and hegemony or an uncritical celebration of survival strategies that have no real impact on capitalism (Castree 1999; Samers 2005). This is an important caution because it does no good to inspire people to take imaginative action without also preparing them for the very real challenges to activism. Embracing conceptual openness should not blind us to the power, logics, and systematicity that exist in the world. People are, in fact, not free to simply choose a new economy out of a grab bag of alternatives, and they are certainly not equally free to do so. As Marx famously wrote, "Men make their own history, but they do not make it as they please; they do not make it under self-selected circumstances, but under circumstances existing already, given and transmitted from the past" ([1852] 1999, chap. 1). In Colombia, as elsewhere, these circumstances involve a highly unequal distribution of power structured along differences of class, race, ethnicity, region, and gender. These power relations are maintained and contested through patronage, politics, pesos, and pistols.

The value of Gibson-Graham's analysis in Colombia—"where a handful of elite families are thought to monopolize control of the media, politics, and the nation's (licit) economy" (Roldán 2002, 1)—is not to deny power but to emphasize that power does not correspond to a single, monolithic, and inescapable logic of capital. The prime beneficiaries of Colombian socioeconomic relations are these "leading families," who may identify primarily as capitalists. However, their power is not exercised exclusively through and for capitalism, and it creates and depends on a range of noncapitalist practices. Even the capitalist elite actively participate in noncapitalism. While there is a logic to the relations of power in Colombia, it is not the logic of capital, but rather the logic of an elite. Or, to be more precise, of an elite operating in the dynamic environment of the war system, in conflict with other elites and nonelites.[3] Thus, there are always contradictions and counterforces within and beyond the dominant hegemony that modify the workings of power.

In what follows, I describe the interwoven dynamics of regional cultural politics, diverse economies, and violence in order to contextualize today's barter projects. This analysis illustrates barter organizers' motives, the material and symbolic resources that they draw from, and the relations of power—both material and sociocultural—that they are working within and against.

## Paisa Economies and the Hegemonic Bargain: From Peacefare to Warfare

Despite assumptions to the contrary, widespread violence is a fairly recent phenomenon in Medellín and the surrounding region; it resulted from twentieth-century political and economic expansion mapped onto racist ideologies, rather than a timeless "culture of violence" or intractable partisan differences (Roldán 2002). In fact, as Roldán writes, for much of the nineteenth and twentieth centuries Paisas stood out for their pragmatic, economistic opposition to war and social division:

> There was little in Antioquia's past to suggest that it should have become an area hard hit by partisan violence during *la Violencia*. Neither the province of which Medellín is the capital nor Medellín itself was associated with violence in the Colombian imaginary. A stereotype existed of Antioquia and its inhabitants, but it was one that characterized *paisas* as the nation's sharpest businessmen and pragmatic technocrats, a region of aggressive colonizers. . . . Many a joke was made targeting regional inhabitants as too obsessed with making money to spare the time to take part in politics. When forced to choose between going to war . . . and arriving at a negotiated solution that would . . . allow business to continue unimpeded, the region's inhabitants were perceived as usually opting for the latter. (Roldán 2002, 10–11)

Regional identity and a strong entrepreneurial ethic functioned as a form of "peacefare" (Wolf 1987; Fox 1995). As Wolf described, new possibilities for war emerge with changes in the mode of production, especially changes in the logic of natural resource exploitation, the ability to generate surplus and centralize power, related alterations in social organization, and the emergence of new technologies. However, just as the mode of production is related to warfare, so is it related to peacefare. Different manners of organizing society create different mediating mechanisms that favor peace over war. In Wolf's words, "organized peace becomes a possibility alongside of organized war" (1987, 141). In Antioquia, peacefare was driven by the thirst for economic growth, in combination with social links established across class and party lines and among different elite factions, relations maintained via kinship ties, patronage systems, and joint economic ventures.

This dynamic of peacefare was not, however, an Edenic state of equity and justice. Early Antioqueño society was characterized by a "hegemonic bargain" in which the ruling elite maintained peace, order, and basic social supports for their underlings in exchange for obedience, hard work, and cultural conformity (Roldán 2002). This cross-class alliance hinged on a racial project (the social construction of all Antioqueños as a separate white race characterized by hard work, autonomy, individualism, and fierce pride) and a civilizing mission that together naturalized racial difference and ideas of progress and modernity (Escobar Villegas 2009; Restrepo 1988). However, the racism and regionalism undergirding the hegemonic bargain eventually tipped the system toward war. As Paisas colonized new regions in the 1920s and 1930s, they encountered recalcitrant Others—Afrocolombians, Indigenous people, and others who did not fit Antioqueño standards of "civilization" and were unwilling to concede power to the self-righteous colonists. The expansion of agriculture and mining—organized along subsistence, feudal, and capitalist lines—into frontier regions filled with "less human" beings set the stage for violence.

Prolonged violence may have remained unlikely, however, without other shifts in the socioeconomic relations of peacefare, particularly the emergence of a new political class focused on nationalist (rather than regionalist) alliances and fears of solidarity among urban workers, rural peasants, and progressives (Roldán 2002). With the hegemonic bargain threatened from numerous angles, violence emerged as a means of consolidating power. Inspired by regionalist, do-it-yourself attitudes and traditions of extralegal political and economic organizing through patronage networks, competing elite factions formed paramilitary groups to assert control over frontier regions and political institutions. The level of violence overwhelmed the peacekeeping powers of the regional elite and local police forces, but prideful autonomy left the region isolated from national military forces. The result was extremely high levels of "selective and concentrated" violence during the early 1950s, leading to some of the country's highest rates of murder, massacre, and displacement (Roldán 2002, 9). La Violencia came to an end only when the nation's elite, alarmed at the economic consequences of prolonged civil war, forged an unprecedented power-sharing agreement, but the end of La Violencia did not mean the end of violence. The national state remained weak, rule over frontier territories and populations continued to generate conflicts, and the socioeconomic relationships and cultural imaginaries that had once facilitated peace were more fragmented than ever.

The contemporary economies and politics of Medellín and the region grow out of these colonizing searches for subsistence and wealth, the cultural traits that are proudly maintained as part of Paisa identity, and the new dynamics of violence. Although the "ethnological heresy" of the Raza Antioqueña ignores regional diversity and depends on fallacious arguments about race and ancestry (Parsons 1968, 3), it persists as a powerful source of local pride, as do the old stereotypes of Paisas as energetic entrepreneurs. The successes and failures of barter activism are largely shaped by these historical characteristics, particularly do-it-yourself entrepreneurialism, disrespect for the state and central authorities, traditions of patronage and passive followership, and cultural conformity and a fear of difference more recently exacerbated by red baiting. This history of peacefare and warfare seems far removed from contemporary realities, but we see these dynamics in the everyday economic actions of many barterers, such as Santiago.

## Living the Diverse Economy (*Written with Santiago*)

Santiago wakes to his daughter's alarm clock. Even now, at five o'clock, his hillside barrio is coming to life with the clanking of pots and pans and the rumbling of buses shuttling people to downtown. While their daughter prepares for school, Santiago and Beatriz try to catch another hour of sleep until the sun rises over the Aburrá Valley. Finally, Beatriz gets up to prepare breakfast while Santiago uses stored rainwater to wash yesterday's clothes. After breakfast, Luz Marina leaves for school and Santiago takes his daily walk, during which he visits the Financial Cooperative Cotrafa. Santiago and Beatriz have savings at the cooperative, which he uses on this day to make an electronic payment for the water bill at his second home.

This second home—located in a rural area on the opposite side of the city—is Santiago's newest response to the violence and turbulence of the *barrio popular* and his family's economic needs. For the last three years, he has tried to establish a peaceful home and micro-farm on land that he purchased using his own savings, informal loans from family members, and a loan from a second credit cooperative. But this hasn't been easy. While his wife and daughter stay in their city home, Santiago travels to the other side of the city every weekend and during the nights to work on the land and house. Now, after three years of work partially alone and partially with his wife, daughter, and brother, they've completed a simple home of wood and cement block, they have a garden for home consumption, and they're generating a modest income from spinach, *yacón* (an Andean tuber), *uchuva* (gooseberries), and passion fruits.

Here we already see how livelihoods are constructed through the interweaving of diverse strands of ownership, labor, and exchange. Consider the complexity of Santiago and Beatriz's homeownership. Until 2003, Santiago was living in a small apartment on the second floor of his mother's house. He and Beatriz pooled their money and built their current house as a place to start their own family. Technically Santiago's mother still owns his old apartment, but he collects the rent from it to pay his family's food and utility bills. In short, he has transitioned from gifted housing from his mother to a collectively owned private house of his own, and he also benefits from the informal right to the surplus from his mother's apartment, which he redistributes to his family as a whole.

A closer look at Santiago's new farmhouse also reveals surprising articulations between capitalist and noncapitalist economies. The Cotrafa cooperative was established in 1957 by employees of a capitalist textile company, as an extension of their informal, solidarity-based savings program. Thus, in paying his water bill (to a public, noncapitalist, but profitable utility), Santiago is engaging with a noncapitalist (but formal-economy) cooperative that developed out of a noncapitalist (but informal) savings group that emerged because of a formal capitalist corporation. The farmhouse also involves significant noncapitalist exchanges. For example, his brother plans to build on the property as well—a way of recovering the loan he extended to Santiago and expanding the family's collective labor.

In terms of labor, Santiago and Beatriz share one of the most transparent and democratic households I have seen, maintaining largely separate finances but communicating openly about how they and their daughter will contribute monetarily and nonmonetarily to the household. Their household labor is highly visible and carefully negotiated to maximize the freedom and well-being of each family member and the long-term stability of the whole. Whoever is at home at midday is in charge of cooking, though everybody hopes it will be Beatriz because her food is the best. To compensate, Santiago does more of the washing. While Beatriz prefers to use city water for washing, Santiago takes advantage of collected rainwater. He sees the economy as a more-than-human space and has made care for the environment (and appreciating the free gifts of nature) a guiding pillar of his life, along with barter and support for democratic grassroots governance through neighborhood assemblies (Juntas de Acción Comunal, or JAC).

Constructing a family workspace is only one aspect of Santiago's diverse economic portfolio. His livelihood is primarily based on community service and work as an artisan. Interestingly, these developed together and reinforced each other. Examining the intersections among these multiple projects—and their relationship to other economies and the broader context of violence—reveals the range of value systems he enacts. The majority of these do not involve private ownership, private decision making, and the use of wage labor to produce privately owned surplus. His economic activities and value systems are thus far beyond the capitalist tip of the economic iceberg.

In high school, Santiago began obligatory community work with a literacy program in a nearby neighborhood. This became a really fun process with an intergenerational group of residents, so he continued the work in his own neighborhood. He joined the barrio's JAC and created a youth group, a *natillera* (a traditional collective savings group that pools money throughout the year), and joined an association named Convivamos. Through Convivamos he and Beatriz learned beadwork, which is now central to their livelihood along with macramé, crochet, cross-stitch, and other needlework. Becoming producers has helped them sustain themselves economically and allowed them to appreciate barter as a possible life way. Unfortunately, Santiago's involvement in these community processes created "envy" in the neighborhood, and he began receiving death threats. After a while, he decided the risk was serious enough that he abandoned his work and fled to live with a cousin.

For many years Santiago avoided community work in his own neighborhood, but in 2006 he was invited to join the new municipal program in participatory budgeting. The participatory budgeting process yielded three scholarships for professional study in exchange for community service. At first, he was hesitant to apply because higher education seemed overly abstract and impractical, but he decided to use this program to study business administration at a private university. "First of all," he said, "I wanted to be a good example to my daughter. And also, it was nearly free. I really struggled with the bureaucracy of the university and their lack of interest in real community-oriented and solidarity-based businesses, but I finally managed to graduate in 2012. As difficult as it was, I'm happy I did it, and I always tell people that I got my degree by way of [government-sponsored] barter." At that same time (in 2006), Santiago helped establish a non-profit to promote community economies and manage a collective workshop in his neighborhood.

This community service work allowed Santiago to study the JAC and the potential for local community governance, which eventually led to paid work as an advisor to the JAC. "From 2006 to 2008," says Santiago, "I had a lot of community work. I helped create a center to sell products from that sector of the city, which we established but were never able to make sustainable, and I also helped create a gym and sauna and an automotive shop using participatory budgeting monies. For security reasons, though, I had to abandon work in my own barrio yet again. So I began working as an advisor to JAC and I dedicated myself to finishing my degree. Today, my community service consists of two main tasks: my voluntary work with [my nonprofit] and my paid work as a consultant."

To a large extent, Santiago combines paid and volunteer work to create a meaningful existence within the context of violence and unpredictability. His nonprofit began slowly because he was occupied by other community work, but after renewed threats of violence in 2008, he stopped this other work and had more time to dedicate to his own organization. In this way, a diverse livelihood portfolio has provided him with not only economic resilience but also emotional resilience in the face of disabling and dehumanizing violence. Pursuing all of these lines of community work with the "entrepreneurial spirit" characteristic of Paisas, he has opened a surprising number of new opportunities. "I completed short courses in solidarity economics, which brought me into contact with barter, and I began doing mini-barters in [my organization]. As a result of these contacts and this work, we took on subcontracts from the city in 2009, 2010, and 2011 to spread our knowledge of barter to public and private entities, primarily through the School for Solidarity Economy. I use barter to bring the solidarity economy into my livelihood and my professional work," and in the process he formed new contacts to facilitate future work. Santiago's consultancies to the JACs have also put him in touch with organizations around the city. Some scholars might describe these as insignificant economic activities that exist at the margins of capitalism, to serve capitalism, and at the whims of capitalism. But the household economy of Santiago and the urban economy of Medellin are too complex to be reduced to capitalism. Santiago's activities are more significantly tied to public decision making than corporate imperatives, and they are based on noncapitalist economic subjectivities, habits of mind and emotional instincts that are tied to public and shared property, nonwage labor, collective decision making, and the generation of social rather than personal wealth.

When we wrote this description of his personal economic history, all of this work was on hold while a new municipal administration rewrote the city development plan. Santiago was waiting for the plan to be approved so the city could establish new projects and contracts; he was eager to learn if he would find opportunities in the new plan. In the meantime, Santiago remained unemployed. With characteristic optimism, though, he told me that "this isn't so bad, really. Since I haven't had an income, I've been able to invest more time in our micro-farm. Our household revenues have been lower but we've managed to sustain ourselves from the rent of my mother's apartment and the handicrafts that we sell. Plus Beatriz and Luz Marina are big savers. This makes us very frugal, but it means that we don't go hungry. On the contrary, we have no debts and no hardships."

This sense of sufficiency that Santiago establishes through his diverse economy—another example of how barterers are beginning to defy the logic of scarcity—is reflected in the balance of his day. After getting exercise on his walk to the cooperative, Santiago returns to the house to finish some woven sandals that another barterer requested and then delivers those to her workplace at yet another cooperative. Returning home, he sets to work on two projects that Beatriz began: jewelry for a woman who is experimenting with exports to Italy and a backpack that a neighbor ordered for purchase. After Beatriz returns from theater practice and her errands, the couple sets off to deliver these handicrafts and then go to the nonprofit for the late afternoon. The office is a large space with lots of corners to hang out and work, but it is usually vacant now. Their goal is to always have a productive project that can generate income for whoever is staffing the site during the days, but they haven't been able to maintain this. Beatriz and Santiago use the walk to their nonprofit as a rare moment together and also to deliver a number of products that they'll trade at the organization's barter fair the following weekend.

At the end of the day, once Luz Marina has finished her schoolwork, they all leave to spend the night at the micro-farm. Although the farm is located in a village known for violence—one of the reasons Santiago was able to afford it—it feels markedly more peaceful than their barrio, "where neighbors are stacked up on top of one another and the noise and pollution fill every second of the day." Because of the demands of country work, everyone in the village goes to bed early to rise early and beat the midday heat. Santiago, Beatriz, and Luz Marina follow suit. Tomorrow they have weeds to pull and peas to harvest. They're just starting to figure out how to make the farm work in this climate and without being present to provide constant care, so they want to get in a full day's work.

You can see how complex Santiago's livelihood is. In one day he manages various types of labor: unpaid labor for his family, unpaid labor shared with his family, as well as paid, unpaid, and bartered labor from his garden and handicrafts. He normally depends on paid work as a contractor, which he does via nonprofit organizations whose goal is to serve the public and via government entities, utilizing public money (collected from the citizenry via taxes). To achieve all of this, he uses personal assets, but also a wide range of public assets (streets, water, light, and the significant investments in his education) as well as the assets of private businesses and cooperatives. He owns his property due to informal financing from family members and formal loans from credit unions (of which he is a member and therefore a partial decision maker), as well as from private banks (where he has no democratic role). So does he live in a capitalist economy? A subsistence economy? A cooperative economy? Following Gibson-Graham, I would argue that Santiago lives in a diverse economy and manifests material and cultural characteristics that reflect this diversity. References to "our capitalist economy" and "our capitalist culture" obscure this diversity and the many economic logics, goals, and value systems we engage with or pursue in our day-to-day lives.

"My household economy," Santiago says, "may be really limited compared to some people, but compared to others it's really rich, so I would say that our family economy is perfectly satisfactory. We're relatively good, or rather, we don't struggle looking for work or making ends meet, which means that we are really able to take advantage of life. There was a time in 2004 when our savings hit bottom and we were forced to seek wage work to reestablish our savings, but from then until now we have never suffered that kind of insecurity again and I don't think we're in any rush to return to that. I like to live in peace and calm and have no debts, and to know that what we have is ours and it's not loaned to us or owned by others. I don't like to live by making sacrifices in terms of food and recreation, and we really try to enjoy nature and travel, especially since we're in a megadiverse city and country. And ultimately I hope that all of my work contributes to a country with less corruption and a more fair distribution of wealth, because in our city and our country, very few people have a lot while a lot of people suffer with little."

## The Diverse Economies of Medellín

Santiago's story shows how one family weaves together multiple economies as part of their pragmatic pluralism and their pursuit of other ethical ideals. Now, stepping back to the city as a whole, we will see how substantial noncapitalist economies are across Medellín and how commonplace pragmatic pluralism is. As you might expect in a city with nearly 20 percent unemployment, 30 percent underemployment (Escuela Nacional Sindical n.d.), and an infamous illegal sector, capitalism is not the only game in town. Most economic activity is non-capitalist and most households depend heavily on noncapitalist practices. I analyze some of the most important economies in Medellín—the conventional capitalist economy, the government sector, cooperatives, petit commodity production in family businesses, household labor, and the informal sector—by asking how labor is mobilized, how transactions are enacted, and how surpluses are distributed in each of these economies. These different economies articulate through everyday practice, when people like Santiago bring materials, labor, value, knowledge, and social relationships from one "type" of economy to another. Through these articulations, they forge an economic subjectivity that is deeply pluralistic. As we saw in Santiago's story, the precarities within each economic sector further reinforce this pragmatic shifting from one to another.

This analysis highlights one motive for barter—to compensate for an economy that denies large segments of the population an adequate livelihood—and reveals the material and social relationships and subjectivities established through the conventional, diverse economy. These latter aspects are the wellspring of barter, but as I describe in chapter 6, they also present significant challenges to creating barter as an ethical-political project. In this section, I especially focus on the period since 1994, when Medellín's first barter fair was established, and during the recession of 1999–2002, when barter saw a second wave of expansion.

It will help readers to understand that Colombia has had one of the most stable economies in Latin America. Renowned for slow but steady growth of 4 to 5 percent per year, Colombia largely avoided the stagnation, inflation, and debt crises that plagued other Latin American countries during the "lost decade" of the 1980s, and it reported positive economic growth from the Great Depression until the recession of 1999. Employment in Colombia is relatively sensitive to macroeconomic changes, but unemployment has been fairly low in comparison with the rest of the region, reaching a low of less than 8 percent in 1994. However, with economic liberalization and contraction in the second half of the 1990s, unemployment peaked sharply, rising to 20.5 percent in September 2000, its highest level in modern Colombian history (Bernal and Cardenas 2003, 7).

Colombia's GDP has continued to grow steadily since 2001, especially as improved security attracts foreign investment. The global economic recession interrupted growth in 2009, but the country recovered quickly. This growth has been achieved through processes of industrialization and economic restructuring that amplified inequality, and in combination with patterns of violence that exacerbated this trend. By some measures, Colombia is considered the ninth most unequal country in the world, surpassed in the Western Hemisphere only by Haiti. The wealthiest 20 percent of households hold almost 25 times as much wealth as the poorest 20 percent (*Economist* 2011). In 1998, 16.1 percent of Medellín's residents were not able to satisfy their basic needs

(Restrepo Mesa 2000, 141), and in 2012, more than 37 percent of the national population lived below the poverty line (a figure that has decreased steadily in recent years) (World Bank 2012). To the extent that economic development continues to follow a model of "modernization" and increased efficiency, Colombia will continue to show a "paradox" of "growth without employment" (Gutiérrez 2007, 5–6). Nonetheless, life expectancy is high, at seventy-three years, and the country's Human Development Index is just below the regional average and improving (UNDP 2011; World Bank 2012).

## Capitalist Economies: Formal and Informal Work

The formal labor market—and all of the businesses, sales, and profits it supports—is what people most commonly identify as "the economy," but in Colombia this formal market is nearly inextricable from an informal economy of equal or greater size (Ochoa Valencia and Ordóñez 2004; Uribe and Ortiz 2006). The Medellín Chamber of Commerce estimates that 49 percent of the city's businesses are informal (Gutiérrez 2007), and the national statistical bureau reports that slightly more than half of the nation's employed people work in the informal market (4,624,000 people, compared to only 4,356,000 in the formal market) (DANE 2010). Micro and small enterprises can be seen as "the core of the Colombian economy"; in 2005, large corporations accounted for only 1 percent of all registered businesses, while micro-enterprises accounted for 75 percent (Rosenbloom and Cortes 2008, 722). Thus, although I have grouped the formal and informal sectors as "capitalist economies," we should actually expect to see a range of owner-worker relationships, forms of payment, and types of surplus appropriation. From our perspective—thinking of economic change as a material and cultural problem—this range of decision-making, control, and value systems is highly significant.

The inadequacy of the formal labor market may be its most notable and enduring characteristic. Alongside rising employment, the city has seen a growth in informality, self-employment, and temporary or contract labor. Formal wage work is especially limited for the poor and people without a high school education but can be scarce even for college-educated people like Santiago who lack family connections. The National Union School (Escuela Nacional Sindical n.d., 1) argues that Colombia's high unemployment, underemployment, and informality and the limited coverage of social security protections stem from "a structural problem in the national labor market in terms of the generation and protection of dignified work conditions."

Worker dissatisfaction is reflected in public opinion polls, in surveys of "subjective unemployment" (employment that is inadequate or inappropriate to one's training), and in total incomes: 34.6 percent of workers earned less than the minimum wage of $230 per month, and 40.9 percent earned between one and two minimum wages. Women are particularly disadvantaged in the labor market; they are more likely to be engaged in informal or temporary work, and, partly as a result of this, their average incomes are only 78.4 percent of the average man's income. Child labor is also not rare in the city: about 4 percent of children between five and seventeen years old were working in 2007; and 10 percent of children overall, and 40 percent of working children, do not attend school (Escuela Nacional Sindical n.d.). However, these problems are not universal and have changed over time. As Farnsworth-Alvear (2002, 17) notes, "Because Colombian [textile] manufacturers maintained wage-levels that allowed for workers' participation in a modern consumer economy, and because they cultivated employees' loyalty by providing health care, recreation, and other benefits, workers' experiences in Medellin [were] roughly comparable to those of their counterparts in North American and European manufacturing," at least during the middle half of the twentieth century when that industry was growing and labor conditions remained strong.

The extremely precarious situation of low-income households (reflected in Table 2) contributes to high levels of violence (McIlwaine and Moser 2003) and interest in economic alternatives. Informality may itself be a highly exploitative and violent condition because it implies exclusion from legal safeguards. On the other hand, escaping the regimented, inflexible legal and financial requirements of banks and government agencies can permit solidarity-oriented forms of ownership, labor, surplus management, and decision making, as we saw in Santiago's flexible home finance and labor relationships. If barter is well

**Table 2**
**Precarious labor and livelihoods among low-income female and male workers in Medellín, Colombia, 2005**

|  | Women | Men |
| --- | --- | --- |
| Education (years) | 10 | 10.1 |
| Had paid employment | 34% | 40.4% |
| Days worked per month | 11 | 14 |
| Had a formal job (with benefits) | 7% | 12% |
| Had a job contract | 7.2% | 10.6% |
| Hours worked per week | 23 | 30 |
| Monthly wage earnings (primary job only) | $42.14 | $60.57 |
| Monthly self-employment earnings (primary job only) | $7.33 | $15.66 |
| Total earnings (primary wage and self-employment jobs only) | $49.47 per month $1.65 per day | $76.23 per month $2.54 per day |

SOURCE: Data from a large survey of stratum 1 and stratum 2 workers by Attanasio et al. (2008). The Colombian government classifies households and neighborhoods according to six socioeconomic strata based on factors such as property value, average neighborhood income, and access to public services. Stratum 1 is considered "low-low," and stratum 2 is "low." Taxes, utility rates, health fees, and many legal penalties are adjusted to an individual's stratum, with people from strata 1, 2, and 3 paying lower rates.

designed and marketed, people might more easily use it as Santiago did: to complement these solidaristic activities and fill some of the livelihood gaps left by scarce opportunities in the conventional market.

For the most part, however, public and private initiatives to support precarious households have focused on increasing formal employment or formalizing businesses in the informal sector. As the Global Entrepreneurship Monitor concluded, "A very large percentage of the [Colombian] population creates businesses, but not because it's their best option, rather because they have no other" (Múnera et al. 2009, 103). Informality is, for many small business owners, a reasonable response to extremely slim profits that cannot realistically be shared with a state that rarely seems to serve them and may actually impede their work. The historical absence of the state has contributed to a "culture of evasion," which reinforces the individualistic pursuit of "favorable results at whatever cost to whomever" (108). This may be one of the most damaging impacts of informality, that it can undermine the sense of a social surplus that can be collectively created and managed for the public good.

Micro-enterprise has been one of the local government's main responses to unemployment and underemployment. Municipal administrations have tended to believe that employment policy is largely the domain of the federal government. Thus, municipal policy has "been limited to asking the private sector to have more business social responsibility by generating quality employment, helping micro-businesses, establishing agreements for the training of independent workers and developing programs for entrepreneurship, among others. And it is entrepreneurship that has become the main employment policy" (Gutiérrez 2007, 11). In many ways, the municipal administration's business promotion plan during my research period—the Cultura E (Entrepreneurial Culture) program, support for micro-businesses, formalization of the informal, and the provision of small loans via the Banco de las Oportunidades (Bank of Opportunities)—sought to incorporate the masses into the circuits of finance and traditional capitalism. However, these projects, which emerged from a development plan entitled "Medellín Productiva, Competitiva y Solidaria" (A Productive, Competitive, and Solidaristic Medellín), present alternative possibilities as well. These programs support the creation of not only small *private* businesses, but also collective enterprises, solidarity associations, and groups capable of taking advantage of the city's small participatory budgeting process. Unfortunately, these types of programs have often been politically motivated and short-term in nature and have not instituted the structural changes necessary to support innovation, technology, research, development, and competitiveness (Múnera et al. 2009). Many students of the School for Solidarity Economy also complained that they did not address their biggest challenge: finding markets favorable to micro-enterprises.

In short, the formal economy articulates with an informal economy that supports it (keeping wage laborers alive between jobs) and siphons resources off of it (using products, infrastructure, taxes, knowledge, and other resources established through the formal economy for informal and noncapitalist ends). As Yanagisako (2002) and García Canclini (1993) argue, these complex and varied articulations between capitalism and noncapitalism reflect local cultural processes and generate new forms of economic culture; they also draw heavily on Paisa pride in an entrepreneurial identity blending both ruthless selfishness and family solidarity. When we speak of a Colombian worker or businessperson, or a capitalist, we must therefore examine the informal and noncapitalist values, sentiments, and desires that are interwoven with their formal capitalist ones. And as activists, we want to look for ways that these values might be leveraged for justice and sustainability.

## Alternative Capitalist Economies: Self-Employment, Cooperatives, and the Narco-Economy

Between the capitalist and noncapitalist realms lie a number of alternative systems of production and trade that share some capitalist values, logics, and material processes but deviate from these in meaningful ways, such as the San Andresito markets for stolen and used goods and a growing number of "fair trade" markets meant to support peasant producers of ecologically sustainable foods. Microcredit organizations and mutual savings associations provide alternative, collectivist financial systems, though sometimes as appendages of patriarchal, capitalist firms. And Colombians also have a number of traditional economic practices—such as *mingas, convites,* and *mano cambiada*—through which labor is pooled and exchanged through immediate or delayed reciprocity. The most significant alternative markets in Medellín, however, are in self-employment, cooperatives and the "solidarity economy," and the narco-economy.

First, nationally, approximately 60 percent of informal workers are self-employed; 32.1 percent of Medellín's workers govern themselves. These workers may not be free from exploitation, but theirs is of a different type. They control their own means of production, the labor process, and the surplus value that they create. A large portion of these workers must suffer from economic privation—in addition to lower and less predictable incomes, they are four times more likely than formal workers to lack social security and other job-related benefits (DANE 2010)—but if the barterers that I describe in chapters 3 and 5 are any indication, a sizeable portion of this population was not relegated to self-employment but actively chose it because of a desire to escape capitalist relations of production.

A second alternative market sector can be found in the solidarity economy, which in Colombia is composed of cooperatives, mutual associations, and employees' funds, with cooperatives representing 78.5 percent of solidarity businesses (Confecoop 2010). Santiago's daily rounds give a sense of how ubiquitous cooperatives are, especially in the financial sector. Together, these businesses—which are supposed to be democratically run—have an enormous economic impact. In Antioquia in 2009, for example, 1,030 such organizations generated 15,684 jobs and 4.4 trillion pesos in profits for their 1.3 million members (Confecoop 2009). Antioquia's solidarity economy is heavily concentrated in Medellín, which was the source of 90 percent of cooperative earnings and 85.5 percent of members (Confecoop-Antioquia 2010). However, cooperatives often fail to achieve their democratic ideals. Santiago and other barterers, despite their above-average desire to have a voice in economic affairs, find it difficult to make meaningful contributions to cooperative governance and often represent the "solidarity economy" as an expert-led, nongrassroots alternative economy.

These institutions have substantial multiplier effects as well, distributing profits to educational programs as required by law and to other social programs according to the interests of their members. For example, in 2010 alone, the financial cooperative Cooperativa Financiera John F. Kennedy, Ltda. contributed 4.6 million pesos toward government and nongovernmental education programs, including school grants, adult technical training, and environmental education, plus an additional 20 million pesos for cultural programs and 453 million to support other nonprofit organizations (Confecoop 2009). The solidarity sector grew steadily from 2004 to 2009, outpacing the economy as a whole and suggesting that alternative systems of ownership, financing, and surplus distribution are economically competitive (Confecoop-Antioquia 2010). It is clear, however, that not all of the enterprises technically included in "the solidarity economy" actually generate liberatory or transformative political economies (Satgar 2014; Vásquez-León et al. 2017).

Solidarity economy promoters in and out of government have tried to strengthen the sector by designing cooperative business clusters and local economic circuits. These business alliances and alternative markets share many of the goals of barter, including building local economic synergies beyond the conventional market, building economies of scale and reducing business costs, and strengthening a noncapitalist economic identity (Zabala Salazar n.d.). Unfortunately, government programs to support the solidarity economy at the grassroots—including the School for Solidarity Economy with which I volunteered and the program for Solidarity Culture—have suffered from lower funds than conventional business development programs, as well as corruption and poorly focused management.

In many ways, the drug economy exemplifies unfettered free markets. I have included it as a third alternative economy, however, because the dynamics of illegality and violence make the narco-economy qualitatively different than other ruthlessly competitive economies. Data on the extent of drug production are notoriously poor and ideologically inflected; for example, while the United Nations Drug Control Program estimates the drug trade's value as 8 percent of global trade, other reasonable measures place it at 1 percent or 0.1 percent (Thoumi 2005). Nonetheless, it is clear that the violence, institutional weakness, and capital flows associated with the narco-economy significantly affect Colombian economic development. The drug trade, violence, and corruption have undermined legal business activity, discouraged foreign investment, destroyed trust and confidence necessary for effective economic organization, and reduced GDP growth by as much as 2 percent per year (Holmes et al. 2008; Thoumi 1995). Drug violence negatively affects employment, monetary policy, land ownership and inequality, and legal exports (Holmes et al. 2008). At the same time, the industry creates numerous economic opportunities for coca growers, traffickers, and gunmen and has substantial multiplier effects through money laundering operations in contraband, land acquisition, and construction. Between 1980 and 1995, the drug economy accounted for 5.3 percent of Colombia's GDP, more than coffee (4.5 percent) and petroleum (1.9 percent) (Safford and Palacios 2002, 315). Illegally acquired money was so important—and so distortionary—to the formal economy that President López Michelsen (1974–1978) created the "sinister window" for converting foreign currency into pesos, no questions asked, at the Banco de la República. Some cartel leaders, especially Pablo Escobar, were famed for investing huge sums in social development programs, low-income housing, and community recreational facilities.

We can thus see how the narco-economy shapes other economies: "Other sectors also profit—indirectly via a multiplier mechanism—from the employment, income, and demand created by the drug business. The purchasing power in these sectors has indirectly created hundreds of other employment opportunities in legal sectors. Capital goods, such as agricultural equipment, chemicals as well as consumer goods and services (banking, legal advice) are offered increasingly in the remote coca cultivation areas. This 'trickling down' also represents a distribution of the drug profits" (Maurer 1992, cited in Fleming et al. 2000, 397). The articulations go in the other direction as well. As Chomsky (2000) points out, Colombian small farmers began planting coca and opium poppies in part because multinational corporations undermined the G77 countries' efforts to stabilize agricultural commodities in the 1970s. Stabilization of commodity prices would have made Andean peasants less vulnerable to fluctuations in global coffee, grain, and fruit prices. Absent these protections, however, they found in coca and poppies more lucrative cash crops characterized by relatively stable demand but a host of undesirable "externalities."

In short, the narco-economy generates tremendous suffering but articulates with formal and informal economies in a range of contradictory ways, with benefits accruing to different social groups at different times. Without appearing to praise the narco-economy, it is worth providing a specific example of how it can nurture democratic systems for generating and distributing surplus. When an international corporate consortium wanted to build an electrical plant in Barrancabermeja, the local Fuerzas Armadas Revolucionarias de Colombia (FARC) command—strengthened militarily and economically by cocaine money—followed the familiar path of imposing demands on the firms involved. Rather than extracting protection fees, however, the FARC negotiated for the construction of a $2 million vocational school for local youth and $150,000 to generate jobs. "What is interesting," writes Richani, "is that the community actively participated in the wheeling and dealing of the negotiations between the guerrillas and the companies involved" through the local Junta de Acción Comunal (2002, 80). In this particular case, cocaine-driven militarization thus helped deepen popular democratic control over transnational capitalist enterprises. Richani reported similar experiences in several other cities.

## Noncapitalist Economies: The Public Sector and the Home

One of the most important noncapitalist spheres is found in the state sector. Medellín's municipal governments established a local economic model that combines "creative forms of local state ownership and control of key enterprises" with support for micro-enterprises and solidarity economy businesses (Bateman et al. 2011, 2). For example, city ownership and very effective management of the public utility Empresas Públicas de Medellín, which has now expanded its presence across the Americas, provides significant funding for economic and social development; 30 percent of EPM's profits go to the city budget.

Employment is one aspect of the state's economic role. From 2001 to 2007, the number of direct government employees decreased from 6.8 to 4.2 percent of the total workforce (Gutiérrez 2007, 8). These workers' experience of employment is quite similar to that of their private-sector peers, but it is not capitalist. Instead of using private property to produce private profits, they use public resources to produce goods and services for the benefit of all. Thus, their labor is owned and controlled, at least de jure if not de facto, by all of the citizens of Medellín. Because these workers are also part of a broader labor market, it may be more accurate to consider this as part of the alternative market sphere; however, I have included them here because of other aspects of government spending.

The full impacts of public expenditures in the economy extend well beyond employment. At the same time that direct government employment has decreased, government contracts to private firms and especially nongovernmental organizations have reportedly increased (based on interviews with NGO representatives), generating a hybrid system of privatized, but nonprofit and noncapitalist, provision of public goods and services through the mobilization of a mix of public and private capital and exploitation of labor at higher levels than the government itself could perform.

To offer one example, the 2011 municipal budget—which includes direct employment, subcontracts to businesses and NGOs, capital purchases, and redistribution through subsidies and social support programs—pumped just over 3 trillion pesos (approximately $1.5 billion) into the local economy. Five percent of this budget is directly managed by neighborhood councils through Medellín's "participatory budgeting" process, the same process that allowed Santiago to pursue higher education. While the outcomes of this innovative process are complex and varied, it has in many cases devolved into what I call "paramilitary budgeting." Demobilized right-wing groups (and, to a lesser extent, left-wing organizations) have used participatory budgeting to provide jobs and services to their support base, effectively capturing public money. Still, the participatory budgeting program does seem to have increased the public's sense of ownership over municipal resources and, by channeling armed or formerly armed groups into civil decision-making processes, it may help erode the tradition of clientelism and thereby deepen democracy in the city (Uran 2010).

The source of government revenues reveals the complex articulations among capitalist and noncapitalist activities. While wage labor in a capitalist firm is typically considered the hallmark of capitalism, following the money reveals that even this quintessentially capitalist relation includes significant noncapitalist elements. These are perhaps most visible when examining total labor costs from the employer's perspective. In 1996, nonwage labor costs in Colombia were 52 percent of the worker's salary, up from 42.9 percent in the early 1990s. These nonwage costs included severance and unjustified dismissal pay, other workers' rights, contributions of 2 to 3 percent for employee health care, 13.5 percent for worker pensions, 2 percent for labor training by the Servicio Nacional de Aprendizaje (National Learning Service), 3 percent for social welfare programs administered by the Instituto Colombiano de Bienestar Familiar (Institute for Family Wellbeing), and 4 percent for family subsidies managed privately by *cajas de compensación* (business employees' coalitions) (Bernal and Cardenas 2003, 2). In other words, a substantial amount of the surplus generated by wage laborers was redistributed neither as workers' wages nor as capitalists' profits but rather as a social surplus to be managed by the state. The capitalist enterprise, then, is not only a site of exploitation and accumulation but also a node in more varied processes of redistribution.

To see government spending as the democratic distribution of a social surplus is both useful and misleading.[4] It is useful in that it highlights how government spending is distinct from strict capitalist practices and how it can be made more democratic. But it is deceiving to the extent that it clings to a democratic ideal without adequately considering the real networks of influence that skew government expenditures away from genuinely social processes. Politically connected families and institutions have disproportionate impact on government spending, both in Colombia and elsewhere. In Colombia, significant inequality, the war system, and the legacy of the hegemonic bargain certainly pave the way for institutional capture and the privatization of public decision making.

While the formal, informal, and public sectors account for most of Medellín's visible economy, they represent only a small portion of overall economic activity. Only slightly more than half of the national population works for pay. With the exception of a small number of fully dependent children, elderly, and infirm people, the remaining 42 to 52 percent are not economically inactive but are engaged in types of work that are unrecognized and uncounted within "the economy."

Many of these workers are part of a second noncapitalist sector, perhaps the largest in the country: the unvalued but very real labor of mostly female home workers. According to a 2010 study, 63 percent of men and 92.4 percent of women spent time in unremunerated work for social reproduction (López Montaño 2011). On average, unremunerated work accounted for 21 percent of men's work (13 hours per week) and 44 percent of women's work (32 hours per week). While it is difficult to accurately value this work, it is common for unremunerated household work to account for at least 15 to 39 percent of GDP (López Montaño 2011), or perhaps as much as 46.3 percent (in a Canadian study, Chandler 1994), and to compose more than half of total hours worked (Ironmonger 1996).

Research in Manizales, Colombia, estimated the magnitude of this unpaid work (Table 3). If valued at market prices, domestic work (excluding child care) would exceed the combined value of manufacturing, agriculture, and commerce; remarkably, this was true in Colombia's coffee heartland. Even according to conservative estimates, household labor accounted for 45 percent of Manizales' GDP and, if remunerated, would have offered monthly incomes of several times the national minimum wage.

It is difficult to generalize about what type of surplus appropriation occurs within the home because household power dynamics vary tremendously and defy easy categorization. What is clear, however, is that household labor is not capitalist; it may be slavery, feudalism, or some form of collectivism. Housewives and other homeworkers are clearly engaging with the capitalist economy (through purchases, for example), but they are not workers within a capitalist system and hence their subjectivities and politics should be understood as distinctive. Their politics may sometimes align with (typically male) worker politics but can also differ, such as when women contest their exploitation by male household heads by demanding "wages for wives" (Raynolds 2002).

**Table 3**

**Two estimates of the value of household labor in Manizales, Colombia, 2000**

| | Per Household | Citywide | Relation to Manufacturing | Relation to Agriculture |
|---|---|---|---|---|
| Value of domestic work (calculated based on market prices for value added) | $741/mo. | $722 million/yr. | 2.6 times | 1.93 times |
| Value of domestic work (calculated based on self-valuation by the worker) | $339/mo. | $330 million/yr. | 1.22 times | 0.88 times |
| Minimum wage | $148/mo. | | | |

SOURCE: Data from Loaiza Orozco, et al. (2004).

## Economic Subjectivities in the Diverse Economy

Understanding Medellín's diverse economy and the significance of noncapitalism is essential for appreciating the context barter activists are working with, not least the cultural context. People in Medellín typically do not distinguish among the different types of economic practices that they conduct on a daily basis. This was especially evident in the School for Solidarity Economy workshops, when would-be micro-entrepreneurs routinely discussed their household and business finances in overlapping terms and misunderstood trainers' exhortations to treat the business as a separate sphere. Since people do not separate out and label these different spheres, they easily adopt the dominant language of the economy as a primarily capitalist space. However, as the above analysis suggests, they regularly engage in a remarkably wide range of practices, only some of which involve capitalist relations of production.

Paisas have approached such diverse economic possibilities with their characteristic energetic entrepreneurialism. I argue that the historical experience of negotiating this diverse economy has led to the emergence of an economic logic characterized by "pragmatic pluralism." Theirs is not a capitalist subjectivity oriented around private property, individualism, private processes of appropriation, and competition, nor is it an anticapitalist subjectivity, but rather a diverse economies subjectivity with its own set of logics and values. Santiago's daily routine, his linking of different economic sectors, and his vision of well-being represents this pragmatic pluralism, though his economic subjectivity is also informed by a clear anticapitalist ideology.

Economic subjectivities are also highly influenced by the specific local experience of poverty. People from the lowest social strata in Colombia describe poverty as much more than a material lack. They associate it closely with "discrimination, the situation of women, low participation [in civic life], environmental impacts, insecurity, violence, the use of free time, drug addiction, the lack of solidarity, the lack of organization, the lack of spirit [or faith], machismo, vulnerability and the lack of power" (Restrepo Mesa 2000, 153). Fear and frustration are also important consequences of and contributors to poverty and violence. Many participants in the city's School for Solidarity Economy expressed low senses of self-worth and capability. This internalized self-devaluation is a formidable obstacle to conventional economic development and alternative economic experimentation.

## The War System

Before concluding, I want to return to the issue of violence. Gibson-Graham's theory of change may leave the impression that economic activists can concern themselves with *economic* subjectivities, identities formed through economic relations, and questions of needs, desires, consumption, surplus, and commons. People are, however, significantly more complex than this. Their identities and subjectivities are constituted through economic processes in interaction with other aspects of their everyday environment. In Colombia, and perhaps particularly in Medellín, violence is a strong sociocultural force.

In Medellín, as elsewhere, violence and economies are inextricably linked and mutually constitutive (Lutz and Nonini 1999), and both shape activists' projects and subjectivities, as well as the society that they seek to change. Anthropologists have argued that violence is not an exceptional or pathological condition, and that it is not merely destructive, but that it also produces new social relations, norms, meanings, and ways of being (Scheper-Hughes and Bourgois 2004; Scheper-Hughes 1992; Kleinman et al. 1997). One of the most powerful effects of violence is not physical harm but the "culture of fear" (Green 1999), "radical uncertainty" (Moodie 2010), and "epistemic murk" (Taussig 1987) that it creates.

Following Richani (2002), I refer to the political economy of violence in Colombia as a war *system*. From this perspective, the country's armed groups are seen not as independent entities with distinct motives and logics, but rather as fully interacting components of a larger dynamic that they create and respond to, sometimes in ways that subvert their original intents. In Richani's analysis, the national military and leftist guerrillas reached a "comfortable impasse" in which both sides benefited more from protracted war than they would have from victory or peace. The army and guerrillas established a "positive political economy" for war, deriving significant profits and political power from militarization and the weakness of civilian government oversight. Among other effects, this political economy of war led to an agrarian counter-reform achieved through land purchases and the forced displacement of millions of rural people into Colombia's cities, especially in Antioquia (Reyes Posadas 2009). The emergence of the narco-bourgeoisie and paramilitary forces and the escalation of violence toward the end of the 1990s destabilized this mutually beneficial system by fracturing the elite and increasingly exposing them to the negative costs of war. The moment seemed ripe for a negotiated peace, but the U.S. government's Plan Colombia provided the military with enough money and arms to decrease their incentive to compromise, thus nudging the war system back toward protracted conflict. Ongoing compromises between paramilitaries, state forces, guerrillas, and drug traffickers suggest that the lucrative business of war continued for many years to detract from a politics for peace. The recent peace accord between the Colombian government and the FARC shows how the growth of a transnationally focused elite shifted the balance of power toward peace (Stone 2016).

The war system—even if weakened by this realignment of the Colombian elite—remains important for its extensive and intensive effects on everyday lived realities in Medellín. Forced displacement drives many of the dynamics of informality and exclusion that I described above, leading people to invent creative strategies for survival and to participate in highly exploitative capitalist and noncapitalist processes. Most importantly, "violence, security and poverty interrelate in the eyes of the poor, often in causal ways" (McIlwaine and Moser 2003, 113). Many marginalized urban dwellers view poverty and violence as mutually constitutive and see both as tied to lack of opportunities, general social breakdown, and a deep-rooted lack of respect for others. In Castellanos Obregón's (2009) terms, poor young people are "produced for" and "seduced into" the war as they negotiate their options for achieving viable and dignified lives. This interconnection between violence, poverty, and humanizing respect is central to the barter project.

Social breakdown and the war system create a context in which people may long to assert their personhood and establish social connections, but where they are constrained by fearful conformity and political temerity. Collective projects in Medellín are viewed with suspicion and the basic communication and organizational skills that they depend on are largely lacking. The historical political economy of violence, displacement, distrust, and atomization is a major impediment to the construction of barter collectives and barter economies built on trust and solidarity. Finally, as the anthropological literature suggests, decades of violence have forced people to develop strategies and sensibilities for a world of "deep ambiguity and uncertainty" (Penglase 2014). People often respond to this precarity by normalizing uncertainty and developing strategies to navigate it safely and effectively (Scheper-Hughes and Bourgois 2004). This desperate flexibility in response to violence is, in many ways, similar to the pragmatic pluralism cultivated by economic uncertainty, and the two reinforce each other to make pragmatic pluralism a more obvious, unquestioned form of common sense.

I want to close this chapter on the personal level, with a story about the very real entanglements between diverse economies, violence, everyday life, and subjectivities. This story, which will be extremely troubling to most readers, is by no means representative of all of Colombian society and economy, but nor is it unprecedented. I offer it here as an important counterpoint to the primarily hopeful story that is my focus in this book. It shows what barterers are working against, as well as the socioeconomic and cultural context that makes their project so difficult.

Several months into my research, two women came to my solidarity economy study group angry. They were appalled—though not entirely shocked—by the craven disregard for dignity that had passed through their neighborhood that week. The men, they said, walked the neighborhood in broad daylight, on a weekday, in clear sight of the shopkeepers and the unemployed, leaving a simple one-page flyer on each doorstep. It listed the prices of girls' virginity by age. Six-year-olds fetched the highest price, though girls of any age were lucrative. With a few phone calls to the anonymous gang that everyone knew ruled the neighborhood, parents and guardians could turn a quick profit and ease the pains of chronic underemployment. Just a few phone calls to pay off their debts at the corner store, pharmacy, or funeral home, or even the debts they owed to the gang itself in exchange for the license to sell used goods from their front stoop. Just a few phone calls to make money for the electric bill or school expenses.

Imagine the calculus. A grandmother is trying to figure out how she will feed four or five children and grandchildren, how she will afford her husband's medications, how she will find the long-overdue rent money to avoid eviction. Her thirteen-year-old granddaughter is already hanging out with those wannabe thugs, drinking and smoking at the corner store, and who knows what else. It's only a matter of time, thinks the grandmother, until she does something stupid, gets herself pregnant just like her aunt, just like the neighbor's girl, and then what? Only more problems: another mouth to feed, one less pair of hands to help around the house, and if they do get evicted, a newborn to worry about. It's horrible to think like this. The grandmother shakes her head. It's shameful. But she's not the only child she has to worry about. If it's only a matter of time. . . .

The commodification of girls' virginity is only one of the most disturbing examples of a common process of turning bodies into items for the market, but girls are not the only victims of violent commodification. Urban guerrilla camps, paramilitary movements, failed demobilization programs, and the explosive growth of the drug trade have created a tremendous economy of low-level violence in the city. Teenage boys become hired guns, their bodies useful only as long as they can pull triggers, and otherwise disposable. Murder for hire is big business, accounting for 47 percent of the country's murders in 2010, and there's a market for every price point down to $25 (*El Tiempo* 2011). Of course, all of these children would love to sell themselves as high-value, high-skilled laborers, maybe even university-educated professionals, but opportunities for advancement are limited and the edgy bravado of the streets barrages children with messages that are both louder and more realistic seeming than the handful of public service announcements about going to school.

One cannot ignore the psychological impact on the child, the fundamental assault on the dignity of the entire family, and the way these simple acts feed a broader social dynamic of domination, violent dehumanization, disempowerment, and fear. The facts of supply, demand, and profitability do not easily justify the free flow of commodities whose very nature is morally repugnant to many people and whose social costs are so obvious. It is even harder to justify these markets when the "facts" of supply and demand are created through systematic intimidation, exploitation, and impoverishment.

Not every family in Medellín is touched so directly by these horrific markets for boys' and girls' bodies, but nobody is immune and nobody is blind. Faced with these tragedies and nearly constant news reports about government officials embroiled in scandalous relations with multinational corporations and paramilitary groups, the people of Medellín view the economy from a very different perspective than most people living in the United States. They see what goes on in the market, what happens behind the scenes of the formal economy. This doesn't mean that they are entirely displeased. Many still support the economy, but they are under few delusions. Critique comes more easily, and the search for alternatives seems more obvious.

In this context, Olga's search for a market that creates "real security" takes on greater significance. She—and virtually all of the other barterers—is asking a vitally important question: can barter heal the social fabric by helping people "to get to know each other, to begin to recognize each other [as fellow humans], and to create true trust"? Following Wolf, I would add a second question: can barter become a form of peacefare based not on an oppressive hegemonic bargain but on social and economic relations that help us opt out of economies of violence? Or in Escobar's words, could it help construct "peace—understood as a set of economic, cultural, and ecological processes that bring about a measure of justice and balance to the natural and social orders" (2008, 17)?

## Conclusion

To understand barter activism in Medellín, we must first understand the broader economic landscape out of which barter grows. This chapter has discussed several of the key economies of Medellín and shown how one barterer, Santiago, integrates these diverse market, labor, financial, and value systems into his everyday life. Drawing from Gibson-Graham, I have shown that these economies articulate in complex ways, with often-unpredictable justice out-comes. While some scholars might argue that capitalism is the dominant economy—and that it has the power to permit noncapitalist economies to oper-ate as long as they are nonthreatening—the scale and cultural and historical importance of alternative capitalisms and noncapitalisms suggest that we might interrogate economic articulations in a more open-minded way. From an activ-ist standpoint, the challenge is to identify which articulations present viable political openings.

Economic activists face one fundamental constraint: they must build the future out of the social and material conditions of the present. Medellín's bar-ter activists do not have the luxury of starting from scratch. They live in a world of multiple economies, each with its own logic, values, and social and material relations. The people of Medellín have grown up in these economies. They know what is expected of them, what success and failure look like, and they almost instinctually envision how to fulfill their desires through these economies. Their familiarity with the already-existing economies of the city is one of the greatest frictions against new barter economies. It creates a pragmatic plural-ism that obscures the distinctions between economic spheres, complicates ethi-cal interrogation of them, and militates against a singular alternative.

On the other hand, these already-existing economies are also resources. In fact, they are the main resources that barter activists have at hand. They pro-vide the raw materials for noncapitalist imaginings, practices, social relation-ships, and identities. This includes the possibility of revealing that capitalism is neither inevitable in the future nor even totalizing today. To continue with Marx's introduction to *The Eighteenth Brumaire*, "The tradition of all dead gen-erations weighs like a nightmare on the brains of the living. And just as they seem to be occupied with revolutionizing themselves and things, creating some-thing that did not exist before, precisely in such epochs of revolutionary crisis they anxiously conjure up the spirits of the past to their service, borrowing from them names, battle slogans, and costumes in order to present this new scene in world history in time-honored disguise and borrowed language" ([1852] 1999, chap. 1). The tradition of dead generations does indeed weigh heavily on the minds of barter activists. The Antioqueño hegemonic bargain remains alive and well today, deepened by the conflation of nonconformists with leftists, and hence with guerrillas and terrorists. This system of war and terror, bound up as it is with capitalist development in the region and with other economic rela-tions (Reyes Posadas 2009; Richani 2002; Ross 2003), is a powerful impedi-ment to activism.

Yet the nearness of violence also provides a sharp urgency to barterers' work, and a deep longing for humanity. As we will see in the coming chapters, many participants see in barter an opportunity to "revolutioniz[e] themselves and things." They cling to pieces of the past for inspiration—to Indigenous traditions of barter and salt currencies, to *campesino* traditions of shared labor, and to family rituals of collective savings—and they look to the diversity of Colombian and international alternative economies for the same. Masked in the old, they march toward the new, struggling to create, adopt, and embody the spirit and language of barter, to replace avarice with mutuality, greed with sufficiency, competition with solidarity, exchange-value with use-value, and dehumanization with humanity.

# 2

# The Birth of Barter

Many barter activists in Medellín proudly declare that their work recuperates a pre-Columbian tradition of moneyless exchange. The Aburrá Valley that is home to the Medellín metropolitan area was a trade hub linking Indigenous groups in a circuit that stretched northward to Mesoamerica, southward to the Incan Empire, and east to Tayrona and present-day Venezuela. The region is also rich in post-Conquest traditions of noncapitalism, ranging from highly exploitative ones like slavery and feudal haciendas to more solidarity-based ones like systems of collective labor or labor exchange that are still occasionally practiced today, and the *natillera* savings clubs of extended families and friends.

While organizers may find inspiration in Indigenous traditions or hope that claiming these historical roots will bolster their cause, there is little continuity between pre-Columbian, colonial, and postcolonial systems and today's barter systems. Rather, contemporary barter grows out of entirely new movements for community building, economic experimentation, and in some cases ideological opposition to capitalism and the monetary economy, and actual barter practice is informed more by transnational knowledge flows across solidarity economy networks than by transgenerational inheritance. In most cases, Medellín's barter projects began as simple experiments or one-off events. As communities increasingly embraced them, however, organizers began to elaborate a broader vision for barter as an alternative economy and culture, showing "co-revolutionary" spread from one sphere of life to another (Harvey 2010b).

The full scope of the barter project really hit home while I watched Santiago present at the Solidarity Economy School. The SES was a government program to promote entrepreneurialism across the city. It especially targeted the poor based on the premise that solidarity would enable them to start small businesses. In this sense, it represented the prevailing global trend of neoliberal poverty-relief programs, framing the poor as autonomous individuals who must manage themselves as a business, cultivating their capitals and capacities so they can help themselves via more competitive market entrepreneurialism (Bateman et al. 2011; Ferguson 2015; Gershon 2011). This is a stark contrast to alternatives that would see the poor as rights-bearing citizens or members of broader communities that can organize collectively to change the rules of the game and promote substantive equality. However, neoliberal programs like the SES are "fundamentally polyvalent," creating the possibility of challenging neoliberal values and materialities by reemphasizing solidarity, localizations, and counterglobalizations that are (at least partially) empowering (Ferguson 2010; Freeman 2014; Honeyman 2016).

Throughout August and September 2010, I worked with five barter activists to lead the school's short course on barter systems and community currencies. Our nine workshops covered the history of money and trade, international experiences with alternative currencies, how to administer a barter market, and alternative economy project design. We hoped to identify people interested in alternative economies and equip them with the knowledge and skills necessary to expand barter across the city. During the fourth session, Santiago was explaining how to run a barter system. Participants already had a good idea of how barter and local currencies could be used to facilitate economic transactions, so he wanted to complement this with a general framework for thinking about effective and ethical organizing. Introducing participants to concrete strategies that had already been tried in Medellín, he especially wanted to stress the importance of collaboration, communication, and consensus.

By way of introduction, Santiago drew a simple chart to illustrate the diversity of tasks that confront any group of barter organizers (Figure 2). He stressed that markets are only a small part of the picture. In an ideal system, each market should be complemented by regular newsletters to deepen people's understanding of barter and alternative economies and provide a list of members and their products. Each market should also begin with a meeting during which participants and organizers hash out the rules and discuss any issues that arise, as well as regular assemblies to work through bigger issues and long-term goals. Behind the scenes, all of this should be managed by an administrative team of three to twelve people who conduct trainings, manage finances and facilitators, maintain an institutional history, set norms for ethical behavior and product quality, publicize the system, encourage active participation, and help new members become practiced barterers.

As workshop participants questioned Santiago about each of the administrative tasks, it occurred to me that the same visual could be used to describe the processes and institutions that support the conventional Colombian

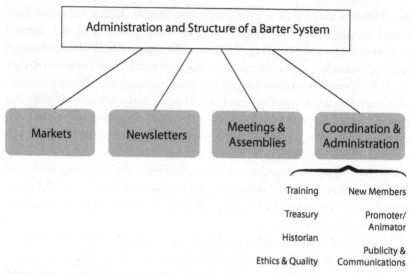

FIGURE 2 Santiago's vision of the tasks required to effectively administer a barter economy.

economy. The conventional economy works through a network of physical and virtual markets at which people exchange goods, services, knowledge, and money. Their exchanges are also shaped by particular beliefs about what the economy should look like and information about the supply and demand of goods and services. Barterers' newsletters play the same role as business journals, magazines, newspapers, television programs, schoolbooks, business directories, and other media of basic economic enculturation and communication; they are the *Economist* or *Dinero* of the barter world. The meetings and assemblies of the conventional economy are perhaps less clear, but we can imagine much legislative activity as playing this role. Most important, though, is the behind-the-scenes coordination and administration of the economy by central banks, government regulators, national treasuries, finance ministers, corporate conglomerates, marketing agencies, international trade negotiators, and thousands of others who make a living by managing the economy. And we should not neglect the role of consumers themselves as active shapers of the economy (Miller 1997).

Every economy—conventional or alternative, visible or invisible, hegemonic or counterhegemonic—is created through constant material, social, and cultural action by individuals, communities, and institutions. The Colombian state-capitalist economy relies on the daily work of thousands of people from the government, business, academic, and civil society sectors, as well as the collaboration of millions of consumers and investors. The resulting economies are made by recognizable "institutions" as well as more subtle cultural practices; for example, massive corporate downsizing has become valued in part because of investment bankers' ways of praising one another, engaging in workplace competition, and responding to their own job losses (Ho 2009). Barterers are trying to create many of the same institutions and cultural practices that undergird the conventional economy, but repurposed to advance an alternative logic and ethics.

However, barterers did not begin with such a well-defined project. In this chapter, I describe how barter emerged in Medellín first as a community-building response to violence and social breakdown and later as a form of economic and political activism. I chart the rise and fall of the city's first three barter experiments, detailing how organizers refined their ideologies and strategies through these experiences and how their decisions, theorizations, and practices framed later activism. Today's barter projects began with three unrelated experiences: the Barter Days in Bello (a municipality in the northern part of metropolitan Medellín), the barter fairs at the Altamira residential complex, and the Barter Bazaars and Local Exchange System in Pajarito (a small rural village on the edge of the city). The earliest barter projects generated a surprising amount of interest, which organizers leveraged to garner public and private support for spreading barter across the region and even to other parts of the country. This put barter on the map as a recognized possibility for social development and solidarity economy but raised dilemmas about the appropriate scale of an alternative economy, the speed at which it can or should grow, and the trade-offs organizers should accept in order to proliferate their idea. We'll see how Medellín's barter expansionists were forced to "thin" their vision in order to make barter more legible for people still committed to mainstream economic values, while committed localists maintained a "purer," more radical vision of alternative economies, but at the cost of seeming isolated, parochial, or unrealistic.

## Medellín's First Barter Experiments

### Bello's Barter Days

The first experience with contemporary barter systems in the metropolitan area was the Barter Day in Bello, a *municipio* of half a million people located to the north of Medellín. The first Bello Barter Day occurred on June 21, 1994, as part of an effort to reestablish broken social ties and "rediscover joy." The 1990s were a dark time in Bello. Drug violence was at its peak, and while it had taken a particularly frightful, unpredictable turn from the perspective of the middle and upper classes, it assumed a monotonous brutality in working-class neighborhoods where children were integrated as messengers, traffickers, and assassins from very young ages. For many people, violence, silence, and fear were everyday expectations. Turf wars divided communities and constantly altered patterns of mobility. Children grew up thinking not that they lacked a promising future but that they lacked the very promise of a future; they were quite literally disposable and would frequently turn up floating in the Medellín River.

But especially for older generations who had known other possibilities, this pain also sparked a desperation to create something else. Luis Alberto Jaramillo, the exuberant organizer who first told me that there are no barter systems in Medellín, reflected on that era in Bello:

> This environment was also one of searching, of constructing options, of "they can take everything from us, but not our happiness." There was a hope for happiness and dignity, an urgency to smile . . . that was unbreakable. A great urgency to look into the eyes of the other and to once again feel accompanied, to give meaning to . . . well, to every second, with every friend, with every memory, with whoever you shared ideas with. . . . We had this disposition. We came [to barter], first of all, in our search, with our questions, and also out of the need to meet one another, for the urgency of caring, because to share and the gift—the gift, this anthropological category, right?—the gift was there. This . . . these distinct manners of giving meaning to everyday life and giving meaning to the future.

The artistic community of Bello responded to violence and social collapse with play. They held campfires and youth art projects, assembled musical groups out of the strangest mix of instruments, built sculptures out of trash, planted trees on the mountains—whatever they could do to create spaces for celebration.

Barter was one of these spaces. The barter days began with ten to fifteen friends, most of whom had grown up in Bello and become artists, but who were gradually falling out of touch as jobs, family obligations, and violence pulled them apart. They would pass in the streets or see each other in bars, but life was dividing them. And so, to counter this slow disintegration, they decided to host barter days as a way of committing to come together for a day of real sharing every two to three months. Bartering was to some degree an excuse, but it also responded to a sense that each of these friends had so much to share, so many talents and capacities, but they rarely got to enjoy this wealth. Immersed in the monetization of human life in the always-imperfect wage labor market and the devaluation of human life in the narco-economy, these friends found comfort in celebrating their own value on their own terms.

Their ties of friendship and their creative, bohemian spirit proved essential for kick-starting the barter days. As one founding member said, "This came to pass because . . . we were all friends or acquaintances." The key to sustaining it, however, was mutual accountability. The friends pressured one another to come out for each festival, to help organize, to lend a hand. This group ran the events for many years and provided many of their own resources to make each day an exciting and dynamic festival. Recalling the Bello barter days, participants often underscored how transformative it was that this collective experience unleashed sharing: of food, time, knowledge, sights and sounds, and dancing partners.

Over the course of seven years, diverse residents of Bello and neighboring municipios met four or five times a year in a local park in what eventually became a large celebration centered on the direct exchange of products and services, without the use of conventional or alternative monies. Participants shared coffee and a collective lunch, enjoyed artistic and educational activities (workshops on how to make kites, origami, and music; displays of antique scientific equipment; painting, music, and poetry readings), and celebrated the wealth of resources in the community and the chance to gather publicly. The only cost was a thousand pesos for lunch. Trading was minimal—reportedly reaching only a hundred fifty trades per day—but became increasingly important.

The barter days quickly expanded to include over a hundred people, and it became one of only a few social spaces that integrated the entire family across multiple generations. The Casa de la Cultura, a government entity whose director was part of the initial circle of friends, provided logistical and economic support for these fairs, which it saw as an important element in a broader campaign to promote a *cultura ciudadana* (civic culture), to stimulate *convivencia* (living together peacefully), and to support the municipio's unusually large population of artists. As time passed, the organizers began reflecting on the project in new ways, appreciating not only the social benefits but also the economic potential of alternative exchange in a city with high rates of unemployment. Thus, the initial response to social alienation and dehumanization took on a co-revolutionary contagion. Organizers also increasingly imagined it as a response to the problems of capitalism and a possibility for "responsible consumption based on necessities rather than fashions."

Interestingly, these early barterers' response to violence was surprisingly similar to that of postgenocide Mayan widows in Guatemala. Just as Bello's artists used barter to claim public space that was usually off limits, Mayan widows used "development projects, their own bodies, and . . . evangelical worship to reinvigorate community and kin networks by pushing the limits of permissible spaces in a militarized society" (Green 1999, 171). And both groups began to see recuperation from violence as necessarily involving the restoration of social relations and cultural values that "regarded survival as a collective enterprise," though admittedly more so in Guatemala than in Bello.

Luis Alberto was especially inspired by barter. He envisioned this project as part of a broader solidarity economy social movement and created a newsletter to educate people about barter. *Truequiando* (later renamed *Al Trueque*) was published on a semiregular basis between 1999 and 2005. It informed readers about community events, included classifieds for businesses that accepted barter, and taught readers about the transnational solidarity economy movement.

As the years wore on, the organizing team gradually unraveled. A conflict about the nature of barter days was part of the problem—some organizers were increasingly passionate about the economic potential of barter, while others rebelled against this sense of "seriousness" and importance. They also faced the usual challenges of organizing. The increasing demands of organizing barter fairs and its lack of novelty eroded some organizers' passion at the same time that the regular stuff of life—job offers in distant cities, the increased family responsibilities that come with children, changes of residence or the need to care for elderly parents—presented other obstacles. Also, the system lost a key ally when a change in government brought a new director into the Casa de la Cultura, someone with a much more conventional view of the arts. The resurgence of armed groups in the area and their increased intervention in local politics further discouraged organizers and participants. In 2001, the group finally ended the barter days. The idea of bringing barter to a broader public and expanding its economic impact never bore fruit, at least not in Bello.

This was not the end of barter, though. The seeds that these events had planted continued to sprout through the work of individual participants. The former director of the Casa de la Cultura organized several annual barter fairs at the technical school where he now worked, and many of the artists continued bartering among themselves, sometimes for significant services like school tuition and therapy. More importantly, though, Luis Alberto shifted his energy to Medellín, where he had come into contact with the organizers of the city's other two pioneering barter systems. Far from a failure, Bello's Barter Days were, in the words of one organizer, "one of the most important social laboratories where this solidarity practice with ancestral roots could be tested, and although it was sometimes viewed as utopic, it proved its value and projected its possibilities into new processes developed in other realms" (Vásquez Montoya 2005, 46).

## Altamira's Barter Fairs

Independently of the organizing in Bello, residents of Altamira initiated barter fairs on May 23, 1999. Altamira is a mega–apartment complex in Medellín's Robledo neighborhood that houses over six thousand middle- and lower-middle-class residents. The apartments were initially built for schoolteachers and professors, but the population has diversified over the years. Altamira did not escape the violence and disorder of the 1980s and 1990s; the neighborhood's public spaces became flophouses for drug abusers, and some apartments were operating bases for drug traffickers and assassins. Not surprisingly, the social atmosphere deteriorated as many inhabitants moved out and the remainder withdrew into the safety of their homes and nuclear families. By the end of the 1990s, however, security within the complex was improving and residents reemerged to reestablish social networks.

In this context, four neighbors discovered Argentina's Redes de Trueque (barter networks). One of them, Guillermo Moyano, was an Argentine living in Colombia. Intrigued by the possibility of acquiring goods and services without money, they decided to see if barter would work in Altamira. Rather than the simple, direct exchange of goods and services used in Bello, Altamira's organizers adapted the Argentine system of "multi-reciprocal barter" using a "facilitator." They created their own currency, known as Altamires, to facilitate trade. These Altamires were simple paper triangles with values of one-half, one, five, and ten. On the day of the fair, each participant would report to the organizers' table, where they would present the full line of products they wanted to trade. The organizers and trader would negotiate a value for each product, and the organizers would give the participant Altamires in exchange for these products, thus putting Altamires into circulation and bringing all of the products under the central control of the organizers. Once all products entered the system, the organizers would display them with their corresponding prices and participants would use their Altamires to acquire the products of their choice. Clearly, this system was much more formal than Bello's and quantified value in a monetized way.

Before organizing their first fair, the organizers wanted to pique community interest and sow the undercurrents of their own ideological orientation. They hung small fliers around the complex that said simply, in large letters, "Adios al vil metal" (Goodbye, vile metal). A month later, when they figured that the curiosity had lingered long enough, they hung a second set of fliers in the same locations announcing that the "Altamira barter club" invited the entire community to a barter fair on the following Sunday. Early in the morning on May 23, they set up the first barter fair on a shady lawn. With a few tables of used books, movies, and music and a stack of Altamires, they waited.

Children were among the first to arrive. Wandering by as they romped through the neighborhood, they asked about the books and movies and were surprised to learn that they could have anything they wanted if they simply brought something in exchange. Many returned home to pick through their old books and toys, selecting the ones that they would trade for Altamires so they could acquire other goods at the fair. The kids, reported organizer Carlos Alberto, were proud of their trades. They felt empowered, "like adults with the means in their pockets to acquire whatever caught their fancy." Although the organizers insisted that Altamires didn't share the pernicious qualities of money, the children certainly approached the currency as play money with real benefits. Suspicious parents soon followed to see how their children had gotten the new books and toys they were bringing home, and the barter fair gained steam.

By the end of the day people were still coming, asking that the trading not stop. They had exchanged three thousand five hundred objects that would have cost an estimated 15 million pesos (nearly $9,500) in the formal market, and the unifying effect of this simple activity was impressive (López López 1999).

Surprised by their success and inspired by the interest of children, the organizers hosted another fair in October centered on Halloween costumes and the exchange of toy weapons for nonviolent toys donated by a recycling cooperative. In the land of magical realism, it only made sense to use an alternative currency to demilitarize playtime among six-year-olds. Trade increased to four thousand five hundred products in this second market, and then to seven thousand in the January market, which saved residents approximately 35 million pesos (approx. $19,000) on school supplies and textbooks (*Semana* 1999). They also used the barter fairs to inventory the supply and demand of services and knowledge in the apartment complex, with the goal of creating a directory of traders. Through these events, they hoped to demonstrate that barter was an "extremely viable alternative to lighten the economic burden of normal households' expenses" (Echavarría n.d., 19) and to form a permanent barter group in Altamira.

While a continuous, daily trade of goods and services never developed in Altamira, the barter group continued to organize two to four thematic barter fairs each year, the most popular of which was always the annual textbook barter, and their efforts prompted informal bartering. Carlos Alberto—an organizer who was particularly energized by his antiauthoritarian distaste for state-led currencies, wage labor, and bank debt—twice managed to pay his overdue condo fees by repairing and painting the fence surrounding the apartment complex and helped other tenants do the same. Throughout my fieldwork, he continued to provide tutoring services to high school and college students, some of which he negotiated via barter. In addition to the economic benefits, quantifiable in terms of reduced household expenditures, the fairs increased community integration and "convivencia" between children, young adults, and adults. They also gave children an opportunity to develop their own leadership skills. Several youth began to organize their own fairs with their own facilitator, the Altaminiño (roughly, "Altakids").

By 2006, Guillermo Moyano, the Argentine organizer, had turned his attention to promoting barter in other parts of the city, so the core barter group decided to test how much Altamira's residents had embraced barter. They announced that they would not organize any new fairs on their own but that they would assist anyone who picked up the mantle of leadership. When nobody stepped up, they concluded that there was not enough support to continue. If the community wanted to be only passive beneficiaries of others' work, Carlos Alberto told me, then the philosophy of collaborative construction and *protagonismo* (protagonism, or a sense of agency) was falling flat. In 2008, a new community group began bartering in a relatively closed circle, and there have been numerous calls for Carlos Alberto to reinitiate barter fairs. He has responded with occasional events, but without the participation and frequency of the early years.

Altamira's adaptation of the Argentine multi-reciprocal barter model remains one of the most popular—and most problematic—ways of bartering in Colombia. Altamira's organizers liked the Argentine use of facilitators because it made trading easier and faster. Also, this system ensured consistent pricing and established an equivalence between the total value of products and the total value of the community currency. Since facilitators were circulated according to the exact value of products, this effectively eliminated the scarcity that drives so much exploitation in the conventional monetary system. Because of this equivalence, if everyone followed the rules, the market day would end with all products in new hands and all Altamires back with the organizers. If products remained because nobody wanted them, it was the organizers' responsibility to either auction those products for the remaining Altamires or save them for the next barter fair. In Altamira, the organizers wanted to open barter fairs to the entire community, rather than restricting them to members as was common in Argentina. Also, they chose a thematic focus for each barter fair to simplify the markets.

Reflecting on this style of barter, Carlos Alberto argued that it was useful as an early stage of experimentation because it allowed a lot of people to try out barter, but that it should not be replicated in other areas. He described multi-reciprocal barter as a "monster" (*malcrianza*) that corrupted barter exchange by putting organizers in the middle of each trade. Because traders never interact with each other, trade relationships become depersonalized, products lose their full histories, and traders are able to maintain their conventional mentality as consumers using a different type of currency but shopping just the same. Other barter systems have also found that the simplicity of a thematic barter is easy, but the reduced diversity of goods inevitably makes thematic markets less useful. Still, the centralized control of multi-reciprocal barter is alluring when introducing barter to new communities, and its similarity to conventional shopping seems to help newcomers trust more in multi-reciprocal barter than other types of exchange. As a result, it has been carried around Colombia as a handy way of demonstrating how barter and alternative currencies could work, and it remains popular in barter trainings.

## Pajarito's Local Economic System

Also in 1999, while residents of Altamira were organizing their first barter fairs, an energetic and experimental new Junta de Acción Comunal took office in the village of Pajarito. The JACs were legally designated in the 1950s to stimulate local development and grassroots democracy, and though they have had mixed success and been the target of paramilitary violence, this particular JAC decided to fully embrace these original goals. Pajarito, home to about two thousand people at the time, is located in a rural sector of Medellín that was extremely isolated. There were no paved roads into the village, and at night it stood out as a dark patch amid the sparkling lights of the city's western mountains. Most families in Pajarito had lived there for generations, and some older residents went to the city so infrequently that they had supposedly never seen a stoplight. Village politics had long been run by the same few families, but a group of university-educated newcomers shook things up.

Julio, a hydrologist at the Universidad Nacional, and Clara, an engineer, moved to the area seeking a quieter and more connected community. They were astounded by the warm reception from their new neighbors and the safety of the area. They could leave doors unlocked and walk the hills at night—even in this corner of one of the world's most violent cities—and if they left their clothes drying in the yard when a rainstorm came, they could rest assured that the neighbors would bring in their laundry. Although they were certainly not seen as natives, this strong sense of community heightened their commitment to the village. Thus, when they learned of plans to locate a garbage dump in the community, they used their backgrounds in hydrology and engineering to educate their neighbors about potential impacts and led the charge against the project.

Later, when municipal funds promised to fulfill many residents' dream of finally having a paved road network through the village, Julio and Clara suggested that they think twice. They were worried that the roads would change the character of the village and bring violence from adjacent neighborhoods. But they didn't want to simply resist the hopes of their new neighbors, nor did they want to single-handedly oppose a project that would enrich a powerful local family, so they framed their challenge as a series of questions and conversations. It turned out that other neighbors shared their concerns but longed for the ease of movement that roads would provide. At first, rejecting roads seemed crazy, absolutely counter to visions of "progress" and the economic opportunity that would come from better access to the city. Through the conversations, however, people remembered the long-abandoned network of trails that crisscrossed the village and they eventually voted to recuperate the trails network rather than approve road construction. These two political actions mobilized the community in new ways. People began to envision themselves as active participants in local politics, as owners and caretakers of their community, and as capable of planning their own development.

Some of the community members asked Julio and Clara to run for the JAC, and they were elected with the hope that the community might determine the shape of local politics, rather than vice versa. The new JAC dedicated itself to a series of community projects: ecological work parties, a new local theater group, special programs for youth and the elderly, and a fresh take on the local economy. Julio, now the JAC president, asked a fellow professor about local development strategies for Pajarito. The JAC eventually commissioned María Alejandra Múnera, one of Professor Gabriel Awad's students, to study the issue. Her undergraduate thesis concluded that a LETS-type system might significantly strengthen Pajarito's local economy, so they decided to try it out. Many people were doubtful that the project would work, but they were willing to try. As one eighty-year-old man reportedly told Múnera, "Your idea is really nice. I'll help you, but it's not going to work here." Julio explained that the real problem "was the newness, because the money system already has so much strength but these alternatives are unknown." After an initial attempt, the LETS experiment went on hold while Julio and Clara took a one-year fellowship in Italy, but when they returned in 2000, they found renewed interest in making the system work.

For the next seven years, the Pajarito Sistema de Economía Local (Local Economic System, or SEL) operated as a core group of twenty to thirty members who used their own accounting system to trade goods, services, and knowledge without the use of conventional or alternative monies. These members, most of whom were local residents and active members of the JAC, traded among themselves on a regular basis. Each time two of the members made a trade, they noted the details of the transaction in a small checkbook-type registry. These trades were then tabulated in a centralized accounting system. For example, when Doña Marta gave *arepas* and tomatoes to Clara, both would record their trade. Doña Marta would then receive a credit that she could redeem by accepting items from any member of the system and Clara would receive a debit that she could eliminate by offering goods to another member. Thus, while products are exchanged directly from one person to another, the debits and credits are to the system as a whole. This restructures the economy as a collective rather than personal venture. It gives all members a stake in helping each other succeed as producers and consumers.

Because Pajarito was rural but near the urban edge, its residents had a large diversity of products and services to offer. The SEL's directory—a simple, stapled packet of wallet-sized papers—advertised over one hundred goods and services including food, garden supplies, gardening and home repair services, transportation, nursing and first aid, and educational assistance (Table 4). The system was a valuable source of everyday household needs, occasional and emergency services, and educational and recreational services.

A second component of the Pajarito SEL was a quarterly bazaar open to the entire city. These bazaars were intended to show a broader public that barter was a possibility and to promote trade between the city and the country but with prices set so that rural people could access goods that were typically beyond their means. Julio explained, "In the conventional economy, if I compare a shirt and beans, it takes a lot of beans to come to an equivalency. So we created a

## Table 4
## Goods, services, and knowledge offered in the Pajarito Local Economic System

**Food**
- Arepas
- Garlic
- Herbs
- Bananas
- Onions
- Party platters
- Traditional foods for special events
- Fruits and vegetables

**Odd Jobs (*Oficios varios*)**
- Hauling of small loads
- House cleaning
- Assistant for general work
- Carpentry
- Electrical work
- Painting
- Plumbing
- Shopping
- Shipping and deliveries
- Trips to Medellín
- Motorcycle taxi

**Knowledge**
- Computer training
- Handicrafts classes
- Household appliance repair classes
- Basic English
- Elementary education tutoring
- Solidarity economy seminars

**Gardening**
- Compost and soil
- Garden work
- Pruning
- Fertilizers

**Services**
- Help with productive projects (especially agriculture)
- Construction consultations
- First aid
- Agricultural consultations
- Yoga classes
- Song composition
- Child care
- Architectural design
- Blood pressure testing and healing
- Sewing

**Other Goods and Services**
- Sewing machine repair
- Bags
- Photocopies
- Construction materials
- Educational materials
- Newspaper publicity
- Recycled paper

new system of equivalences that had nothing to do with 'socially necessary labor.' . . . For example, we'd value one kilo of beans at five thousand pesos and one pair of blue jeans at five thousand pesos. That way farmers could have more value in this system and actually acquire the things that were hard for them to get otherwise." The bazaars used multi-reciprocal barter with facilitators as their core mode of exchange and established a parallel space for direct barter for people who didn't want to use facilitators and for goods that were not accepted for trade by the main organizers. These bazaars would draw hundreds of people and led to the exchange of over 1.5 million pesos ($700–1,000) worth of goods.

Unlike some barter fairs that operate today, they banned all monetary exchanges because they saw those as "a form of pollution."

The permanent members of the SEL met regularly to review their accounts and discuss imbalances in the system. Like the conventional economy, the SEL required constant monitoring and adjustments. Organizers helped members learn to balance their production and consumption to avoid the overaccumulation of credits or debits, and some members always needed reminders about how the system worked. Clara once recalled an old farmer who loved the system. After a lifetime in the country, he could build or repair just about anything and was thrilled when the SEL helped him share these talents with neighbors. In the spirit of rural solidarity, however, he always thought of these as gifts rather than trades. He was happy to help a neighbor fix their roof or install an irrigation system, and while he may have expected some sort of delayed reciprocity, he didn't feel the need to maintain strict records of transactions. "It was a bit contradictory," Clara said, "since the goal was to move away from a calculating economic mentality and he was already doing that, but I always had to remind that farmer to record the services he provided so he could benefit from the system and it wouldn't fall out of balance."

The university-educated members of the JAC treated the project as a large experiment and constantly brainstormed what might happen if they tinkered with the system in different ways. The constant self-evaluation and adjustments helped refine the system, but also generated a degree of cliquishness or hierarchy within the barter group based on people's interest in theorizing and critical reflection; some participants felt excluded. Toward the end of the SEL experiment, the group decided that barter needed to go deeper than exchange, intervening directly in production. They established seven community gardens to deepen solidarity and grow the produce that would back their currency, but never fully developed a community production system before problems emerged.

When I first met Julio, tucked in the corner of a busy café, he described the SEL with such excitement, such passion for what they had accomplished, that even its collapse seemed like only a minor setback. Julio and Clara had known from the beginning that their days were numbered. Even before they joined the JAC, an urban development plan (the Plan Parcial Pajarito) had dictated that a hundred thousand people from one of the city's roughest neighborhoods would be relocated to housing projects in the village. "Pajarito could never sustain such an influx of people," he said. "When the newcomers arrived, they brought guns and illegal economies along with their furniture, and they regarded the barter bazaars with suspicion. These newcomers didn't understand the barter philosophy and many weren't interested in learning." People left the markets feeling insulted if organizers rejected some of their products or cheated if they couldn't find products they liked in exchange, and the organizers simply could not explain that the market belonged to the whole community and was not solely their responsibility. Julio said,

> Brian, we never thought it would get this far. When we were doing this we never thought that it would be something that would continue forever. All of these things started to take on a political meaning. "Why are you doing this without money? What is your problem with money? Why won't you take my money?" We never wanted it to be political. We knew that it *was* political, but we never wanted to proselytize and we didn't want to get involved with [political] parties, to compete with parties, to compete with people with guns. We also rejected funds from the city because we figured any funds that came in from outside would come with conditions, and we didn't want any conditions imposed on us. All of this was one big social experiment, and we wanted to maintain it as long as it was fun, as long as people approached it with happiness and enthusiasm. But when the moment came when that enthusiasm diminished, we stopped.

Julio leaned closer to me and lowered his voice to a whisper as he told me about this turbulent ending, and his eyes dampened. One day people came to the market with guns to make demands. Around the same time, one of the most active members of the SEL, a "hippie kid" who had grown up in Pajarito and was loved by everyone, was killed after he twice defied a local gang's orders to cut his hair. And then Julio received a phone call one night summoning him to a meeting with the leader of an armed group that had flowed in with the new residents of Pajarito. He went, and he was fortunate enough to return, but that was the end of the SEL. This, explained Julio, is what violence does: "A big part of the violence is simply to destroy collectives. . . . The damage to the social fabric is the worst. The destruction of collectives is hard to repair."[1]

The Pajarito system was never perfect. Trade levels remained lower than desired and the bulk of trade was concentrated among a handful of participants, as is common with LETS systems and indeed with all alternative trading systems. Nonetheless, and despite its nonproselytizing approach, the Pajarito SEL continues to remind many people in Medellín of the possibility of constructing solidarity economies that have both economic and community-building impacts and that achieve the regularity of everyday exchange. Julio said they never foresaw the impact it would have. It was "revolutionary" and remains "unforgettable . . . an experience that we will repeat if conditions change." We learned a tremendous amount, he said. "Parallel economies are not substitutes for the normal economies. We already knew this. But we learned that there *are* alternatives, that there really *is* a possibility to do things differently. At the beginning, we never would have imagined what we ended up achieving. [But these alternative economies require] sympathy in the broader society. They require people who understand, who believe, who cooperate." In Pajarito, that proved the most difficult obstacle. In the context of Medellín's ongoing war for economic and territorial control, broad sympathy was impossible. "Everything started to take on a political meaning."

Each of these experiments approached barter for slightly different reasons, drew on different inspirations, and developed their own mode of bartering. None of the three initial experiments continues to the present day, though their influence goes on. As Julio noted, they demonstrated that barter is a real possibility and that people can create their own economies rather than simply resigning themselves to the economies they were born into. These projects also helped barter organizers articulate their own alternatives to development, in which well-being was centered on rehumanization, *convivencia*, and fun. In this model, barter was an important tool for peacefare because it generated people-led economies that reestablished social relations, emphasized collective and collaborative interactions rather than controlling and competitive transactions, and re-embedded the economy in a different set of norms. This inspiration energized individual barter promoters, who vigorously spread the message and practice of barter across the city and even to other parts of the country and beyond. The nature of barter today is a direct outgrowth of their efforts.

## The Spread of Barter

While Medellín's early barter experiments were established independently, they came together for the first time in 1999, when Pajarito's Gabriel Awad, Altamira's Guillermo Moyano, and Bello's Luis Alberto Jaramillo sat on a panel with Argentine barter activist and scholar Heloisa Primavera. The meeting had little impact on Pajarito's organizers, who were staunch in their desire for a purely local project, but it transformed how Jaramillo and Moyano worked. As Jaramillo said, "The two of us didn't separate again after this time." They began to advance a vision of barter as a much larger political and economic project that could be developed across the city and the region.

Luis Alberto launched the Bello barter newsletters as a way of articulating this vision to himself and others. A few months later, when Guillermo Moyano couldn't travel to a barter event in Buenos Aires for personal reasons, Luis Alberto went in his stead. The monthlong trip offered glimpses of his dream made real. He bartered for airplane tickets, traded his way across Argentina, visited some of the largest barter markets (which, at the time, hosted thousands of barterers), and saw what he called "a noncapitalist world." There were shortcomings, including a lack of clarity and consistency in what the Argentines were creating, but he found it incredible to see that we could in fact create our own economies.

When he returned to Medellín, Jaramillo was obligated to present his findings to the Comfenalco *caja de compensación* in exchange for the airplane ticket they had purchased for him.[2] Jaramillo realized he "needed to learn to tell the story of barter." He had to put words to the vision. So he immersed himself in barter, traveling wherever he saw the word, talking with friends and strangers about it, developing his newsletter and educational materials, joining the Pajarito group and attending their meetings, and probing ancestral forms of barter and similar projects like permaculture and agroecology. Suddenly barter seemed conspicuous across the landscape—a woman in Medellín was bartering out of her garage with a dozen friends, a Catholic radio station in Bogotá featured a barter and solidarity economy show, the Colombo-Americano cultural center traded free English classes for labor, and Comfenalco itself had a textbook exchange. As Jaramillo began viewing barter as an economic project and not merely a form of community building, he realized that it is also an ontological project. "Establishing barter systems," he explained, "actually permits us to live in a different world." If the conventional economy is built on the valuation of goods and services, and people gain prestige based on how much they can acquire or display, barter offers a different world. We become multifaceted humans with inherent value. The goods and services he traded in Bello were mere surface phenomena: "The true reality in barter is our knowledge, skills, and capacities, qualities that are inherent in everyone, and the mutual recognition of our value as humans."

Moyano and Jaramillo established a biweekly forum known as the Minga Nutibara, where people could develop a barter philosophy and exchange goods. Because of his connections with Argentina, Moyano was probably more aware of the economic potential of barter. He became a grounding force for Jaramillo's dreaming and proved very adept at finding support from city and state governments and solidarity economy institutions. Moyano secured a number of contracts that turned barter organizing into a job for himself and, occasionally, his friends. These two charismatic figures—the college-educated Argentine hippie and the local, self-taught Marxist artist—began to formulate and passionately spread the gospel of barter. (See one articulation of barter's values in Figure 3.)[3]

## Bartering across Antioquia

Surprisingly, the first major government support came not at the local level but at the direct request of the departmental governor. Governor Guillermo Gaviria (2001–2002), intrigued by barter's potential to support grassroots development, prioritized it as one of the solidarity economy activities that his government would support.[4] As a result, the Institute for the Development of Antioquia (IDEA) invited Moyano and Jaramillo to implement the Truequeando por Antioquia (Bartering across Antioquia) project as part its "social strengthening" program. By this point, both organizers had networked with other solidarity economy experiences in Latin America and had experience conducting

# PRINCIPIOS Y VALORES
## en los que se sustenta

**1.** El trueque es una forma de economía solidaria, donde nada se pierde, nada se regala : todo se recicla, todo se valora.

**2.** La participación es libre, abierta y plural. Quien quiera participar debe estar dispuesto y dispuesta a renovarse en valores como la reciprocidad, la comprensión, el apoyo mutuo, el bienestar común, la solidaridad, el respeto, la confianza, la responsabilidad y la equidad.

**3.** Truequiamos teniendo en cuenta los intereses, necesidades y gustos nuestros y de los otros y otras. Por lo tanto es un ejercicio que requiere permanentemente el diálogo y la concertación.

**4.** El trueque es una experiencia de vida: la vivimos en los eventos como las ferias y encuentros. La idea es que cada vez más haga parte de nuestra cotidianidad.

**5.** Sostenemos que es posible reemplazar la competencia estéril, el lucro y la especulación por la reciprocidad entre las personas.

**6.** Los productos y bienes que disponemos en este espacio deben ser de buena calidad, estar en buen estado. Si son alimentos que sean agroecológicos o sanos, tener utilidad real y que no refuercen el consumismo.

**7.** Multiplicar los beneficios y la importancia de esta practica en nuestras comunidades y organizaciones.

**8.** Destacar los valores de usos y los beneficios de los productos y servicios que se dispondrán al trueque. Así habrá también intercambio de saberes. Por ejemplo_uso de una semilla.

**9.** Con el trueque NO buscamos promover artículos o servicios, sino ayudarnos mutuamente a alcanzar un sentido de vida superior, mediante el trabajo, la comprensión y el intercambio justo.

**10.** Vivir esta experiencia de intercambio como una posibilidad de REINVENTAR LA VIDA en el mismo acto de reinventar el mercado, a partir de la construcción de nuevos vínculos sociales desde el interior de los pequeños grupos.

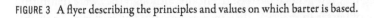

FIGURE 3  A flyer describing the principles and values on which barter is based.

workshops, trainings, and discussions about barter. The project, which continued into 2004, promoted barter as a tool for solidarity markets and "for the development of community-focused local governments" (Vásquez Montoya 2005, 53). In this sense, it represented both a scaling up and a new co-revolutionary process of barter as democratic polity building.

The team planned regional workshops to teach government officials the philosophy and practice of barter and methods for establishing permanent barter nodes in their community. To complement the workshops, they organized barter demos using multi-reciprocal barter with currencies named after ecological or cultural features of the hosting municipalities. By this point, they had the methodology down to a science: their training materials show exactly how the market area should be designed and describe several different roles for the dozen or so market organizers that they recommend for each fair.

During the project's first year, 2003, Moyano and Jaramillo report conducting more than thirty trainings and fifty-six barter fairs in thirty different municipios of Antioquia, including thirty-one markets focused on textbooks and ten on harvests. To make a case for barter according to conventional economic metrics, they estimated the total savings generated by these fairs: more than 436 million pesos ($156,000). These events permitted the exchange of fifty thousand products using at least twenty new local currencies. Fourteen took place in schools, universities, or neighborhoods of Medellín, and several were held in other departments of Colombia. The project extended the idea and practice of barter into dozens of partner organizations including government agencies, universities, cooperatives, development and pro-peace NGOs, and museums.

The project also prompted them to create the more or less monthly e-newsletter, *No Nos Llamamos Plata* (We're Not Called Money), to advertise their events, promote other alternative events (especially those related to nonviolence), and detail the philosophical underpinnings of barter. They found inspiration in thinkers as disparate as Jesus, Karl Marx, Manfred Max-Neef, Muhammad Yunus, Thomas Jefferson, and Amartya Sen, though they located the core of barter in the creation myths of their "Amerikan ancestors" who "through the millennia have known how to cultivate life in abundance, without exploiting or doing harm."

The IDEA renewed the project for a second year and especially encouraged mayors, school boards, and principals to hold textbook barters "as a way of responding to the difficult situation and the lack of money that many parents face when it comes time to buy supplies and books for their school-age children" (IDEA 2004). In 2004, Moyano and Jaramillo therefore focused on textbooks, organizing very few general barters. Ironically, although they were delimiting the utility of barter in practice, they increasingly pitched barter as a valuable marketing option for small businesses. They were attempting to extend the project to other parts of the country (informally changing the project name to Truekeando por Colombia and proposing a Colombian Barter Network) and to link it to other alternative projects like permaculture and ecovillages.

An interviewee who was well positioned to observe these activities suggested that Moyano and Jaramillo vastly overstated the number of trainings and markets they organized. It seems relatively clear that, despite calling their workshops "How to Develop a Permanent Barter Node," they devoted relatively little energy to the follow-up activities necessary to establish sustained and diversified barter systems. Many of the barter fairs and barter groups remained short-term, declining with changes in community commitment, the political composition of the local government, and especially once the IDEA project ended and money for workshops and promoters dried up. With a few exceptions, they had not nurtured the local-level organization necessary to "develop a permanent barter node." This is the background to Luis Alberto Jaramillo's lament that *sistemas no hay.*"

Nonetheless, the impact of the program cannot be denied. It drew significant attention to barter as a form of marketing and established a precedent for supporting barter within many of Medellín's most important solidarity economy organizations, such as Confiar and Comfenalco, and in universities and government agencies. Within Medellín, this spawned barter groups in two urban areas (La América and Carlos E Restrepo), the rural area of Santa Elena, and the neighboring municipio of Envigado, and it enabled organizers to spread their experiences to other parts of the country, including the departments of Cundinamarca (Bogotá, Cota, Zipaquirá, and Chia), Santander (Vélez), Vaupes (Mitú), Tolima (Ibague), and Caldas (Manizales), and to other countries. Some communities continued to pursue barter, such as in the municipio of Bojayá, where a farmers' association won a grant from the Pan-American Development Foundation to increase farm production and barter the surplus within the community. Finally, working barter into departmental and (later) municipal development plans established an official channel for government support.

On the other hand, by so thoroughly pushing a single modality of barter—the multi-reciprocal barter markets employing local currencies and often focused on a single theme—the Truequeando por Antioquia team framed barter as a rather rigid and limited economic alternative rather than a flexible tool filled with possibility. Thus, Carlos Alberto's description of multi-reciprocal barter as a "malcrianza" is reminiscent of James Scott's (1998) argument for why many centralized, state-based welfare projects have failed. For administrative purposes, they depend on "thin simplifications" that "can never generate a functioning community, city, or economy" because they are too removed from the rich, complex, and collectively embodied "practical knowledge" of real life (Scott 1998, 310). They don't allow people to use their pragmatic pluralism to craft their own well-being. Many people in the solidarity economy formed their opinions of barter based on the foundation laid by this project, and they complain that barter is not practical because it is too radical in its opposition to money, is too rigid, and does not touch a broad enough sphere of the household economy. Combining these perspectives, we see that grassroots movements are not immune to the allure of "thin simplifications"; at least some currents of the barter movement also created a model of barter that was too simplified to be practically useful or culturally transformative. Nonetheless, broad thirst for a socially and economically rewarding alternative economy fueled the continual emergence of new barter systems, and in some cases the persistence necessary to sustain them.

### Community Markets: Carlos E Restrepo, Santa Elena, and La América

On July 12, 2003, as part of "Bartering Across Antioquia," the Junta de Acción Comunal of Carlos E Restrepo and the neighborhood's "group of friends of the elderly" organized the first barter market in that liberal and culturally active community. The JAC saw the market and associated cultural events as a way to build neighborhood solidarity. In December, they secured support from the Secretary of Social Development and the Corporación Antioquia Avanza to push this further, organizing Merkados de Intercambio Solidario or Merkados de Trueke as a complement to the already-existing, monthly Merkados Verdes, which offered fair trade links between small-scale, sustainable farmers and urban consumers. The markets featured more than fifty booths, and a report from the April 2005 market estimated that the total value of bartered projects was 750,000 pesos ($300).

The Carlos E group continued to organize barter fairs even after the IDEA project ended. In August 2006, after having held eight barter fairs and with support from the Corporación Colombia Sostenible (essentially the same organizers behind the IDEA project), they formed the Permanent Barter Group of Carlos E Restrepo. They remained more or less active until 2008, when a new JAC began to restrict the use of public spaces. While some informal bartering continues to take place at the produce, arts and crafts, and book fairs that are common in the neighborhood, no organized barter system has reemerged in recent years.

Following the model of Carlos E, the Corporación Colombia Sostenible sought assistance from the Secretary for Social Development to organize a barter group in Santa Elena. Santa Elena offers an interesting mix of small farmers whose families have worked the same land for generations, middle-class and wealthy urbanites who spend their weekends and vacations in the cool upland landscape, and hippies, artists, and other "strange bugs" who have decided to permanently settle in the area. Like Pajarito and even more than Carlos E, Santa Elena is widely considered an "opportune environment" for alternative economic activities like barter.

The Corporación Colombia Sostenible organized Santa Elena's first barter fair and a series of workshops on October 14, 2005. They continued to convene local farmers, artisans, and artists over the following months and consolidated Santa Elena's Permanent Barter Group in December. From December 4, 2005, until 2016, with only one exception (when federal elections prohibited public events) this group organized a barter fair on the third Sunday of every month. They also printed three barter directories that included residents of Santa Elena, urban Medellín, and various other municipalities who were willing to trade goods, services, and knowledge. The barter fairs always included cultural activities (at a minimum an open mic and sometimes more planned activities like concerts or literature readings) and sometimes appropriate technology workshops known as Festivales de Ideas Productivas Solidarias (Festivals of Productive, Solidaristic Ideas). The organizers even formed an alliance with the local bus company to accept their alternative currency, the Floricambio, as partial payment for bus fare on several routes. The Santa Elena fair, which I describe more fully in the next chapter, demonstrates the importance of creative experimentation with barter models and persistent organizing.

The neighborhood of La América attempted to follow Santa Elena's lead, dedicating money to barter in the participatory budgeting process. After a brief conflict about who would execute the project—an environmental organization or a college—they managed to form a small group that developed informational materials and held three community barters. The people from La América forged links with Carlos E and Santa Elena, and all three systems agreed to accept one another's currencies. When the La América group dissolved, however, those members who had money left over flooded the Santa Elena market to spend their money. Because they didn't bring any new products to contribute, this created an imbalance in the Santa Elena market that prompted inflation and resentment.

All of these systems moved away from the multi-reciprocal barter system, functioning instead as typical markets. Producers had their own booths where they could display their goods, and while sales in pesos were often forbidden, producers engaged in face-to-face trades in exchange for local currencies or other goods, and they negotiated their own values. This flexibility and decentralization likely contributed, in large part, to the importance of the markets. In Santa Elena, where the monthly barter market continued for over a decade, organizers repeatedly adjusted the rules of trade to reflect "practical knowledge" and people's lived realities. As we will see in the next chapter, virtually all participants mix direct trade, trade using facilitators, trade on credit, and some sales for pesos.

## Proliferation across the Solidarity Economy

Barter markets have found their way into schools and universities, theater groups, environmental NGOs, agroecology training programs, multiple government agencies, some of the city's largest cooperatives and microcredit organizations, the charitable foundation of the Éxito chain of grocery stores, and the municipal and state development plans. To my knowledge, this proliferation of barter makes Medellín fairly unique globally. Many of these groups engage in one of the least demanding modalities of barter: once-a-year, thematic events. While these events do not constitute diversified economic systems that

significantly affect socioeconomic vulnerability, they can significantly contribute to household economies and show real promise for scaling up (see
chapter 4).

Several organizations stage their own barter events, separate from the work
of Medellín's main barter activists. The largest of these is the annual textbook
exchange coordinated by the Comfenalco *caja de compensación* and the Fundación Éxito, the charitable arm of the Éxito grocery store chain, owned by the
French multinational Éxito Group. Since 2001 Comfenalco has run an
extremely well-organized exchange of secondhand textbooks during the first
month of the school year. As the program has expanded across the country, it
has grown to serve fourteen to sixteen thousand people per year and to generate
annual savings of 700 million to 1 billion pesos (approx. $300,000–500,000,
depending on exchange rates; statistics provided by Comfenalco). These are
extremely important figures given that numerous researchers have concluded
that a leading contributor to the school dropout rate is the scarcity of family
resources and the high cost of supplies, which can exceed the monthly minimum wage in the month that school starts (Díaz Tafur 2005 and other articles
in the special issue of *Economía Colombiana*; Reimers 2000; Rodríguez and
Valenzuela 1998). Barter thus reduces short-term financial stresses and long-
term economic vulnerability by permitting increased investment in education.

A second independent program with similar results is the Programa Canje
(Exchange Program) at the Colombo-Americano Cultural Institute. In 1990,
the Colombo-Americano began to implement this labor exchange program
inspired by the director's experiences in the United States. The Colombo-
Americano offers perhaps the best English-language instruction in Medellín,
and large numbers of people were applying for grants to study for free. Through
the Programa Canje, students work forty hours per month in exchange for four
to five weeks of free English classes, free entry to the institute's movie theater,
and library membership. The program has allowed them to make English classes
available to lower-income people, but "without supporting a culture of *asisten-
cialismo*" (dependency or welfarism). It also ensures that students are seriously
committed to their studies and supports the functioning of the institution. The
economic, educational, and employability benefits to students are tremendous,
but the benefits to the institution are equally large. The program brings a diverse
group of highly skilled workers into the Colombo at no expense to the organization other than the cost of administering the program. They have had up to
a hundred twenty Canje workers at any given time (the equivalent of thirty full-
time staff), and thirty of their permanent employees began working with the
Colombo-Americano as Canjes.

In addition, after the relative success of the IDEA project, barterers began
to find support from the city government of Medellín, through the Secretary
for Social Development, the Juntas de Acción Comunal, and participatory

budgeting. This led to a range of spin-off projects. In 2004, the city department of sports and recreation (INDER) asked Moyano and Juan Carlos Ortega (another collaborator on the IDEA project) to organize a youth barter fair focused on toys, an activity that the IDEA has replicated on their own every year since, with thousands of donated toys and over a thousand participants. In an interview, one of INDER's directors explained that barter "allows children to access toys without having to pay for them, and they come to understand that there are other types of economy. [Also,] the children who participate become businesspeople . . . and they learn to see the world in a different light." Her celebration of businesspeople stems in part from a noncritical stance on capitalism, but it also represents pragmatic pluralism and signals that the programming of capital-friendly states can be multivalent, teaching forms of entrepreneurialism that can be channeled toward capitalism or noncapitalism.

From 2004 through 2006, the San Pedro Cemetery-Museum used a social development grant from the municipal government (worth more than 35 million pesos) to hire Moyano, Ortega, and a team of anthropologists, psychologists, social workers, and public relations personnel to conduct Bazares de la Vida (Bazaars of Life). Located in the poorest and most violent sector of the city, the San Pedro Cemetery-Museum has a strong public outreach mission. Barter markets were meant to create a safe space for community celebration, heal the torn social fabric of the area, provide opportunities for *convivencia*, and offer a marketing possibility for small businesses. After a long process of twenty-one trainings and three practice barter fairs, they held the first Bazar de la Vida on June 12, 2005: 193 small business owners and over a thousand other participants traded 1,386 products for a total value of 5,746,500 pesos ($2,400). The process brought community leaders together in new ways, and the workshops revealed how desperately people needed to speak about violence and social disintegration.

These projects are far from perfect. For one thing, they have involved huge infusions of government funding, infusions that have often eclipsed the estimated economic benefits to participants. INDER's barter fair depends on nearly 9 million pesos of "seed capital" per year to purchase new toys for the market as well as workers' salaries and an additional 3 million pesos in event costs. Some barter organizers have critiqued the INDER barters for emptying barter of its true transformative potential: they argue that children are turned into mere consumers, and the sense that they could be producers, active contributors to an economy, and participants in a face-to-face trade is lost. This critique clearly illustrates their theory that alternative exchange is not noncapitalist unless it provokes a change in worldviews and values. It also hints at the deeper transformations they aim for—which I will discuss in later chapters—related to production, a sense of agency, and ethical negotiation. Finally, working with these activist ideas from the perspective of "revolutionary . . . pero" highlights an important lesson about contemporary governmentality. The INDER project (like many of these government-sponsored barter initiatives) may have the result of disseminating neoliberal ideologies through "antipoverty" and "community-building" projects. The very same projects, however, may have the effect of mobilizing communities on a path toward alternative production and social relations. Clearly, we have to look well beyond official discourses and intentions to ascertain the real effects of potentially neoliberal (or potentially radical) projects.

The Bazares de la Vida had similar shortcomings. While participants there did engage in more direct forms of barter, the project included huge labor costs. INDER and the Museum-Cemetery argue that the benefits of these events, particularly for postviolence social reconstruction, justify these expenses. As the director of the Museum-Cemetery said, she is fine with the large investment because people have learned that "they're not going to go hungry for lack of money" and "they continue to barter in small groups and among neighbors," without the formality of an organized market or system. Periodic events can actually have longer-term payoffs than we sometimes realize, she argued, and these initial imperfections might be justified on that basis.

What all of this barter activity means is that barter has taken on breadth rather than depth. Far from constituting an enclave economy, it has seeped into other realms of social development and solidarity economy. The occasional and intermittent barter events sponsored by this array of organizations are building institutional knowledge of and acceptance for barter. They are creating a broad base of people who understand barter as a potentially useful economic option. Among other benefits, these activities may be laying the foundation for more effective coping in times of major economic crisis, as occurred in Argentina in the early 2000s. And they offer experiments that barter activists can study as they develop their own theories of economic and sociocultural change.

However, it is important to question what exactly participants are learning about barter, and what they are learning to see as barter. The Truequeando por Antioquia project and spin-off events fall into a common trap for barter organizing in Medellín: in order to convince a large public that barter is a real economic possibility, and in order to show participants that it can be easy and pleasurable, organizers teach people styles of barter that are far from their ideal of sustained, diversified, and community-run systems. They also raise unrealistic expectations by modeling barter through events that require huge investments of money and time. And perhaps most importantly they fail to transform market participants from consumers to "prosumers" (producers + consumers), which means they have little impact on people's sense of economic agency, personal value, or the separation of production/consumption that undergirds a logic of scarcity. Many observers from other solidarity economy organizations in Medellín have lost interest in barter. They want to see more practical and quotidian barter systems operating at a realistic scale—much like the system in Pajarito—before they can be convinced of barter's value.

## The State of Barter Today

Barter organizing changed significantly at the end of the 2000s. Guillermo Moyano and Juan Carlos Ortega moved to Venezuela to promote barter as part of President Hugo Chávez's Ministry of Popular Economy; their absence decreased some of the momentum of barter while also opening spaces for new ideas and styles of organizing. Luis Alberto Jaramillo continues to be a key referent for barter, though his main activities fall more in the realm of speaking his dreams than putting them into practice via community organizing. The off-the-cuff, bohemian, and ideologically radical style of many of these original organizers and the resulting lack of follow-up have led many people to discount barter as a "serious" economic possibility.

The task that Santiago outlined in our workshop—establishing a parallel economy complete with new markets, news sources, and governing institutions—is a formidable challenge. Medellín's barter organizers have faced numerous obstacles maintaining *campesino* interest, establishing links along an entire product chain, resolving transport costs, and maintaining fluid communication and collaboration among organizers. These challenges and shortcomings are common across the world's alternative economy systems. Efforts to establish barter systems—like much community work—often fall on one or two people rather than becoming collective initiatives. As a result, organizers often end up working reactively, spending the majority of their energy conducting or trying to win support for small, disarticulated projects rather than developing a larger vision for socioeconomic transformation or a more fine-grained focus on making alternative exchanges feasible on a day-to-day basis. Also, as Julio made clear, there are severe limitations on politicization and alliance building in Colombia related not only to contemporary violence but also to the institutional and cultural legacy of violent political conflict. Barterers are working against concerted efforts to "destroy collectives."

And yet, many people remain hopeful about barter. The Santa Elena barter fair continued for over a decade to provide a living example that community-organized barter can be valuable. The Programa Canje and Comfenalco textbook exchanges continue in full force, a new barter theater has formed in the city center, an agroecology organization includes barter in their massive annual festival, and other events spring up from time to time. And the Solidarity Economy School proved a major boon to barter organizing, providing fresh resources and a forum for spreading the barter vision. In 2009 and 2010, the city government contracted barter activists to facilitate parts of the curriculum.

Organizers used these contracts to support existing barter groups, activate dormant ones, and conduct additional demonstrative barter fairs in new neighborhoods, essentially casting a wide net for new barter groups. In their trainings and barter fairs, they advertised the breadth of barter styles, promoting options beyond the centrally controlled multi-reciprocal barter. During that time, several community groups expressed interest in forming permanent barter groups, but they seemed most focused on organizing periodic barter fairs as in Bello or Altamira. Organizers frequently discussed the need for a permanent network modeled on Santa Elena's directory of barterers, but made few efforts to create and activate this network. Groups who first encountered barter at the Solidarity Economy School began organizing their own barter markets after my fieldwork, and have continued through cycles of activity and inactivity. The demand for convivencia has not flagged, nor has the belief that economic alternatives are a necessary tactic of "peacefare." Figures as disparate as Governor Gaviria, Luis Alberto, and Julio stress the importance of generating economies that not only sustain livelihoods and combat structural inequalities but also reweave social relations and cultivate alternative values.

In the next three chapters, I narrow my focus to the Santa Elena barter fair and the social, economic, and subjective impacts of barter on participating households and individuals. Initiated as a series of experiments in the mid- and late 1990s, barter has gone further than anyone expected. The informal, diverse, and constantly changing group of barter organizers—a group that has included housewives and engineers, hippies and *campesinas*, university professors and self-taught Marxists—has exploited numerous opportunities to spread the idea that alternative economies can ameliorate social and economic problems in Medellín. In doing so, they have stretched the local notion of "solidarity economy" beyond the most conventional sectors, opening space to advance less institutionalized, people-led economies. As we will see, they have struggled with the challenges of collaboration, and their project seems to include some deep-seated contradictions, but it also stands out as an enduring, genuinely grassroots project to rethink the economy.

# 3

# A Day at the Market

## Barter Livelihoods, Ethics, and Pleasure

Santa Elena's barter market was a delicious retreat from the clamor and grime of Medellín and the grind of the conventional, competitive economy. On the third Sunday of every month, traders took over the town's plaza, turning the empty concrete circle into a festive ring of orange-topped market stalls. This was a place for dancing, singing, visiting with old friends and meeting new ones, breathing in the fresh air, trying new foods, displaying one's skills, complaining about politics, and, of course, trading. Barterers from across Medellín joined traders from Santa Elena and other rural areas to enact other ways of practicing the economy and re-embedding it in social life. The plural here is important: although they were all involved in the same market, there were meaningful variations in the ways barterers used that market, integrated it into their household economies, and understood what it means to challenge economic conventions.

The range of goods on offer was impressive. Strolling around the circle one could almost always find a handful of stands offering local fruits and vegetables (though never enough to satisfy everyone), plus an assortment of juices, popsicles, wines, and marmalades derived from them. The organizer of the market, a gourmet baker and caterer, supplied the economic community with breads, empanadas, cakes, and the occasional lasagna. Another longtime barterer came up from the city whenever he could spare the bus fare to make *gelatina*, a taffy-like treat that went quickly. And a family that joined the market during my time there quickly recognized an open niche in cheap sandwiches. Aside from food, the market featured used clothing; handmade toys and home decorations in wood, bamboo, and other materials; handmade sandals, shoes, and clothing; henna tattoos; soaps, shampoos, lotions, and massage oils; a wide range of jewelry; used books, CDs, and DVDs; and homemade holiday decorations. New and occasional traders added high-end leather bags, homemade chocolates, Belgian waffles, salsas, and rabbits and chickens.

Perhaps more admirable than the range of products was the market's persistence. Nearly any project can garner attention for a few months, particularly when participants are guaranteed an interesting time with potentially large economic bonuses and when the city covers their costs. In Medellín, as elsewhere, electoral promises yield a steady stream of pet projects that survive for a few months or a year before disappearing into the archives of some local cultural center, giving rise to a problem of *cortoplacismo* (short-term-ism). By contrast, the Santa Elena market's eleven-year duration demonstrates a rare continuity. It survived the departure of multiple organizers and spanned several departmental and municipal administrations. More importantly, it continued to hold the interest of many participants (including some who stopped attending because of other obligations) while also attracting a steady stream of newcomers. During my time there, each month's market brought together a mix of people who had been trading there for four to six years, another group who began participating around two years earlier, and a handful who joined within the previous year. Some had extensive knowledge of barter and had participated in markets across the city, while others had never tried it before visiting Santa Elena. Their familiarity with barter and their conceptualization of barter as a political project also varied significantly, based largely on people's length of involvement.

The barter market, however, was far from perfect. Initially, when the idea was fresh and government funding covered farmers' transportation costs, the plaza overflowed with sixty to eighty stalls and a bounty of farm goods. It was difficult to maintain high levels of participation, though, leaving barterers hoping for more products, especially foodstuffs, basic household supplies, and raw materials for their own production. Also, despite three editions of a barter directory, daily trading never gained steam; barter remained primarily a market-day affair, not the permanent "system" that Luis Alberto Jaramillo and the organizers in Pajarito aspired to.

Even with these shortcomings, the Santa Elena market was the core of barter throughout my research, the "most important living laboratory we have" according to one organizer. In this chapter, I describe the monthly barter market from a variety of perspectives so readers can appreciate the diversity of barterers, the ways they approach trading, and the qualities of barter that bring them back despite the market's imperfections. I also analyze several approaches to trading that challenge economic generalizations about barter and money, and the ethical norms that barterers are developing for their collective practice. Most importantly, though, I offer readers a sense of how markets look and feel, and what types of sociality they produce. To fully understand these laboratories, we have to examine markets not only as spheres of economic exchange, but also as phenomenological and social experiences.

Given that barter emerged out of hopes for reweaving the social fabric, it is not surprising that many barterers value the social experience of barter markets as much as they do the economic benefits. By providing an escape from the ordinary, barter allows people to come together differently and to recognize and value one another (and themselves) in new ways, ways that are not mediated by money or conditioned by the competitive rush of the business day. In this sense, barterers have already accomplished one of their main goals: to re-embed the economy in society. Or, more accurately, to recognize that the economy is always already socially embedded and therefore subject to our own changing imaginations and actions.

The *experience* of the market is so important because barter is primarily a politics of everyday life rather than a formal political project. There are no barter rallies, and few barterers actively advocate that politicians reconceptualize urban development through a solidarity economy lens. Rather, barter activism occurs through the day-to-day workings of the market, where we see a collective (if often informal and uncoordinated) attempt to develop a new ethic. This emerging ethics is fashioned out of barterers' efforts to negotiate what barter means to them, what place it has in their livelihoods, and how barter transactions and a day at the market should look and feel. As barterers debate the rules of the market, formally and informally sanction one another, and decide what types of trades are fair and desirable, they are developing a barter ethics around values of satisfaction, egalitarianism, and solidarity. This ethics is also related to—and reinforces—a different worldview, one that emphasizes the links between production and consumption, individual and collectivity.

Getting a feel for the market and its traders thus helps us appreciate three key aspects of alternative economies activism: the extent to which the lived, sensual, and social experience of the economy affects activist outcomes as much as ideology does; the extent to which alternative ethics emerge through practice rather than (or, in some cases, alongside) predefined deliberation; and the extent to which alternative economic and political projects demand regulation and enforcement, not merely feel-good collectivism. In the end, these experiences, emergent ethics, and informal regulations all revolve around complex negotiations of value, including use-value and exchange-value, moral values, and a number of alternative economic values such as good-use-value and social-value, which I describe below.

## Going to Market

Santa Elena is only thirty minutes from downtown Medellín, but it feels like a different world. Within minutes the bus whisks you out of downtown up into the hills, and then just as rapidly out of the city entirely, free from the hustle and bustle of the traffic and a thousand meters above the hot, smoggy air of the urban core. The road rises through densely packed neighborhoods out to the urban fringe, where miniature coffee fields are interspersed with houses and shops, and then zig-zags across the mountainside, offering alternating views of the city below and spring-fed waterfalls against the lush hillside.

The mixture of passengers reveals the town's character: an old campesino returning home with chicken feed that he purchased with some savings as well as the profits from the flowers and herbs that he took to market; a young middle-class family with their camping gear; a group of university students looking for an adventurous and perhaps romantic day outside of the city; a couple of hippie artisans with their bags of jewelry to sell; a semiprofessional daughter making her weekly visit back home; and an anthropologist taking mental notes about the whole affair. Santa Elena has long been both a part of and apart from the city.

The large expanse of forest and fields is home to only twelve thousand residents, most of whom live on extremely small plots of land (*minifundios*) and have survived, until recently at least, by combining subsistence and market agriculture. Officially part of the Medellín metropolitan area, Santa Elena has long been important not for agriculture but as a trade corridor and a getaway for the urban elite. Through the first half of the twentieth century, Medellín's wealthiest families would hire porters to carry them up the mountain in *silletas*, wooden chairs strapped to the carrier's back and forehead. In recent years, the town has become accessible to a broader swath of city dwellers through more conventional transport, including a gondola connecting one of the city's poorest neighborhoods to an ecological park. Santa Elena is promoting eco- and agrotourism as a way to capitalize on its abundant natural resources and Medellinenses' nostalgia for an agrarian past. Every weekend, tourists stream into the most accessible parts of Santa Elena, and large numbers of middle- and upper-middle-class families have built weekend or permanent homes in the region, attracted by its relative safety and accessibility.

Santa Elena's romantic image hides the social and economic challenges that its residents face. Although Santa Elena has fared better than Medellín's other rural townships, farmers have struggled to make a living on their small plots from crops like potatoes, blackberries, garden vegetables, and flowers. Increasingly, farm production serves as a minor complement to other income sources, and many young people are fleeing to the city. Tourism and the subdivision of farmland to make space for urbanites' homes provide short-term boosts but further reduce long-term farm viability. They also lead to new tensions with outsiders and fears that Santa Elena will become a bedroom community of Medellín. The township has attempted to slow growth and control the rate of land fragmentation, but with mixed success.

Santa Elena has also not been immune to violence. Although murder rates have been relatively low, this has come largely through undisputed control of the region by key narco/paramilitary leaders rather than through genuine security. A sizable number of new residents came to Santa Elena fleeing other areas, and violence has woven its tendrils into locals' lives here as well, shaping their mobility, residential choices, and social activities. As the bus winds through the fog-shrouded outskirts of Santa Elena, however, it's easy to forget that you are not, in fact, escaping these pressures.

As in most Colombian towns, the social center of Santa Elena is its plaza, which serves as a marketplace and meeting place, the place where people do their Sunday visiting on the way to and from downtown or the local grocery store. It is a stopping-off point for tourists on their way to the ecological reserve, their family getaways, or the quaint towns in Antioquia's famous Oriente region. It is a place for political rallies and town celebrations. And it is the home of the barter market.

But stepping down from the bus, you can't help but notice that this particular plaza is strange. It is not an orderly square from which Simón Bolívar presides over a church, government buildings, and small bars blasting *cumbia* over their sound systems. Instead, it's an aloof little circle carved into the hill. Amphitheater-like stairs rise from the plaza on one side, and a small road—more like a driveway—curves around it, rising up to the stone-and-brick church that crowns the hill and then continuing down the other side and back to the bus stop and the main road out of town. Government offices are tucked around the corner, out of the way. The statue presiding over the town center is not that of the Liberator but rather a couple of *silleteros*, campesinos carrying their flowers to market on one of the traditional chair-shaped carriers. The semicircle of shops surrounding the plaza includes the standard corner stores and liquor shops, but also a cute Italian restaurant and café, an art gallery, and a cooperatively owned storefront housing an environmental NGO, community restaurant, and artists' cooperative.

Santa Elena is at once city and country, a place for work and living and a place for retreat and recreation. The waves of artists, artisans, hippies, and other urban escapees who have migrated to Santa Elena in recent decades have given it a unique character. As in other areas, community participation and social mobilization remain difficult, but there is a common perception that people there—even some of the older campesinos—think differently, that they may be more open to experimentation and less hopeful for Progress and Modernity than people in other parts of the city. An organizer from a different part of town noted, enviously, "Santa Elena is a propitious environment for barter."

I typically got to the market early to catch other happenings and side conversations. Walking toward the nearly empty plaza, I would pass a handful of men drinking coffee and chatting at the corner store and a clutch of *artesanos* gathering at the plaza's entrance to sell jewelry to tourists and churchgoers. A few barterers would be slowly starting their day. While several of us hauled the heavy wooden market stalls from a town-owned storage room and cobbled together the mismatched pieces of these supposedly standard, government-provided tables, others looked on, chatting as they arranged their products. The next few buses—and maybe a car or motorcycle or two—brought the remainder of the barterers, and before long the plaza was abuzz with activity. Olga, the market organizer, arrived in her trademark hat: an enormous straw affair. An energetic forty-something, she circulated through the market to ensure that everyone had a stall, to greet newcomers, and to sort out the questions or complaints of the half dozen people demanding her attention. People put the finishing touches on their stalls, and with the plaza full and the sun burning off the last bits of morning fog, the market rumbled to a start.

## The Barterers

The plaza's circular shape lent the market a community feeling. All of the barterers shared the same view into the open center of the market. They could easily see the action and regularly joked and teased with other barterers across the circle. The simplicity of this layout was nice for visitors as well; a single lap provided a sense of all that was on offer. A quick look at the types of barterers in Santa Elena provides a sense of how barter fit into their economic portfolios and social lives. I have grouped the producers into loose-fitting categories based on their products and personal histories, though many barterers defy easy categorization.

### Artesanos

Perhaps the most unsurprising group of barterers was the *artesanos*. Most travelers to South America have walked down tourist streets fringed with blankets showcasing paintings, small sculptures, and necklaces, earrings, rings, belts, and other accessories made of beads, seeds, stones, feathers, and a mix of metals. The salespeople often sport hippie garb and are generally viewed with slight disdain by the traditional upper classes and politicians. These folks are great for tourists and supply a huge percentage of Colombians' jewelry, but they hint at deviance: a bohemian lifestyle of late nights, marijuana use, nomadism, and general irresponsibility. Worst of all, they represent the most threatening manifestation of informality, for there is a sense (true in some but not all cases) that they were not born into poverty and informality but voluntarily chose it as a way of opting out of the system.

The *artesanos* were the type of people—along with more traditional artists and musicians—who helped start the original Bello barter fairs, and they played a major role in Santa Elena. Less enamored of the fast life, expensive consumer goods, and wealth, and more concerned with living well and establishing meaningful connections, these artists and *artesanos* frequently bartered among themselves, even outside of formal barter systems. Of course, they could not avoid the demands of a monetary economy, but compared to other workers, their art and handicrafts offered them more control over their own work and social lives.

The six or seven *artesanos* who frequented the Santa Elena market defied many of the common stereotypes. Flor was a good example. A middle-aged woman, she lived in the city with her husband and daughters. Her husband was a taxi driver, but after car payments and fuel, his income was not enough to support the family, so her earnings were essential. A proud Indigenous woman (the only barterer I met who self-identified as Indigenous), she ran her own business selling intricate beaded jewelry using traditional and modern designs. She spent every weekend at one of the city's craft markets, often accompanied by her daughters or mother. Flor's work was expensive, time-consuming, and of a very high quality, and her prices reflected that. She knew that attending barter markets instead of additional cash markets might be economically irrational, given that market sales were her livelihood, but barter did offer material benefits. Flor typically left with a large bag of vegetables and clothes or books for her daughters, as well as cash from sales to nonbarterers. Plus, she occasionally made a big trade for something really valuable, like the stove that I discuss later in this chapter. But the biggest attraction was that "there is something special, almost indescribable" about barter markets, something different and slightly more enjoyable and relaxing. Returning home, she was always far more excited to show off her trades after a long day of barter than to discuss what she sold at the conventional markets.

Most of the other *artesanos* were in similar situations. They treated their work as a full-time job, not simply idling in bohemian celebration but carefully planning their next project, gathering the right materials, designing and making products, and devoting many hours a week to markets or street-side vending, in addition to the task of running their homes and raising their children. Their work supported families who were neither extremely poor nor comfortably middle class. The barter market offered useful household goods and contacts with clients for future cash purchases, but it also offered a different social experience and a way to blend economics with recreation. Carla, a jeweler, explained,

C: I sell *artesanías*, and when someone arrives at the [conventional] market, all of us are like, [hurriedly] "Someone came, a customer came." The vision is

totally different. When we're at the barter market, we all visit with one
another and there's not that pressure of "Someone arrived. Whose booth
did they go to?"

BB:   So in the other markets there's a lot of competition?

C:   Of course, of course. Obviously. And there's jealousy, the jealousy that . . .
that . . . that why does *that* person have so many people [at his booth], what
are they checking out, what's he got that's so great? This is different from
what happens at the barter markets.

Other *artesanos* agreed that barter offered a less competitive environment
where they could hang out, exchange ideas, and be friends without constantly
sizing one another up and second-guessing their own business strategy.

Still, art was their livelihood, so they had to think carefully about the economics of barter. Several *artesanos* adjusted their strategies for the barter market. Flor, for example, usually left her finest pieces at home because they were
simply too valuable, and she generally could not find something of equivalent
value for which she would like to trade. Carla had a different strategy for her
most valuable pieces. At first, she seemed to advertise that half of her booth
was for barter and the other half for sale, a practice that sparked resentment
among other barterers. When I asked her about it she quickly interjected,

No no no. It's that, how should I put it? I've been learning. Now I say, "Okay,"
[picking up a necklace] "this can be traded," right? But I give it a value that
disincentivizes that. If I tell you "a set [of earrings and a matching necklace] for
a hundred Floricambios" you say, "Huh? Wow. Really?" I didn't tell you "No,
I won't trade it to you." Give me the hundred Floricambios and it's yours. . . .
But the other ones are valued at eight, ten, twelve and it's because the level of
work allows me to offer them at those prices. When I tell you that the others
are worth more it's because they're difficult materials, they require truly
difficult work, that it is really valued much higher. And this is what I live off of.
Really barter is a one-day project right now. It's not for the rest of the month.
I wish that I could take home from the barter fair what I need to live for the
rest of the month, but since I can't then I have to disincentivize trades in this
way. . . . It's my means of sustenance, the means of sustenance for my whole
family, so I have to conserve these [expensive] materials. I have to conserve
them but without giving up on [barter].

This was a challenge that all barterers face: how to pursue their economic interests without violating the ethics of barter, ethics that are rarely explicit and
that are still under construction as participants interpret concepts like solidarity
and fairness. This forced barterers to negotiate various forms of value: the value
of their own labor, exchange-value in the conventional market, exchange-value

in barter, use-value, the social value of participating and belonging, and moral and political values.

Flor's and Carla's experiences reflect most *artesanos'* production systems and barter strategies. They are dependable and enthusiastic participants, eager for the social and economic opportunities at each market and hopeful that barter will expand further, but also careful about how they incorporate nonmonetary exchange into their livelihoods. Nonetheless, the *artesanos* were not always seen favorably in Santa Elena. This is partly a result of lingering stereotypes and fears of *viciosos*, *marijuaneros*, and *peludos* (druggies, potheads, and long-hairs), prejudices that contagiously come to affect the market as a whole, but the economic impact of *artesanos* was probably most decisive. A number of former barterers complained that the fair had become a "monocrop of handicrafts" and was short on basic household goods. One woman went on to explain that an excess of *artesanos* created a "double-price system" of cheap farm goods versus expensive handicrafts; this divide made trades difficult. During my year as a barterer, however, the short supply of farm products gave campesinos a comparative advantage. It's to them that I turn next.

## Campesinos

Many Colombians assume that campesinos are the most active barterers; they identify the countryside with premodern traditions that preserve community and simplicity. Describing my research to people in Medellín often prompted long responses beginning with statements like, "Of course, the campesinos and the *Indigenas* still do that all the time. . . ." The truth, though, is that it has been difficult to sustain campesino participation because of their economic precarity.

Three of the market's regular barterers came from traditional farm families. They were the last of the few dozen Santa Elena "natives" who had once participated in the market, and they helped with organizational tasks over the years. It is important to note, though, that all three are older women whose farm and gardening work supplemented their families' primary livelihood activities; their barter strategies reflected this.

Dolores, for example, prepared for the markets on Saturday night. With her sisters and cousins, she harvested vegetables and herbs, packaged them into market-sized bundles, and sometimes made a batch of marmalades, soy products, chocolates, or other prepared foods. When the *campesinas* arrived at the market, its entire dynamic changed. Food was in such high demand that there were special trading rules for the *campesinas*: unlike the rest of the barterers, they didn't have to pay a small fee to rent their stall because they weren't at the market long enough to justify this. As soon as they arrived other traders lined up to get a share of produce before it ran out. The *campesinas* traded quickly, preferring direct trade to Floricambios because they had "already filled up with those little papers," and they couldn't always find things to spend them on. Because they accumulated so many Floricambios over the years, their trips to market were often a blend of trading what they had and shopping for clothes or jewelry with their reserves of facilitators.

The high demand for food seemed to present a tremendous opportunity. As one barterer pointed out, "Food is almost like money. You can basically fix whatever price you want for the food because almost nobody produces it." In fact, many barterers would have paid a premium for bartered produce because, much like fair trade or organic shoppers, they valued the social conditions of production and exchange. But the *campesinas* never seemed to respond to these market signals either by demanding higher prices or by bringing larger quantities of food to fill unmet demand. In fact, when I harvested several dozen oranges in my neighborhood and experimented with offering them at higher than market exchange rates, other barterers seemed content with those higher prices, but I received a stern "that's very expensive" from one of the *campesinas*. She wanted me to know that I was violating unspoken norms about valuing products reasonably and tempering a profit motive. The sad irony, however, was that by using conventional market prices as the standard for what was reasonable—rather than intentionally skewing it as in the Pajarito SEL—they maintained the double-price system that undervalues campesino labor.

Beyond raising prices, there are other ways *campesinas* might have profited more from barter. For example, Dolores belonged to a women's group that sold marmalades and other food products at farmers' and tourists' markets. Many campesinos and *campesinas* across the country are in similar associations dedicated to marketing their produce or supporting other economic ventures. I asked Dolores about bartering the group's products:

D:  As a group we can't really participate in barter because it's from the group. We can't barter because the group produces.
BB:  You can't ever, even if you find things that are good for everyone?
D:  Well, yes, if there are fruits for example then we could.

Even after this clarification, though, Dolores resisted my efforts to think about collective trades. In large part, she was thinking only of the use-value of bartered goods—and the difficulty of sharing those use-values—but ignoring their possible exchange-value. If she were to trade the group's marmalades at the barter market (where they are valued highly), she might be able to acquire goods that could be sold at cash markets for a net gain. This type of economic calculation is nearly impossible, however, when traded goods are seen almost exclusively as having a use-value.

If these farmers were not trying to maximize the economic utility of barter, why were they there? Dolores said she barters "because I like this nonsense [*esas bobaditas*]." Her friends teased her about bartering, but it brought her a quiet joy. There was a lot of hanging out and getting to know each other, and sometimes she found "a little luxury" to take home: a really nice scarf or necklace or set of gloves. Dolores also really appreciated the sense of solidarity and the "culture of barter," of each person thinking about the well-being of the others and enjoying the act of exchange in and of itself.

It was not all roses, though. Dolores withdrew from the market for a while because she was turned off by the "sketchy young people" whom barter attracts. Also, because the market didn't provide enough basic needs, she says most participants were like her: "I participate because I like to, but if I was looking for money then I couldn't return." Every trip to the market implies costs. The way barter is right now, "it's only for people who don't need money. It doesn't serve the poor, only if they can find something cheaper [than in the regular market], which sometimes is possible."

Barterers participated, she said, because they had the "culture of barter" and were genuinely interested in exchanging goods, but that mentality—that focus on use-value above exchange-value and social benefits above or alongside economic ones—is uncommon. "This culture doesn't work here, among the natives of Santa Elena. You'd have to make it so they weren't all thinking about money." And to achieve that, you would need to create a "serious" barter market, one that meets basic household needs by providing clothes, shoes, things for school and first communions, and food. There would be butchers and dairy farmers. Campesinos would return if it were improved, she says, but a butcher is not going to come exchange things here without money. Why not? I asked. "It has to be very organized. Very organized." Once the economic benefits of barter are glaringly obvious, though, Dolores thinks that participants would begin to think less about money and could learn the culture of barter, "but you would also have to deal with their complexes," she said. Their complexes? Yes, for example, so that they felt like it was okay to wear secondhand clothes because it doesn't mean something bad about them.

Unfortunately, the economic benefits of barter were not obvious enough to keep most campesinos involved, especially as the city expanded its subsidized farmers' markets. All of the farmers living exclusively from their farms eventually left the Santa Elena market. Like the *artesanos*, they were market people whose sustenance depended on finding the right commercial opportunities.

Former barterers Don Lupe and Doña Beatriz shared particularly eloquent descriptions of their barter experiences. Don Lupe is a sprightly old farmer with a small plot of land and a modest country house. When I explained my project, his eyes lit up. "The first thing you need to know is that barter was a thing of the grandparents." In the time of my parents, he explained, neighbors would trade with each other all the time. "If one person had a bunch of corn but needed beans, they would just go to the neighbor's house or to their *compadre* and ask if they could trade. And they would do it without measuring who gave what because they weren't keeping score." Back then, Don Lupe recalled, people hardly bought anything from the stores because everybody had their own corn, which they would store for a whole year to make *arepas*, *mazamorra* (a sugary beverage), and to feed their animals. "Nobody does this anymore. It was really great. It was a great way to live and a great way to be neighbors, but most kids don't want to do that anymore. It's too much work and they're lazy. They want to do other things and they want to make money. They want the city and technologies and other things."

Don Lupe interrupted his recollections to give me a tour of his farm. Descending past the house into a lush, shaded gully, he proudly pointed out a dozen different trees, each labeled so that children and other farmers who came to his house could appreciate the diversity of local flora and their role in protecting the stream that ran across his property. On the other side, the path opened to a field overflowing in a dense tangle of vegetables. Don Lupe explained that, as he has grown older, he has grown more passionate about the ways of the grandparents. He gave up using chemicals on his land years ago, and he eschews medicine except for what the land provides. Then he pointed out five herbs within ten feet of where we stood that cured upset stomachs, headaches, and skin infections. "Some people would look at this and think it was a mess," he said, "but I think it's beautiful. My father taught me to never depend on just one thing—never have a big field full of corn. There is so much diversity here and it's all safe and healthy, and the plants take care of themselves. See how these squash cover the ground between the green beans, so there's very little weeding? This is what I want to leave people. I want to keep alive the ways of the *abuelos*."

"Oh look," he said, walking over to a bunch of large, arrow-shaped leaves. "I got these from the barter fair." I followed him to enormous yacón plants with tubers the size of watermelons. "A young kid came to the market one time with these roots like potatoes, but crisp and sweet, and you could eat them raw. He said they were an old Inca crop. I loved them, so he gave me some. I planted them here and they just started spreading. Now I share it with people all the time. *That* was the great thing about barter. People came from all over and brought seeds. There were so many things I didn't know."

Don Lupe walked me back to the picnic table and resumed. "So I was telling you how barter was in the time of our grandparents, but recently people came to organize other barters in Santa Elena. The first ones were fantastic. A Venezuelan or Ecuadorian or I'm not sure what [Guillermo Moyano, the Argentine] got all of these farmers together and explained how it would work, and the first ones were really good. There were lots of people, forty booths or more, and people traded everything. People came all the way from Sonsón with plantains and sacks of *panela* [raw sugar], and we brought our goods, and we would trade for things that we couldn't grow here. It was mostly food for food, and it was so nice that we didn't need money. But it started to fall apart because after a while there weren't very many goods that were really useful for us and for other campesinos. Each time there were more artesanias and less food.

"After a little while the Floricambios appeared and people were selling for Floricambios. People would come with bracelets, necklaces, and they would buy our vegetables, but these were all things that we didn't need, and I left with a ton of Floricambios. But I asked myself, 'What am I going to do with these? They don't take them at the store. I can't go shopping with Floricambios.' So they weren't very useful. I still have some, I think, somewhere. But the other parts of barter were just amazing."

Doña Beatriz, who had joined us, was shaking her head. She evidently felt the need to temper her husband's enthusiasm. "They set about breaking it when they decided to only allow Floricambios and not look for alternatives [for the people who needed pesos]. There are costs we have to pay: farm inputs, transportation. We can't pay these with Floricambios. Well, transportation we could when they partnered with the bus company. But you can't just go about trading things and getting nothing in return or accumulating little pieces of paper that aren't worth anything." She paused, considering her thoughts. "At the beginning, people were really excited. The market allowed sales for half of the day and then barter for the second half, and everybody stayed because they were really excited to barter. And when we would meet, the town auditorium was full. People were even standing in the back. That's how excited we were. But when they became too radical and excluded pesos altogether, that's when people started to lose interest. Eventually even Lupe couldn't keep going."

Don Lupe had to leave for a meeting, but Doña Beatriz continued the conversation. She explained that they sell at two city markets each month, a downtown market and a tourist market in Santa Elena. "We go every month. The city subsidizes the campesinos really well these days, by setting up markets around the city, so we don't have to be as worried about money. These markets are great because we don't have to pay for the stalls. We fill a taxi with sacks of food and pay 20,000 pesos. I bring goat's milk, cheese, yogurt, and all sorts of vegetarian food and lunches, and he has his booth where he sells the vegetables. I can make 100,000 to 150,000 pesos in a single market, and then we have his sales on top of that. So we support ourselves with these two markets, and now we're building this addition to the house so we can have a little tourist cabin as well. And we sing at some festivals and I work in an office as well."

I asked Beatriz what would make the barter fair more useful and enable their participation, and she thought for a while. "I guess it would be useful if it provided rice, oil, salt, different kinds of grains like sorghum, quinoa, wheat flour. Sesame—well, not sesame because we have a friend who we buy that from. Peanuts, organic sugar. That's all." And what about other things like soaps or brooms, or services? "Oh yes, that too. Soaps, detergents. But not services because where I work there are people of all professions and they can help if I need something."

Her answer gives more depth to Dolores's response to the same question. Beatriz did not want barter to provide all of her household needs, and she did not want to do away with buying altogether. She bought, borrowed, and traded with a wide range of family and friends, and these economic transactions supported the people she cared about and maintained valuable relationships like her friendship with their sesame supplier. Pragmatic pluralism, it turns out, has important social drivers as well as the basic economic ones. She could envision barter being useful, however, if it provided cheap access to food products that they could not grow or buy from friends, and if it included trade for other basic household needs, including manufactured products like detergents that she never even imagined acquiring outside of the monetary economy. But Beatriz was far less enthusiastic than her husband about the prospects of barter. She was not a romantic. The ways of the grandparents and the possibilities of alternative economies might be interesting, but she clearly felt that the conventional economy works well enough, and you don't have to worry about being left with a pocket full of papers when those papers are "real money," accepted everywhere and for anything.

In addition to traditional campesinos like Dolores, Lupe, and Beatriz, the barter fair attracted a few back-to-the-landers and other new farmers, folks drawn to the countryside in search of a lifestyle that offers more autonomy, tranquility, and connection with nature. These new farmers usually produced value-added products like wines, juices, and shampoos and creams, so I have grouped them with the small business owners that I describe next. However, their ideology and practices borrow from *artesanos*, campesinos, and barter organizers. As farm owners, they benefited from household food production and greater than average self-provisioning, but they were far from self-sufficient. Like the *artesanos*, they sought to escape dependence on wage labor and conventional markets, but they were partly constrained by the need for an income (in cash) and/or an inflow (of goods) to sustain themselves and their businesses. For these new farmers, barter constituted one part of a mixed livelihood strategy shaped by desire, external constraints, and ideological commitments. Barter markets helped them establish new rural livelihoods—much like farmers' markets and community-supported agriculture have in the United States.

## Small Business Owners

The remaining small businesses that bartered in Santa Elena crossed the spectrum from informal operations selling cheap clothes or home décor items in the city's *barrios populares* (poor neighborhoods) to home-based businesses making artisanal wines, breads, and shirts for the middle class and an occasional participant who produced high-end leather bags. Most of these businesses targeted relatively small niches of consumers: the minority of Medellinenses who disregarded the stigma of wearing used clothing; people willing to experiment beyond the fairly sharp norms of consumer culture; and that segment of the middle and upper classes willing to pay a bit more for organic, local, healthy, and natural products that retain more of their social history. As Olga, the market organizer, said, "I am a baker, but I am an elitist baker." She sold her loaves of bread at three or four times the price of mass-produced Bimbo white bread, and part of its value was that it was locally handcrafted using whole grains, seeds, and nuts by a baker whom the consumer could come to know. Interestingly, though, class lines were somewhat blurred at the market, where an anti-consumerist ideal and the distance from the cash-based logic of scarcity led middle- and upper-class people to browse used clothing and lower-class people to enjoy artisanal wines and breads.

None of the bartering businesses had a permanent storefront, but some were quite well established. The baker and wine makers, for example, produced for a regular clientele that included small stores in the city. Two carpenters had been producing for years and sold at conventional markets. Several small businesses, though, were more informal, and some were only occasional ventures rather than full-time operations. Many of these informal businesspeople were using barter to test the market, refine their products, and sample life as an entrepreneur, just as the more established barter businesses did previously.

The most established businesses generally had a relatively focused market strategy. Olga explained that, initially, she never expected to barter much of her bread because of its cost, but her booth would be empty after every market. So she started to think more carefully about it. "I put 25 percent of my profits in barter. My *profits*, not my capital. I brought part of my earnings to the market and I came with a different perspective. This way I didn't have to worry about the market value of things, converting everything to pesos to be sure I was making wise decisions. Obviously I didn't make as much as I would have selling my bread, but what I made was lots of contacts. Lots and lots of contacts. And in the long run I got other things out of it. I got lots of free trips. I got to go see places and stay with people for free and I got to learn a lot from this." Advising a group of micro-entrepreneurs in a city-funded business training project, she explained, "You have to think carefully about how to bring your business to the barter market. You have to think in the whole production chain and in the long run, not in today's pocketbook." Other business owners had less mathematical approaches, but most developed a similar system for deciding which products were barterable and which needed to be sold.

Humberto, the carpenter and toy maker, sold two hundred different products at local markets. He loved barter fairs and often skipped cash markets in order to barter, but he and the other carpenter agreed that it is essential to have

monetary sales as well, because you just could not live off of barter. To emphasize his point, Humberto pulled out a watch that he designed using Japanese
parts and locally sourced bamboo. The parts cost him eleven thousand pesos,
and he had to buy them with cash. He was willing to barter these watches, but
he had to be able to earn money as well, so he sold the watches at forty thousand pesos, which he said was a fair price given how much work went into each
one. Sales then subsidized barter. This is why he thought the current rules
worked so well: you could barter with all of the barterers (and in fact you could
never turn down an offer to barter for Floricambios), but you could also sell
your products to any tourists.

## The Wealthy

The demographic group that surprised me most was the wealthy participants,
people who had no economic need to operate outside of the conventional monetary economy and no self-interested reason to oppose it, but who nonetheless
made barter a regular part of their monthly activities. There were two older
women in particular who came from the upper class. They drove to the market
every month, often accompanied by their adult children. They made a day of it,
attending church in the morning, then setting up at the barter fair to enjoy family
time in the fresh air. But more than anything, they both stressed, they enjoyed
the opportunity to be useful to others. One of these women told me that she had
always been touched by the oft-used barter phrase *lo que a ti te está sobrando a otro
puede servir* ("what's left over to you could be useful to someone else"). Barter
offered these women an uncommon opportunity to truly feel someone else's
enthusiasm for their work and the pride that comes with being useful.

Of course, they also appreciated the economic benefits of barter, the direct
benefits of the foods they brought home, and the indirect benefits that their
children received by advertising the products and services that they offered as
their primary livelihoods. As one of them noted, being wealthy never eliminated all economic concerns. She even withdrew for a while because the cost
of driving to the market was becoming excessive given their finances at the
moment. Thus, the opportunity to combine trading with sales was important
for her as well; it helped her recoup some of the costs of participation.

As we sat in her parlor in a high rise in one of Medellín's wealthiest neighborhoods, she told me unflinchingly about the anticapitalist intentions of the
organizers. She agreed that we should try to work against capitalism, but she
had often gotten into trouble for bending the rules when only barter was
allowed. "You can't be so drastic about things. Drastic formulas don't sit well
with me. I really admire that in Santa Elena there are now three different ways
of exchanging things: that you can do direct barter, or half and half, or sell
things. There are three different modes here that correspond with different
desires. That way everyone can find a way to make it work."

## Other Barterers

These categories are imperfect, but they give a sense of who was at the market, why they came, and how they made barter work for them. One barterer deserves special attention for the way he stretches these categories because his economic practice represents a potentially important type of barter. Santiago and his wife make inexpensive woven and beaded jewelry. Until recently he was primarily a student living off of a government scholarship in exchange for community service (a government-supported form of barter, he always points out). Through his studies and personal pursuits, Santiago has been hoping to blend his passions for barter and social service. He discovered barter about twenty years ago and has tried to ensure that someone from his family is present at every barter-related event since. Barter fills him with hope for alternative economic, social, and political possibilities. He imagines it leading people to "a direct confrontation with their consciences" as they grapple with issues of honesty, fairness, and respect, and he dreams that these principled individuals will come together in a society founded on consensus, justice, and environmental sustainability. These hopes have led him to become one of the most active promoters of barter.

One result of Santiago's presence at barter events across the city is that he can begin to think a bit more like a wandering trader than a traditional producer-vendor. While he emphasizes the need to think in terms of use-value, he is also distinctly aware of the exchange-value of goods. He taught his nine-year-old daughter that you can trade for something that you won't use when you know people elsewhere will want it. These types of traders could become extremely important for integrating urban and rural barter systems and supplying the nonfood products that campesinos require. They can speculate on the value of goods in other places and times, redistributing products to the sites of highest demand. Doing so could make barter markets more useful to the large majority who attend only their local market, make people more invested in barter, and maintain a larger number of permanent participants. Organizers, however, do not seem to be attentive to this difference in rationales and strategies.

## "¿Qué es el Negocio?"

With this diverse assemblage of traders now at their stalls, the market would begin. If they hadn't already, the regulars would make a mad dash for the food, beginning with the vegetables and products that could be taken home, and then Olga's baked goods, before settling in to their own stalls. Each barterer had their own style. Very few traders called out to potential customers as they might in a conventional market (though this practice is uncommon in Colombia anyway). The *artesanos*, who were most accustomed to standing at markets, stayed close to their booths, but others left their products under the supervision of neighbors to circulate through the market. Humberto, the toy maker, was one of the most active advertisers, though his sales pitches were as much play as propaganda. Mustering his best advertising voice, he spent the day celebrating the surreal through his toys: absurdly oversized children's toys, clocks that turned in the opposite direction ("to make you younger"), or small shelves that you could hang on your wall at an angle ("so gravity saves you the work of having to knock things off"). Some vendors took breaks to dance salsa in the middle of the circle. Others gathered on the steps to share lunch and treat each other to coffee, and the organizers often discussed barter initiatives across the city in the sliver of shade provided by a palm tree.

Of course, the main point of the market was to trade, and plenty of that happened, too. Julio, the founder of the Pajarito system and an occasional participant in Santa Elena, always emphasized the diverse trading possibilities by asking anyone interested in his products *¿qué es el negocio?* This question was a conversation starter. He wanted to know the value of things, but also how they were going to be traded, and above all he wanted to underscore the unconventional nature of barter, the fact that the *negocio*, the way of doing businesses, is never predefined.

Julio is a purist. He won't trade anything for money and doesn't think pesos have a place in barter markets. He even finds facilitators distasteful because they are too close to money and leave people feeling too much like shoppers. Whenever a new person came to his booth, he assumed a teacherly role, explaining how barter works and even offering to trade with them in exchange for nothing, on the assumption that later trades would give them Floricambios or products that they could use to complete the transaction. Julio's main concern was not his immediate personal benefit but the larger social benefit of helping people get into the system. His approach was rooted in a lesson that a barter neophyte once told me: in addition to the use-value and exchange-value that economists typically consider, there is also a social-value that is created through the very experience of trading and the relationships it establishes. To anthropologists, this should sound similar to analyses of the gift, Kula ring, and potlatch, all of which stress the construction of social relations—including both solidarities and hierarchies—through exchange (Gregory 1982; Mauss [1925] 2000; Malinowski 1922; Weiner 1992; see Wilk and Cliggett 2018, chap. 6, for an impressive synthesis of this literature). It is notable, however, that Julio and other barterers explicitly discuss and strategize around this social-value, and they do so for egalitarian inclusion rather than the construction of hierarchical structures or indebtedness.

Many trades at the barter market contradicted the widely touted shortcomings of barter that money supposedly solves. According to the conventional narrative, barter is a fine mode of exchange when a small number of people want to trade tangible goods of more or less equal value, at the same time, and—this is the clincher—when there is a coincidence of desires. This makes it pretty inconvenient: as one economics textbook puts it, "In a complex society with many goods, barter exchanges involve an intolerable amount of effort. Imagine trying to find people who offer for sale all the things you buy in a typical trip to the grocer's, and who are willing to accept goods that you have to offer" (Case et al., 1996, cited in Graeber 2011, 22–23). Beyond the individual, this makes barter a major impediment to complex economic systems and economic development because it cannot deal with large volumes, deferred transactions, credit systems, and the like.

It's unnecessary to rehash critiques of the indefensible origin myth of money, but Medellín's barter systems offer yet another example that the supposed shortcomings of barter are overstated. Yes, barter understood as an immediately completed, quid pro quo relationship between two people (Anderlini and Sabourian 1992) is of limited use. However, real living humans (unlike definition-making academics) are simply too creative to get stuck in such highly restrictive forms of trade in the first place, or even to narrow their imaginations to single and separate economic spheres. This is the essence of pragmatic pluralism, and it is also reflected in barterers' deliberations about how to combine barter with their other economic activity.

My first market introduced me to traders' ability to overcome the supposed limitations of barter; under the tutelage of two barterers, I managed to trade on credit and despite the noncoincidence of desires. Trading on credit builds long-term ties by solidifying—and giving material form to—a shared willingness to connect. In the same way, it strengthens a sense of community, belonging, and faith in the barter market as an enduring institution. By extending and accepting credit, barterers are saying, "I believe that this market will continue, that our personal relationship will continue, and that we share enough of a common ethic that I can count on you reciprocating appropriately."[1] However, Medellín's credit-based trades are perhaps more vulnerable than institutionalized credit systems and exchanges that are backed by the power of law and force and "a general ideology of stability [and] predictability" (Narotzky 1997, 55). Because Medellín's credit-based trades are rooted in interpersonal trust, when they go bad they are experienced as deeply personal violations. Absent the formalities and bureaucracies of modern credit, trades depend on clear communication. When people are unable to express their expectations or fail to uphold their part of the bargain, this can quickly spark resentment, defensiveness, and accusations of dishonesty, particularly in Medellín's emotionally charged landscape. This is a real source of vulnerability for emergent alternative economies, but it is also the point. Bringing grassroots morality back into the economy means exposing oneself to collective norms and expectations.

To offer one example, during my time in Santa Elena, Santiago declared openly that he would never trade with Humberto again. Santiago is normally quite placid, but Humberto had struck a nerve. After a couple of previous disagreements, including one when Humberto refused to repair a product, Humberto was now pressuring Santiago to renegotiate a credit-based trade. He wanted Santiago to give him more in exchange for the watch he had made, and he wanted his payment sooner. Fed up, Santiago simply returned the watch and stormed off. He was not the only barterer to experience problems with the joyful and kindhearted, but bad-listening, toy maker.

To be fair, economic historians do not say multipartner trades and credit are impossible in barter systems, just that money is a more efficient facilitator of these practices. Some traders respond that *inefficiency* is actually one of barter's most important virtues—by slowing the economy, barter counters the fundamentally unsustainable dynamics of capitalist growth and consumerism—a claim that we'll return to in chapter 5. However, most of Medellín's barter projects have tried to fight this economic friction by developing their own currencies to stimulate trade. These facilitators assume many of the classical functions of money (acting as a medium of exchange, a store of wealth, and a unit for measuring and comparing value).[2] They are extremely appealing to new barterers because they are familiar and unchallenging; they act like money, look like money, and feel like money. They speak to a world of impersonal abstractions: prices that are preestablished and rules that are easy to learn and require no social negotiation. But, ultimately, they are not the general-purpose money we are accustomed to (Bohannon 1959), accepted everywhere and for any transaction, and that is a critical difference. As a special-purpose money, facilitators have built-in restrictions that are meant to encourage trading only at a local scale, of ethical goods, and via solidaristic relationships. They are subject to rules and norms to avoid the creation of scarcity and grossly unequal accumulation, and they are carefully managed by individual traders (like Olga and Carla) to balance different goals across different spheres of exchange. They are also a direct response to the problems with the reigning general-purpose money: that it permits and promotes unethical relationships, goods, and services; that it exacerbates wealth and deprivation; and that it permits local wealth to leak into wider economies.

This reveals an ironic twist to conventional economic histories. In Medellín it was not the shortcomings of barter that led to money; it was the economic and sociocultural problems with money that led organizers to create their own barter systems, and then eventually to develop community currencies as a midpoint between pure efficiency and moral purity. Many experienced barterers even prefer direct trade to more "efficient" facilitators. Why would they prefer to trade in a more constrained way? In part, facilitators are too limited: much like frequent-flier miles, they are a form of special purpose money that can rarely be used when you most want to use it. If barter markets were held more often and had a broader diversity of goods, or if the facilitators were accepted in local stores, then traders would be more eager to accept them.

There is another reason that people choose direct barter over facilitators, and it is one that economic historians would be wise to consider. Many barterers are more interested in short- and medium-term consumption than storing large amounts of value. If they were to store value, it would be better to invest in useful, durable goods rather than papers that are intrinsically worthless. Investing your limited wealth in a purely social convention like money makes little sense unless you can guarantee that the convention will endure. And this highlights an often-hidden dynamic undergirding our commonsense acceptance of money: it depends on a broad-based consensus, an agreement that some particular form of money will be generally accepted, or officialized. This consensus has almost universally been imposed through political and economic violence rather than negotiated democratically. Much of money's success as one of the most widely accepted social institutions comes not from its appeal to the majority—either because it solves the problems they experienced with barter or works as a much-needed way of storing value—but rather from its appeal to the small minority, the only group with enough raw power to ensure that a social convention is maintained (Graeber 2011).

## The Ethics of Barter

Most market days provoke traders to contemplate barter in terms of their business logic (the baker's formula of bartering 25 percent of her profits), in terms of household provisioning (the *artesanos* feeding their families), and as an ethical-political project. Organizers often frame their proposal in explicitly anticapitalist language, explaining that they are against a monetary and trade system built on scarcity, competition, accumulation, the elevation of profit over social concerns, and the depersonalization of human relationships. They also frame it as a project to construct new economic and social relations. However, there was never a social contract for barter, no constitutional convention at which participants debated the meaning of justice and the true nature of a solidarity economy. As a result, barter organizers and participants do not share a uniform vision of barter as an economic, social, and political project, nor do they agree about barter's relationship to capitalism. All of these definitional and procedural issues are constantly being worked out through the practice of trading. Informal conversations, gossip, shaming, praise, and disagreement help to gradually cement these practices into authorized conventions. This ethical work becomes possible—and even necessary—because barter recasts reciprocity as a question to be interrogated, rather than an answer that is provided by the supposedly autonomous and rational sphere of money and market exchange (Hornborg 2016).

Let me provide an example. One day in Santa Elena, Julio and Clara were bartering a brand-new, two-burner gas stove. Word spread quickly that such a high-value item was in the market and people began approaching their booth to inquire about it. Because so many barterers were interested, they were debating the best way to trade it. Clara listed off a few of the people who were interested, starting with Flor, the *artesana*, who wanted to give her ailing mother a labor-saving alternative to her wood stove. Intuitively, Clara thought she should get it, but before making a decision they wanted to deliberate about what would be "the most just" and "most ethical" way of trading this stove. Clara suggested a raffle and Julio thought about picking straws. When they asked my opinion, I wondered whether one person clearly needed it more than the others.

As we were talking, Olga walked up to inquire about the stove out of pure curiosity. Julio explained their dilemma. A neighbor chimed in, saying that she knew the most just way: clearly they should trade it with Flor because it must be so hard for her mother to collect wood all on her own. Olga chastised her: "No, that's not how it works. You give it to the first person," and then she nearly interrupted herself to say, "actually, you're doing direct barter, not Floricambios? In that case you trade it for the best barter that you find, for whatever products you want most. That's the way barter works. You try to find the best match of value." Julio explained that this self-interested approach was fine, but they were trying to consider who could make the best use of it. Olga guessed that was another way of going about it, but she wasn't entirely convinced. In the end, Julio and Clara decided that the social utility of the stove mattered more than their personal profit considerations, and they traded it to Flor for some of her finest jewelry. They certainly did not need these necklaces and earrings, but they felt good about the trade. It represented a different type of value—the good-use-value that we all pursue whenever we say something is "free to a good home" or otherwise seek to ensure that our goods will be well used.

These types of semipublic deliberations about fair and just trading are part of the knowledge production process of this movement.[3] They are essential for working through the ethics of barter and establishing them as more broadly shared norms. Because they do not arise from collective deliberation at formal meetings, these ethics may be less visible and more difficult to articulate. However, because they emerge from everyday practice they may be more realistic than conference room imaginings, and because they are generated through constant negotiation they may be equally democratic.

Analyzing participants' representations of barter alongside their practices, there seemed to be some broadly shared contours of a barter ethics. The centerpiece of these was that the economy should work *for the benefit of all people*. In contrast to the capitalist economy, the barter economy should not structurally advantage certain people to the detriment of others. It should be an "infinite-sum game" rather than a zero-sum game and a trade regime in which "the satisfaction of one person's needs benefits others," as a popular slogan puts it.

This central precept brings two corollaries. First, it establishes that the most important goal of economic action is *satisfaction*. Satisfaction was a key yardstick for evaluating exchanges and behavior in the marketplace. All parties in a transaction should leave fulfilled. When this is not the case, somebody likely violated the code; they were not respecting the interests of their trading partner, were not valuing that person as a producer and a person, or (in the worst of cases) were interested only in personal profit. Satisfaction was also a criterion for the types of goods that should be brought to market. The rules of most fairs state that goods should be up to date, functioning, and of general interest; many barterers add that markets should not be a dumping ground but a place for high-quality products. Finally, satisfaction was used to contrast barter to the capitalist-monetary economy, as in the saying that "money is the chasm between a need and its satisfactor; barter is the bridge that saves us from this chasm." The more economic action and satisfaction are felt to overlap—the more that production and consumption, needs, and their fulfillment occur in the same spaces and at the same time—the harder it is to contemplate and calculate scarcity.

The second corollary is that, to be of benefit to all, the barter economy must be *inclusive and egalitarian*. There can be no favoritism, no differentiated prices for friends and strangers. The market must be transparent. All goods must be visible to all participants, so that nobody has an advantage. And when a particular product is in limited supply, it should be apportioned to maximize the number of people who enjoy it. This is most common with food. For example, if somebody brings three cakes to a barter fair, they are expected to sell by the slice and to make slices small enough so that most people can have one, rather than sell an entire cake to one person. Everybody should, quite literally, receive their share of the pie. These regulations detract from the apparent utility of the market because, unlike in conventional markets, you can't expect to bring a whole pie home for the family. However, these inefficiencies are justified because they introduce yet another type of value into the economic sphere: social-value, or the value of inclusion.

While the barter economy should benefit all, it is not free. The second major precept of barter morality is that *everybody must contribute*. Barterers like to speak of "dar, recibir, devolver" (to give, receive, and give back), a phrase they borrow from Marcel Mauss. Clearly this has to do with a general sense of fairness and the importance of reciprocity for establishing social ties, but it also has important economic consequences. Reciprocity promotes the flow of goods and services in the market, which is critical because stagnation is a large threat to small markets like these. And morally, this mirrors stages of mutual recognition of people's humanity: I recognize you, you accept my recognition, and you offer recognition back to me (Wilk and Cliggett 2018, 168). But the full significance of contributing can be understood only when one considers what it means for barterers as productive subjects.

One of the most common phrases they use is "we all need something and we all have something to give." This statement resonates so loudly because of what it says about *capabilities*. The fact that we all have something to give is revolutionary for some barterers and one of their greatest pleasures. To be useful, to see how exactly your work or your products benefit someone else, is a profoundly enriching experience, especially for some of the wealthiest and poorest traders. Other people's satisfaction demonstrates one's own value as a producer and as a fully human member of the community; it gives not just economic value but existential value, self-worth. The fact that barterers must contribute means that they are the kinds of people who *can* contribute. This is a powerful shift in identity in the face of the alienation and learned uselessness of a broken labor market or the gender norms of a patriarchally ordered privileged class.[4]

Of course, barter markets are also key sites for violating barter ethics, and organizers must sometimes police the markets, a reviled but inevitable practice. Their main policing strategy is to establish the general rules of exchange: if and when money is allowed, with whom you can sell and with whom you must barter, and how exchanges will be made. Restrictions allow organizers to skew transactions in favor of their moral and ideological precepts. For example, many facilitators expire after each market day so there is no possibility of accumulation or gross inequality and participants are forced to trade until all are satisfied. When the monies are accumulable across several months, organizers sometimes establish other rules to ensure that people don't come "just to shop," without contributing to the market. Such practices force reciprocity and combat accumulation without production. If "we all need something and we all have something to give," it is also true that we all must give in order to have our needs met. There are no free riders in the ideal barter market.

Barterers themselves also promote noncapitalist practices and sensibilities by demanding rules changes, exerting social pressure, hurling insults, gossiping, and refusing to trade with people who don't barter properly. Barterers who pressure potential customers are typically looked down on as being too aggressive and therefore more self-centered than mutualistic. The same can be said of barterers who don't respond compassionately when their products break or who change the terms of a long-term trade. The biggest insult is that a barterer is "just here to sell"; these people violate not only the barter process but also the whole range of ethical and interpersonal precepts that underlie barter exchange.

## Fear in the Market

Despite barter's open and affirming philosophy, it is difficult for many people to get started. One day, we were joined in Santa Elena by several participants in the city's Solidarity Economy School. Most were people from quite poor neighborhoods, with little formal education, who were using these trainings to launch businesses that they had been dreaming of. They heard about barter at the school and thought nonmonetary trade might be a great opportunity for their neighborhoods, where money was always in low supply, so they decided to visit.

One student, a fifty-something man named Mauricio, came to the booth I was sharing with Julio. He was very timid and seemed a bit confused or ashamed. Julio started to talk with him, asking if he knew how barter worked. Mauricio said they had explained it to him, but then clammed up.

"That's great," responded Julio. "Did you bring anything to barter?"

"I brought some things from home but I-I-I didn't know that I wasn't supposed to bring used clothing. So no, I don't really have anything." Julio looked down at the plastic bag that Mauricio was hugging to his chest and asked to see what he had brought. Mauricio just stood there and repeated that it was just a bunch of old clothes. He seemed almost paralyzed by shame.

But Julio tried to reassure him: "It's not that you're not supposed to bring old clothing. Old clothing is perfectly fine. What matters is that it be something with use-value, something that somebody else might be interested in. Come on," he said, "let's see what you brought."

Mauricio reluctantly agreed, pulling items out of his bag, unfolding them one by one, and spreading them on the table for us to see. There were a lot of women's shirts and jeans, most of them in very good shape. I commented on how good it all seemed, but Mauricio was silent.

Finally, Julio said, "Listen, friend, here's what I can offer you. Why don't you come over to this side of the booth, and we'll give you some space. You can stand with us and display your clothing and see if people want to trade." Julio had to offer a second time, but eventually Mauricio agreed. He folded his clothes neatly and joined us. Unfortunately, a thunderstorm blew in before he could make any trades.

Mauricio's timidity and fear present an important lesson about how some people react to barter. The same social forces that people were trying to escape by going up to Santa Elena simultaneously made it hard to take the risk of entering such an unconventional economy. Newcomers had to learn all of the skills of the market plus the additional stresses of a wholly different market sphere; the uncertainty was stressful. How could they know what's a good trade? What if someone tried to take advantage of them? What if they couldn't learn the rules? Was the stuff they brought good enough? Would people judge them? What if they didn't fit in? Doubts about personal worth and capacity that often accompany poverty can discourage economic experimentation.

## Wrapping Up

As the afternoon wore on in Santa Elena, the music arrived. A local musician brought his guitar and amplifier so he and Olga's partner could sing the protest songs of their youth. Sometimes others would come, uninvited, to pick up the guitar and play. A few former barterers, people who lived in Santa Elena and stopped to visit with old friends while running their Sunday errands, invariably showed up. Many members and former members brought visitors to the market as a unique outing, and every few months a former barterer brought a class of university students. Occasionally a traveler would come to the market (sometimes with advance notice, sometimes not) and request a stall, and sometimes a literature festival or pet immunization drive would ask to share the plaza.

An old campesino who used to barter often came just to watch. He would sit for an hour or two on the stairs, sometimes talking to young friends he knew from bartering and other times just silently observing the market. He once declared proudly that he was an old silletero. He even had one of his father's original silletas from when they carried summer tourists up and down the mountain. He used it, too, to carry his wife down to the hospital, back around 1970, before there were roads to his house. Now he only carries a silleta once a year, during the Feria de las Flores. Today they use cheap disposable ones that they fill with flowers, carry down to the city, and leave there.

Nonbartering *artesanos* (I always thought of them as poachers) also came to the market in large numbers, standing by the entrance to sell their products to curious visitors. Other spectators came out, too. They sat on the stairs, listened to music, and watched the afternoon turn into night. People of all ages gathered to drink a beer and have a snack. Some of the barterers packed up to return home before dark. Others lingered, hoping to earn some pesos selling to the tourists and locals who were now coming out for the evening. Eventually we had to kick them out so we could put away the booths. And then we paid our facilitators to get on the bus—packed together along with tourists returning home after a day of adventure—to descend back into the smog of the city and the realities of that other economy.

## The Politics of Exchange

Trading in Santa Elena confirms many of the lessons of economic anthropology. Exchange was clearly about much more than use-value and exchange-value;

the value of social inclusion was also extremely important both culturally and economically, as was the value of finding an object's best use. This has been shown elsewhere in terms of exchanges that make no economic sense—such as exchanging identical objects or potlatch exchanges that seem to impoverish the giver (Wilk and Cliggett 2018). People strategize around the ways that exchange creates and solidifies social relations, and Medellín's barterers also considered how general social inclusion expanded the material economic system and enrolled more people in this countercultural project. Activists and academics often portray money as inherently dehumanizing and antisocial, arguing that it dissolves social bonds, makes everything from potatoes to people comparable according to a single measure, and introduces acultural and purely calculative rationalities. As Bloch and Parry (1989) write, this "analysis" probably says more about our own cultural views of the economy than the way actual monies operate. The real question, they argue, is how money is shaped by a preexisting cultural matrix and, I would add, how Medellín's community currencies are also shaped by the political visions of barterers.

In Santa Elena, political imaginaries focused on rehumanization, decommodification, and the creation of just economic systems were translated into market rules and norms. Barterers worked out new rules and norms in two main ways: first, by negotiating the ideology of barter with their practical experiences of exchange and, second, by continually assessing the most ethical and strategic ways of linking different spheres of exchange, such as individual businesses, group businesses, and different barter markets. Barterers' experiments with different regimes of value demonstrate how alternativity and resistance are created through the interplay of material and cultural practices in everyday life. Barterers strive to orient trading toward different measures of economic success, including mutual satisfaction, fairness, inclusion, and nonaccumulation. In suggesting a trade, a barterer sets in place a cultural-political negotiation. She must put forward her own vision for how to achieve these goals, and then refine that vision in dialogue with her trading partner. Failing to achieve a micro-consensus on fairness means, quite simply, that no trading will occur. Moreover, dedication to barter means that traders are renegotiating this repeatedly, through each trading dialogue and through their own inner monologue as they incorporate barter into their household economies and daily production and consumption strategies. As chapter 5 shows, the deepest and longest-lasting changes that we see in barterers occur not just through voluntarism and dialogue but rather various forms of self-compulsion as barterers submit to the rules of the market and the limitations and constraints that economic localization implies.

These negotiations are a central part of what activists imagine as barter's revolutionary impact, for it is here that barterers use their noncapitalist cultural values and measures of economic success to create different regimes of value, and then different economic systems and social relations. This is the critical dialectic that organizers are trying to leverage. Noncapitalist regimes of value are anchored in—and become increasingly useful alongside of—different material relations to property, production, people, place, and exchange. It is this expansion from cultural-political values to trade and then to a broader realm of social and material life that would then permit truly transformative and enduring changes in cultural values. This process is inherently fraught, however, because alternativity often conflicts with hegemonic notions of utility. As we will see, the way activists balance the cultural and material sides of this dialectic significantly shapes barter's impacts, for better and for worse.

# 4

## What Barter Stimulates

### Economic and Social Impacts

> It was amazing. People were able to finish their houses through barter. They were even able to free themselves from debt through barter, by using it to get what they needed [and so reserving their money to pay off debts]. It was really beautiful.
> —Julio, organizer of the Pajarito Local Economic System

> The biggest benefits of barter have been what barter stimulates, not what it provides directly.
> —Olga, organizer of the Santa Elena barter fair

The dynamics and difficulties of barter organizing in Medellín—which mirror experiences from places as diverse as New Zealand, Argentina, the United States, and Mexico—suggest economic and sociocultural obstacles that may be common to all postcapitalist activism. In this chapter, I examine the impacts of Medellín's barter systems alongside global experiences with LETS (local exchange trading systems), the world's most researched alternative currency model. Barter and LETS have had similar trajectories and faced similar challenges sustaining interest, developing large and active trading groups, diversifying the goods and services on offer, and establishing collective governance. At first glance, then, we might not expect barter to have significant economic impacts. Like many other alternative economies, Medellín's barter projects make little impact on poverty, inequality, and vulnerability on a municipal, regional, or national level. However, as the organizers quoted above indicate, Medellín's barter fairs and local currencies significantly benefit participants' households, their businesses, and in some cases their communities. I therefore examine the social and economic effects of barter at the household and community scales, discussing what it provides directly and what it stimulates. But this is, in many ways, the heart of "revolutionary... pero." These small-scale impacts are necessary to test, refine, and reveal how a well-supported and well-developed barter system can transform economic and social relations. They are also essential for generating a depth and co-revolutionary breadth of change at the individual scale. To achieve organizers' "revolutionary" aspirations, barter's impacts must transcend this small scale, but the politics of scale are even trickier than they first seem. As we saw in early efforts to spread barter across Antioquia, scaling up quickly can reduce barter's alternativity and jeopardize its transformative potential.

To tease out the economic and social impacts of barter so we can evaluate the prospects and promises of scaling up, I focus on three questions. First, what impacts has barter had with regard to conventional economic development concerns like household livelihoods, levels of well-being, and support for small businesses? This is the question of greatest interest to policy makers and potential allies in the solidarity economy, who have been patiently observing the trajectory of barter. Second, how do barterers themselves frame the economic impacts of this alternative economy? They focus primarily on their own household economies, but consider those economies in a broader perspective than economic indicators allow. Finally, what are the social impacts of barter? Politicians, NGOs, and everyday folks across Colombia are extremely interested in strategies for repairing a torn social fabric and building the foundations of a peaceful, democratic society. Despite its shortcomings, barter shows promise as a tool for strengthening communities. In this chapter, I have separated the economic and social effects of barter for heuristic purposes, but many of the stories I tell demonstrate their connections. As we will see, deeply integrating economic and social change may be essential for sustaining economies that truly function as alternatives to capitalism and violence.

## International Experiences with Alternative Economies: LETS and Alternative Currencies

The global proliferation of alternative exchange systems during the 1990s sparked hope among radical scholars for the emergence of noncapitalism. Researchers especially followed LETS in the United Kingdom and New Zealand, where national governments promoted them as a form of community self-help and employment generation, and the Argentine Redes de Trueque (Barter Networks), which saw an enormous rise in importance when the Argentine peso and banking system collapsed in the early 2000s.

Scholars have typically discussed these economies as responses to the vulnerabilities created by capitalist development, neoliberal restructuring, and debt- or scarcity-based money. LETS and barter reduce these vulnerabilities by diversifying the economy and livelihood options, localizing the circuit of production-exchange-consumption, and rebuilding social networks. They also address the monetary foundations of poverty by providing a new system for rewarding productivity. Skills and knowledge aren't left untraded—and needs unmet—simply because state-issued money is lacking. Alternative markets that stimulate local production are meant to promote a grassroots version of import substitution industrialization;[1] they are nonstate alternatives to wrest back control over trade and "back stop" conventional economies, standing in the wings until they are called forward during crises (Goerner et al. 2009; Greco 2009; Lietaer 2001; Primavera 2002, 2009; Razeto 2000).

Academic evaluations of alternative economies have been mixed. LETS have been lauded for promoting community-based self-development, fostering alternative labor systems, facilitating localized self-provisioning, developing new skills and abilities among the poor, and incubating small businesses (Carlsson 2008; North 2007; Pacione 1997; Williams et al. 2001). As Aldridge and Patterson (2002) note, however, many early studies romanticized the potential of alternative economies, detailing how they *might* counter the logic of capital but offering little empirical evidence for these impacts. Nonetheless, case studies reported the same difficulties that Medellín's barter organizers face. For example, Pacione's (1997) research on LETS in Glasgow revealed high initial interest followed by low levels of actual trading and severe start-up problems. One of the cases he focuses on was never realized because of low levels of trust in the community and subjectivities steeped in fear and self-doubt: fear of credit, of experimentation, of talking with neighbors and strangers, fear of getting scammed, of getting one's hopes up, of losing government benefits, and fear of defining one's own capacities and desires. While Pacione's second case study is more promising, his conclusion that LETS rebuild mutual aid and counter globalizing capital seems more wishful thinking than coherent analysis.

North (2002) reported a similar dynamic of early hopes followed by false starts and limited trading in New Zealand. There, LETS were promoted by the government as part of a neoliberal welfare plan; Green Dollar networks were supposed to foster community-based social supports to replace the downsized state welfare system. North found that LETS had relatively little impact on the overall economy and on the household economies of most participants, that they were insufficiently diversified and not focused on basic needs, and that they faced major coordination problems. The systems suffered from some of the standard challenges (questions of quality, lack of trust among members, lack of understanding, trade imbalances) as well as unique problems stemming from the dominant mentality of the era, characterized by intense stigmatization of indebtedness and free-riding. Few people were willing to take on debt to the system, which is necessary for trades to occur. Finally, the government's inconsistent promotion of Green Dollars alongside a hard-line workfare program undermined the alternative currencies. In the end, North concluded, "Green Dollars can only be seen as *complementary to*, not a *replacement for* state provision. . . . To be more than prefigurative, they need to develop considerably" (2002, 496).

Aldridge and Patterson countered with an article provocatively titled "LETS get real," which argued that LETS should not be used as tools for economic development in Britain. Although gross data on LETS sound impressive—Williams et al. (2001) estimated that there were 303 LETS operating in the United Kingdom, with a total membership of around 21,300 people—they argued that actual trading levels were insignificant. The inability of LETS to meet their potential derived from *structural* and *sociocultural* constraints: the psychological and material power of money and the difficulty of understanding other forms of money; problems of supply and demand, quality, and transaction costs; organizational problems such as burnout, lack of education, and low community ownership; and low community capacity for such projects, as reflected in low levels of trust, geographical obstacles, and uncertainty or distrust about exchanging services. They concluded that "LETS may prove to have many potential uses, in particular they may be able to make a small contribution to local economic development (perhaps especially for those groups with solidaristic social networks and adequate incomes derived from the formal economy), but . . . they do not provide a cheap or a simple way to alleviate poverty in urban areas" (Aldridge and Patterson 2002, 379).

Aldridge and Patterson's findings are important, especially insofar as they dovetail with North's (2002) conclusions that nascent alternative currencies cannot substitute for the state's provision of basic services. Their desire to "get real," however, leads them to neglect the potential prefigurative importance of LETS systems and how they may build to something larger with time. In fact, there is some circularity to their argument. One of the main constraints on

LETS development is buy-in. Trained in the logic of capitalism and conventional currencies, people have come to see credit as debt; that is, as a dangerous threat rather than a relation of social connectedness. They imagine the economy as a sphere of individual action rather than collective interrelation. And they see themselves as incapable of providing useful goods and services for others. It is hardly surprising that LETS would encounter serious structural and sociocultural challenges; according to organizers, they are *explicitly intended to come up against these challenges* so they can contest taken-for-granted assumptions about the economy and provide new production-marketing-consumption contexts that incentivize different types of assumptions. This chapter shows how barter markets allow traders to evade the structural constraints of capitalism by sparking alternative, noncapitalist modes of production and different ways of mobilizing labor, resources, skills, and investments. In this and the next chapter, I also argue that alternative economies are countering these disempowering structural dynamics in a way that permits new forms of sociality and subjectivity.

These arguments add to North's (2007) comparative analysis of alternative economy experiences in the United Kingdom, Hungary, New Zealand, and Argentina. North argues that, taken together, these experiences demonstrate that alternative currencies can have massive economic implications for large numbers of people (as in Argentina) and over long time periods (as in New Zealand), particularly while the conventional economy is underperforming. Even where alternative economies' large-scale material benefits have been limited, he says, their social and political importance should not be understated: alternative currencies provide concrete evidence that other economies are possible, generate new political communities, and support efforts to build livelihoods around alternative ethical orientations. In combination with part-time jobs and other solidarity economy activities, people "often were able to provide for themselves the alternative, freer form of economy they wanted" (North 2007, 178). Looking toward the future, North (2010) also sees alternative currencies as a valuable tool for confronting peak oil and climate change. Similarly, Hornborg (2016, 91) argues that they may be essential for "radically reduc[ing] the physical vulnerability of humans" to global ecological and economic imperialism. As I discuss in the conclusion, however, achieving these broader goals will require supporting barter systems so they can attain a revolutionary depth and scale of transformation.

## Economic Impacts of Barter

Medellín's barter organizers—like these hopeful scholars—make grand claims about the economic benefits of alternative economies. For example, one barter manual stresses that "barter can help us solve in part our problems of poverty, unemployment and the lack of circulating money." As in the United Kingdom, however, the number of barterers in Medellín is so small and their activity so limited that it would be disingenuous to speak of barter's economy-wide importance. The number of regular traders has never exceeded several dozen families, and trading has rarely taken on a quotidian rhythm, depending instead on monthly markets that are too infrequent to form the basis of survival. In fact, the scale of trading was so low during my fieldwork that I abandoned plans to conduct a quantitative survey of traders. However, in-depth examination demonstrates that those who approach bartering as a serious part of their livelihoods can benefit significantly. Frequent barterers almost universally say they leave happy and come out ahead after every barter fair and that barter permits other patterns of investment and production that would have been unthinkable otherwise.

As Pacione (1997) suggests, it is not enough to look at system statistics and trade figures, and there is no reason to expect an emerging economic practice to have an impact on the national economy. We need to examine these systems at a smaller scale and from a different perspective, focusing not on their exchange-value as measured by contributions to GDP, for example, but on their use-value for participants. This would be akin to taking an emic perspective on barter. Rather than interpreting the low monetary impact of barter systems as a sign of their failure, we might look with surprise and curiosity at why people continue to participate in barter despite these low figures. What is it that they gain? What rewards do they find? And how then does barter affect the structural and psychosocial dynamics of capitalist hegemony?

## Impacts on Households

Based on records of barter, barter with facilitators, and sales at two of Santa Elena's monthly markets, I estimated average earnings equivalent to 100,000 pesos ($55) per month, or $660 per year. This represents 19.5 percent of the monthly minimum wage in just one day and is within the range of earnings that traders reported from other, nonbarter markets. To put this in the Colombian context, these earnings correspond to 6.7 percent of per capita GDP and are roughly equal to household spending on recreation and education combined (DANE 2009). In the international context, this is quite a bit larger than other noncrisis alternative currencies. North and Williams suggest earnings of 2 to 3 percent of GDP in a successful New Zealand exchange (North 2007) and 0.1 percent of GDP in Great Britain's LETS (Williams et al. 2001).[2]

The most common way that barter contributes to household economies is by reducing monetary expenses. Bartering allows cash-strapped households to acquire basic goods like clothing, home supplies, school supplies, birthday and Christmas presents, and food through nonmonetary means. Households are then able to shift their finances to other needs that might have gone unmet, or perhaps to savings, and they are less likely to accrue consumer debts. Observing barter markets—especially thematic ones like textbook or Christmas barters—I initially found little inspiration in many of these small trades. How could barter seriously affect the dynamics of poverty, vulnerability, capitalist accumulation, and inequality if people's participation consisted of little more than trading a handful of books for some used shirts, an old pressure cooker, or a set of action figures? Regular barterers and barter organizers also complain about the proliferation of low-quality and low-value used goods in barter markets and the low levels of new production for barter. To some extent, though, we all risk undervaluing what might be one of barter's most important benefits. More than a quarter of all households in Medellín have formal financial debts, paying up to 27.95 percent interest annually for commercial loans or up to 48.5 percent for microcredit. This doesn't take into account the large numbers who have unreported debts to loan sharks or to paramilitary groups, paying as much as 20 percent interest per month (Jiménez 2010).

It is especially common for parents to take on debt in December and January, when they face the double whammy of Christmas and the new school year. The average Christmas spending in 2010 was approximately $166, and school supplies can exceed $207 per student. In Colombia, as elsewhere in Latin America, increasingly easy access to credit helps poor and middle-class households manage high seasonal expenses and acute financial crises. But the *bancarización* (financialization or bankification) of Colombians—driven by surges in household savings accounts and increases in use of consumer credit by as much as 50 percent per year—create critical household and national vulnerabilities (*Semana* 2011; *Dinero* 2011). By offering nonmonetary access to goods, barter helps stabilize household economies, reduces dependency on credit, and frees funds for investment in long-term household well-being.

Barter, in some cases, also benefits households by facilitating access to goods and services that they would otherwise not purchase. Several particularly enterprising barterers have negotiated trades for costly services such as dental care, legal services, home construction, and counseling and have thereby used barter to increase their overall well-being and household security. In most cases, these trades have taken place outside of the formal barter markets, though they have often been inspired by them and depended on barter-based social networks. In addition, a small group of barterers has managed to pay off debts through barter, such as the Altamira organizer who paid his overdue condo fees by providing services to the community. Although only a handful of barterers have developed the faith in barter and the strategic barter thinking required to arrange these large trades, the Pajarito barter organizer whose quote began this chapter clearly describes how inspiring these experiences were.

Finally, barter permits a different type of household investment. At about the same time that barter organizers and I were self-critically debating how barter could fulfill more basic needs, one of the traders in Santa Elena offered me a very different perspective. She told me that it is actually not such a bad thing that barter does not fulfill all of her basic needs because it provides her with goods that she would otherwise not spend her limited money on:

> I go to invest my Floricambios [the local currency]. [Pause.] It's like this: I say, "Great, this costs me so much money but I have Floricambios. I have them to invest." If I see a product for 40,000 or 50,000 [pesos] in the market I'm not going to buy it because with this money I have to pay for the basic necessities. On the other hand, if I have Floricambios, I say, "Those are for reinvesting and why am I going to save them?" For example for the same product, like an encyclopedia, I wouldn't pay 20,000 but I would pay 20 Floricambios. It's not a basic need. If you're a single mother, the list is the basics. It's fine that barter doesn't fulfill all of my necessities because there are things that one says, "I'm not going to a store to buy these but certainly if I see them in a barter fair, then yes. Yes!" You acquire things like books or encyclopedias that one normally wouldn't buy at a store.

To put this in anthropological terms, having a second sphere of exchange organized around a special purpose money allows barterers to invest differently in order to meet different needs. This is exactly the dynamic Hornborg (2016) proposes when he argues that a government-run alternative currency could be used to meet basic needs, extracting well-being from circuits of commodification, speculation, and scarcity.

This point is not reflected in a purely quantitative analysis of barter earnings and cash savings, but it is important for understanding how barter affects the actual *experience* of poverty. Barter permits a different logic of investment. In the cash economy characterized by scarcity and vulnerability, heads of household must manage their money carefully. Those on the margins are forced into a calculative rationality that prioritizes the short term and the basics and reinforces feelings of chronic stress and personal incapacity. In barter markets, though, even if one's household finances are just as precarious, a mother can think differently; she can consider long-term investments and contributions to well-being that extend beyond the most basic necessities. Why? In part this results from the relative unimportance of barter. Because barter is such a small slice of each household's economic activity, barterers can afford to be a bit less calculating, a bit more carefree in their desires and adventurous in their exchanges. But this different investment logic is also related to the nature of value in barter systems. When value is recognized only in the form of money, it depends entirely on the vagaries of labor, commodity, and financial markets that are far beyond the control of each household head. Value as money is naturally scarce and fickle, and households that fail to treat it as such can suffer tremendously. In the barter economy, however, value derives primarily from the time and capacities of the traders, qualities that are relatively knowable and controllable. Barterers can afford to invest beyond the basics and into the long term because they exercise substantially more control over the production of new value; they are far less at the mercy of distant forces.

In Medellín, barter also supports long-term investments in social development by creating new markets that challenge the wasteful and monopolistic dynamics of textbook publication and resale. The annual textbook barter organized by the Fundación Éxito and a charitable business association saved an average of $50 per user for more than fourteen thousand users (data from Comfenalco). Community-level textbook barters have generated additional savings of $193,000 in thirty events (*No Nos Llamamos Plata* barter newsletters). These are extremely important figures when you consider that a leading contributor to the school dropout rate is the cost of supplies, which can exceed the monthly minimum wage in the month that school starts (Chica Agudelo 2010; Díaz Tafur 2005; Reimers 2000; Rodríguez and Valenzuela 1998). Reducing these household expenditures may help keep children in school longer, indirectly reducing long-term household vulnerability and the social and security problems associated with absenteeism and the lack of job opportunities.

## Impacts on Small Businesses

Barter's largest material impact is probably its stimulating effect on family businesses. While some barterers in Santa Elena traded used goods or products that they threw together on a small scale just for the barter markets, many of Santa Elena's barterers traded products from their small businesses. Olga, the organizer of the Santa Elena fair, explained that her "elitist bakery" benefited primarily from the advertising impact of being in the barter market. Contacts and publicity have been among the most important benefits for small businesses. Many barterers forge connections at the markets that lead to cash sales later on, and these monetary gains help justify the expense of traveling up the mountain to Santa Elena. However, some of the most important connections are not with customers, but with other producers who are willing to share their knowledge: people who can teach you about new crops or products, tourists who share their wine making secrets, or jewelers who are more laid-back and willing to share secrets with competitors. Perhaps most impressively, the barter markets have served as incubators for several businesses.

Roberto and Isabel provide the most obvious success story. Isabel grew up on a farm in Santa Elena, where Roberto joined her several years ago. They are striving to create a life that allows them to enjoy the beauty of Santa Elena and to be connected to the land while remaining essentially autonomous, in charge of their own time and energy. Living in a beautiful, traditional house on her father's small plot of land, they have built gardens for themselves and expanded the house using reclaimed and informally bartered materials. Several years ago they began making wine from a local, wild-harvested blueberry called *mortiño*. At the time, another barterer was making mortiño wine in fairly large quantities, and he helped Roberto and Isabel learn the wine-making process. Once they had refined their recipe, they tried it at the barter markets to widespread approval. Transitioning from production for home use to production for a market, even at such a small scale as the barter market, required increased dedication to wine production and the adoption of more professional processes to ensure even quality standards. Beginning their commercial activities in the barter market, they explained, gave them a chance to scale up slowly and to test their product, marketing strategies, and even minor issues like bottling and labeling in a comfortable and supportive environment.

Having tested the waters, they decided that they enjoyed larger-scale production enough to launch a wine business. They won a government competition for small business training and a five-million-peso grant to construct a professional kitchen and wine cellar. Their experience in the barter fair demonstrated that they were serious producers. Roberto and Isabel have now expanded their range of wines, which they sell in open-air markets and specialty stores in Santa Elena and downtown Medellín. They continue to barter nearly every month, and their booth is busy; they offer free samples to attract new customers, advertise where their wines can be purchased, and easily barter or sell all of their wines long before the end of the day. They also regularly bring garden produce (especially Andean heirloom vegetables) and experimental products such as wine and fruit marmalades to explore new market possibilities. Roberto explained, "I make a living off of my wine, and the big benefit that I've gotten out of barter is that people see the wine and they know about mortiño wine and they try it and later they come and buy it as well."

Considering barter economics via barterers' own perspective means appreciating that wealth, poverty, and economic activity are not purely quantitative concerns; they are first and foremost *experiences*: multifaceted, sensory, and subjective experiences of well-being, self-worth, and social belonging. Numerical indicators provide policy makers the comfort of measurability, comparability, and apparent predictability, but they are valuable only insofar as they reflect people's subjective experiences of well-being. I would argue that policy makers, development professionals, and activists should also adopt an ethnographic perspective that captures these more subtle and subjective aspects of development—Roberto's pride in providing finely crafted Andean goods to the city, our jeweler's sense of freedom and fulfillment when she can provide her daughter with encyclopedias and books, and the sigh of relief that families feel when they are freed of debt. These economic impacts tell us not only how the barter economy feels to people but also what types of innovations and transformations it may prefigure, for they signal exactly the psychosocial dynamics of capitalism that Aldridge, Patterson, and others discussed.

Conventional development research has attempted to incorporate some of these subjective experiences (Collins et al. 2009). However, these efforts often begin and end with academic concepts. As a result, they re-abstract people's perspectives into the languages and institutions of large-scale, professionalized management rather than allowing people's concepts to stand on their own. The ethnographic approach I imagine would more fully honor grassroots knowledge in order to understand not development alternatives, which can be implemented through the same old systems of power and knowledge, but alternatives to development (Escobar 1992). Among other benefits, this would enable us to see market and community as fully interconnected and to recognize diverse conceptualizations of value and well-being, as I do here.

## Social Impacts of Barter

Local literature on barter—like anthropological literature on economies more generally—underscores the connections between economic change and social change. For example, one barter manual describes how "diverse communities have begun to practice this new form of Solidarity and Sustainable Economy because they have realized that there are other ways of relating among ourselves economically, distinct from capitalism, which converts everything into commodities and views people and things from the perspective of money" (Manual del Trueke [Bello] 2008). To change the economy, then, is to build new types of social relationships and learn to see one another differently. In the words of organizers and participants, barter helps promote "mutual recognition" or "a deeper recognition" of each individual as a person. And as Werner observed in a New England time bank, nonmonetary exchange can establish powerful collective identities and "an expanded sense of self, moving from I to we" (2015, 73).

As Olga explained, these changes are especially important for repairing a social fabric that has been shredded by decades of violence, atomization, and the avaricious Paisa mentality of "beat out the other person before they beat you." In Roberto's words, they offer the possibility of creating "real security in communities so that we don't need this 'democratic security' [a reference to the controversial security program of former president Álvaro Uribe]."

This comment underscores what are, locally, considered to be the most compelling motives for building social relations: to repair a broken social fabric and construct *ciudadanía* (citizenship or civic culture). Even Roberto and Isabel, who have used barter effectively for material benefits, see its impact as more far-reaching. Barter, they recognize, has helped them achieve a freer and more enjoyable lifestyle, and most importantly it helps create the conditions for real social healing. When I interviewed them, Roberto began by giving me a tour of their house and wine-making facilities. During the tour, he told me about the growth of their business. But as the three of us sat down to eat lunch, the bulk of our conversation revolved around the challenge of creating community in a context so deeply permeated by violence and distrust. Roberto sees barter as a key to creating *convivencia*, the "art of living together." He sees a deep cynicism in Colombia that has been cemented through a history of dirty and violent politics and that continues to be reinforced to this day. In the week before our interview, reports surfaced that then-President Uribe was planning to pay students to spy on their peers' activities. Roberto explained the consequences he expected:

> This will only create fear, and it will create an arms race on the street. Nobody in their right mind would denounce someone unless they themselves were armed, because to denounce someone is to put yourself at risk. The government is bringing war to the streets. It is enrolling people in the war just like the paramilitary has already enrolled people in the war, and this is going to cause escalation and distrust. [Long pause.] But barter might help reverse the momentum from distrust to trust. Barter is all about getting to know each other and building trust and learning to really see one another. That's a big part of what we've gained from barter here in Santa Elena: relations among community members. Before, people who looked different were called "potheads" or "long-hairs." Anybody with a beard or long hair or a guy with earrings was ostracized, and it was dangerous just to look like this [pointing to himself and to me]. But this has improved through barter, because it brought together all of these different people and gave them a chance to actually interact and to begin to see each other differently. But the problem is that the city is not the same as here. Neighbors don't know each other, even in the most densely populated areas. And the problem is that every social initiative is accused of being socialism, which people think means that it supports the guerrillas, and so they're shut down. What we really need to do is build a different culture here.

Diego told a similar story. Like Roberto and Isabel, he sees barter as far more than an economic enterprise. Being in the market gives him new ideas about how to live more sustainably or in a more rewarding way, and it provides an uncommon opportunity to forge connections with a community of people exploring alternatives. "If you go with the expectation that you're going to find everything, then it's not going to work. You get rich in other ways: socially, spiritually . . . and then maybe on the economic level as well, like with [my] wines. For example, with my dad. He comes up from [a distant town] every month and it's basically the only time that we get to share with him, and now with his new son as well. It's the same with all of our friends from the barter."

Diego, like many barterers, was expressing a different definition of development that focuses on holistic well-being rather than conventional economic and social indicators. The trust, mutual recognition, and connection that Roberto and Diego described are distinct from the social capital so often mentioned in conventional development literature and from other alternative indicators like Gross National Happiness. What they were describing is a basic sense of humanness that provides the grounds for functioning community. Creating spaces and times for sociality is central to this kind of development work.

## Creating the Sociality of Barter

Anthropological literature adds to this grassroots analysis of barter sociality, suggesting that we might expect two types of social impacts—the construction of affective social relations (feelings of connectedness, empathy, or fictive kinship) and the construction of pragmatic social relations (mutual aid, interdependence, or obligation). The stories of Roberto, Isabel, and Diego have already demonstrated some of the social benefits that barter brings, but trust and community building are so important in Medellín that they deserve more attention. Because another anthropologist was studying the construction of social networks through barter in Medellín, I did not make this a central part of my research and cannot detail the numbers and types of networks established and their functions. However, I provide a sense of *how* social relations are constructed in barter markets. What are the actual activities and experiences that lead people to talk, share, lower their inhibitions, and connect with other barterers in ways that they do not connect with other casual acquaintances, and with results that might strengthen trust, conviviality, friendship, and also materially beneficial relationships?

One element of bonding in the market is a simple matter of the time that people spend together. Barterers pass a full day together every month. They admire one another's work, crowd together under tarps to seek shelter from the rain, and ride back to town together in crowded buses. Their conversations may begin with small talk or comments about the market, but they expand into more complex relationships. People start to notice when somebody is sick and check in on them. They share food when another barterer forgets lunch. And they accumulate a body of shared experience so that later, when they see each other at other markets or at small business development programs, they often sit together or stop to talk.

Beyond the simple issue of time spent together, the act of trading itself can establish meaningful commonalities. Barter is often considered a less social form of exchange than gifting or credit because it often involves immediate and exact reciprocity: you give me what I want, I give you something of equal value, and we are done with each other. Forms of exchange that create long-term connections and material interdependence are believed to establish stronger bonds (Gregory 1982; Mauss [1925] 2000; Plattner 1989; Wolf 1972). However, the temporality and commensurability of barter in Medellín are rarely so clear-cut. Many barter transactions lend themselves to long-term relationships. Bartering on credit, for example, implies trust and a commitment to seeing each other again. Also, when farmers exchange seeds at the market or when wine-makers share their wines, these material exchanges also imply an exchange of knowledge that stretches across time. Farmers and gardeners follow up to discuss how plants are growing, they swap information about other farming techniques, and they seek each other out when they have new information or new seeds to share. Vintners check in to see how the new technique worked and to brainstorm how else the process might be improved.

My own experiences as a barterer over the course of just one year showed how collaborations can develop through trading. I typically came to the market with a combination of used items (books, pirated DVDs that I had already watched, and perhaps some clothes or toys that I had acquired at other barter events but couldn't use myself) and food products such as homemade marmalades, salsas, chutneys, vinegars, or citrus gathered from my neighborhood's public spaces. One day, a woman who had previously traded for my salsa sought me out at the market because she wanted more. I didn't have any at the time, but she offered to either barter or buy it from me if I was going to return to Santa Elena over the next weeks and asked me to make some for her at the next market. A woman from the neighboring booth overheard this conversation and asked more about what I made. She mostly traded used clothing but also offered a small selection of marmalades and chocolate candies at each market, and she suggested that we trade recipes and buy jars together so that we could reduce our costs. We did, and in the process met with each other a couple of times, shared life stories, and connected one another with friends who had similar interests. Had I lived in Medellín longer, this collaboration could also have improved our earnings and permitted new production strategies. At another market, this woman's daughter saw my sign offering translation services and approached me seeking advice about jobs. She worked as a freelance translator and wanted to exchange numbers so that we could put each other in touch with potential clients. Later in the year, I explored the possibility of collaborating with a wood and bamboo toy maker to build bamboo bicycles. Again, had I stayed in Medellín longer I would have pursued a small community enterprise with internally displaced people to produce these bikes for both sale and barter. Each of these relationships had both affective and pragmatic components, and each certainly enhanced the network that I could draw on to practice my economy and in case of an emergency.

Most of these exchanges did not *force* solidarity on the traders because we shared neither a legal requirement of long-term reciprocity (as in the case of credit) nor a cultural-moral one (as in the case of gifting). Nonetheless, every form of transaction—as a relationship of interdependence and a demonstration of shared interest in a product—creates an opportunity for mutual commitment. This is as true in the conventional economy as in the barter economy; I had a close relationship with the fruit vendor in my neighborhood because we saw each other every day, talked about what was going on in the city, and began to look out for one another. However, it seems more pronounced in barter markets because, in addition to the common interest in a product, both sides are also manifesting a common interest in the countercultural ethics and politics of bartering. Traders' goal was not "to be done with each other" and then move on, because that produced exactly the type of alienation and commodification they felt in the conventional economy. Ironically, although participants argue that barter markets are not as diversified and materially dynamic as they would like, this "shortcoming" may actually increase the markets' social value. In barter fairs, where people are less driven by a scarcity mentality, they are more relaxed, less worried about every last peso they are spending and saving, and more ready to look beyond the economic.

Finally, barter is undeniably a collective and countercultural political project, and as such it unites participants through their alterity. Barterers are, well, barterers. Because they are such a small minority dedicated to such an unusual practice, they stand out and they know it. "Barterer" becomes an identity, an extremely meaningful one for some of the most active participants and organizers. Even for those for whom it is a less important marker, it still sets these traders apart and binds them together. What is perhaps most impressive about this practice—and particularly in Santa Elena—is that it unites people across the divisions of class and subculture. Elite ladies, smallholder campesinos, poor and working-class families, and bohemian *artesanos* come together in the same space, to engage in a collective and co-constructed practice, and under the same identity. Markers of difference are always apparent—clothing, style, and the types of goods that one trades say a lot about *who* each trader is, and conversations often expose other revealing details like last names and barrios— but these aspects of the social hierarchy seem less important in the barter fairs than they do in the street. Humphrey (1992) argues that barter often establishes links across difference because it involves trading for products that you cannot produce yourself, which often means trading with people from different social or ethnic groups who live in different regions. In Medellín, we see similar effects but sparked by a shared social identity or a shared commitment to countercultural ethics rather than reciprocal material needs, much like the "ideological compadrazgo" that Lancaster (1992) found in revolutionary Nicaragua. Even when barterers chafe under an organizer's heavy hand, or fundamentally disagree about a particular issue, they are still bound together as a minuscule minority engaged in the construction of an alternative. This makes them even more likely to engage in other types of solidarity, like sharing lunches and coffees during barter fairs, sharing rides, or collaborating beyond the market.

## The Community-Economy Problematic

Community is thus, in many ways, an outcome of the barter project, but it is also a necessary ingredient for it. Julio and Clara—who have participated in multiple barter experiments and are particularly attuned to the community-building potential of barter—often wondered how deep these social ties really run. The LETS-style system they founded in Pajarito was specifically designed to build and maintain community cohesion when that small village was threatened by urban redevelopment. When they first moved to Pajarito, Clara was amazed by the strength of the village's community: "You'd hang clothes out to dry and then go down to the city to work and come back thinking, 'Oh no. There was a rainstorm. My clothes are going to be soaked.' But you'd find them hung up inside of your house with no note or anything. People would just do things for each other without thinking of it. It wasn't gifting. It wasn't reciprocity. It was conviviality." Creating a very local exchange system in this type of setting lent itself to collaboration, and the organizers designed barter as part of a broader program to "work with the social fabric." The results were impressive. Once they started to connect barter to other community-wide projects—such as community theater, environmental cleanups, and local governance—people came out in droves. Designed in this way, barter built on a preexisting community in order to activate and strengthen that community. Julio and Clara explained that that's part of what makes barter work: "It has to be the whole thing, about the community, about the cultural events. It has to be about bringing people together. If it's just about the market, then it doesn't work. That's why ferias aren't enough." In their experience, barter takes on extra significance to the extent that it becomes a collective project, and it simply cannot function when the markets are disembedded, abstracted from other realms of activity and conceptualized as a realm of their own.

Unfortunately, they did not see the same degree of community mobilization and community-market integration in Santa Elena's more geographically dispersed barter system. "You can see that people are there just to do it," said Julio, "but not because they want to spend time together with *that* group of friends.... People say there is community there, but I don't see it in practice." Clara was doubtful that Santa Elena's markets could be converted into a deeper, more community-based barter project, but Julio was optimistic. If you started fresh, with a small group of close friends and neighbors, then you might be able to overcome the large distances separating Santa Elena's barterers and initiate activities that extend beyond the market. Some of Santa Elena's long-term barterers have proposed similar ideas: creating a community garden run by barterers, hosting a large event to celebrate World Water Day, beginning each barter fair with some type of ritual, or creating a permanent barter space that could act as a physical node for this community.

I agree with much of Julio and Clara's assessment of the Santa Elena barter group. Even in the absence of a tight-knit community, though, barter is fostering new bonds among subgroups of Santa Elena's barterers. It has deepened friendships among people who already knew each other prior to joining the market, and it has given rise to new friendships, particularly among people engaged in the same line of work or who share a similar outlook on life. Barterers and former barterers occasionally call one another to ask for favors—and the old Santa Elena directory is used most often as a phone book for like-minded people—but it is worth noting that I did not witness the types of strong bonds that anthropologists might expect to emerge from barter: fictive kinship relationships like *compadrazgo* or important, even life-sustaining social networks.

However, I think we are missing part of the picture if we presume that Medellín's social fabric can be most effectively repaired through strong bonds or "practical" social relationships. In fact, there is good reason to believe that relationships with *strangers* and casual acquaintances might be most important for building an atmosphere of trust and respect. Other scholars have made similar arguments. For example, Granovetter (1973) argued that "weak ties" are especially important for weaving together social networks and spreading information and influence, and Lancaster (1992) illustrated how working-class Nicaraguans pursued fictive kinship with more socially distant people as a way of creating a more diverse and resilient social network. However, what Olga, Roberto, Isabel, Diego, and other barterers expressed in their hopes for barter was not (or not only) the desire for new social networks and new communities; rather, they envisioned a different orientation toward others, one that was less closed, was less antagonistic, and therefore allowed for a deeper recognition of our mutual humanity. In Santa Elena's barter market, where diverse individuals came together each month to experiment with something new, despite differences in class, lifestyle, and politics, this humanizing predisposition toward others seemed possible. But barter had these effects not only because it provided "an excuse" for coming together, as some barterers say. Very particular features of the market promoted this humanization, especially its embeddedness in community norms rather than abstract rules, its smaller scale, the fact that it offered an alternative identity to unite these diverse people, and finally some of its inefficiencies, which converted it from a realm of pure calculation to a realm of more relaxed experimentation. In this sense, the "failure" to scale up may actually facilitate some of alternative economies' cultural and psychosocial impacts.

## Conclusion

As a noncapitalist project to build a socially embedded and humanizing economy, barter is fundamentally in tension with the capitalist economy and its social and cultural dynamics. Medellín's political culture forged in violence is one aspect of this, but barterers also have to grapple with an economic culture that celebrates individual self-interest and calculative reasoning while provoking anxieties about credit, collaboration, and free-riding. All of this is undergirded as well by structural, material dynamics. Cycles of economic collapse and recovery drive capitalist investment while repeatedly challenging long-standing social solidarities and new forms of mutual aid like LETS and barter systems. At the household level, continuous processes of primitive accumulation keep grassroots ownership of the means of production to a minimum, increasing dependency on wage labor and credit systems and thereby limiting barterers' ability to fully commit to alternative economies. And finally, the geographic separation of classes and stark differences in skills and education impede efforts to improve market quality and diversification.

These structural and sociocultural dynamics are central to capitalist hegemony. They help lock capitalism in place by making wage labor, private property, and exploitation seem like the obvious choice—or even the only choice—for getting by and getting ahead.[3] However, hegemony is more than the cultural work to define what is thinkable; it is also material and social work to constrain what is practically achievable. The shortcomings that we see across alternative economies in Medellín, Argentina, New Zealand, the United Kingdom, and elsewhere are a clear "diagnostic" of capitalist hegemony (Abu-Lughod 1990). "Getting real" about alternative economies does not demonstrate a fatal flaw; it illustrates precisely how the conventional state-capitalist economy functions to impede alternatives and, therefore, what alternatives must do to overcome these obstacles. Barter is not a fully diversified economy. It does not permit people to live outside of the cash economy. It provides too few opportunities for unemployed laborers, for the exchange of services, and for meeting basic needs. Barter markets suffer from problems of supply and demand, quality (especially with regard to services), high transaction costs, organizer burnout, and low levels of collective action. And in their efforts to expand these systems, organizers also confront uncertainty, distrust, and shame associated with nonmonetary trade, and with other aspects of money's psychological and material power. These production, exchange, organizing, and psychosocial challenges arise from common roots: the creation of multiple scarcities (of resources, time, self-confidence, and a sense of agency) through ongoing primitive accumulation and the commodification of basic needs; the retrenchment of an economic monoculture through support from major institutions, including institutions of the so-called solidarity economy; and the continual separation of economics from other realms of life and realms of value. The question for long-term transformation is whether alternative economies are countering these disempowering dynamics in such a way that new subjectivities, improved participation, noncapitalist production, and economic diversification become increasingly possible with time.

Despite barter's shortcomings, it is clear that people who commit to integrating barter into their livelihoods can gain significant material benefits from it. They use barter to incubate small businesses, test the market, gain knowledge, find customers, and establish a reputation for their business and their products. Barter also provides a boon for their private, household economies, offering a chance to meet some needs without spending scarce pesos or taking loans and permitting forms of long-term investment that might be impossible in a cash market. Diversifying the economy in this way undoubtedly decreases household vulnerability while reducing the extent to which lack of currency impedes labor, exchange, and the production of public and private goods. While many LETS have been critiqued as middle-class hobby economies, Medellín's barter fairs incorporate people from across the class spectrum, including a number of regulars who scramble each month to collect the bus fare to make it to market. As such, the fairs become important sites for expanding business networks, exploring new (classed) tastes and consumer mentalities, and expanding skills. Most importantly from the perspective of some barterers, alternative exchange systems provide material and social resources for the construction of alternative lifestyles and different models of production and consumption that permit more personal freedom and generate less vulnerability and inequality.

In Medellín, the social promise of barter has always been as intriguing as its economic potential. My research suggests that the results are, on the whole, quite favorable. The time spent together in barter markets, the generally festive and carefree attitude facilitated by nonmonetary exchange, and the collaborations that develop through these markets have strengthened friendships and family ties while generating new relationships. The entire Santa Elena barter group might not constitute a cohesive community of close and mutually supportive members, but clusters of friends have emerged from barter. Perhaps most importantly, barter markets offer an unusual opportunity for people to come together across class and lifestyle divides, to interact with and learn to appreciate people who at first seemed quite different and perhaps threatening, and to begin to explore areas of common interest. Fostering a predisposition of mutual respect and mutual recognition—"moving from I to we" (Werner 2015)—may be barter's most important impact. Although this kind of sociality can also occur in conventional cash markets, several barterers noted that barter's difference from the conventional economy made people less competitive and more open to sharing. Barter may deserve more attention than it currently receives in a city seeking opportunities to construct *ciudadanía* and *solidari-dad*. And indeed, this may extend to community economies more broadly.

Grassroots barter organizing has taken hold in the same place where years of violence have generated "fears of anything collective." As Julio whispered to me during our first interview in a small café, people are afraid of collective action, of collaborative thinking, of anything that might be different. It has been "very strongly instilled in people that collectives are different, that they are dangerous." This atomization is one of the main goals of violence, and one of the main requirements for an asocial, disembedded, dehumanizing economy. "The damage to the social fabric is the most grave," he told me. "The destruction of collectives is difficult to repair. But [raising his voice with excitement] *that* is why it's so beautiful that there's still barter in this city." Amid activists' utopian dreams and blistering self-critique, this point stood out clearly: imperfect as it may be, barter is a step toward a society that people long for and a hopeful reminder of grassroots agency in creating alternative futures.

Any time we ask about impacts, though, we should step back to interrogate how exactly we are conceptualizing "impact." Debates about the effects of alternative economies—and the tension captured by "revolution . . . pero"—represent a deep disagreement about the nature of the world we live in and desire. When we are "seeing like a state" (Scott 1998), Aldridge and Patterson's analytic is useful, and we must acknowledge that these alternative economies have not yet been effective in generating employment or meeting basic needs on a mass scale, except in moments of economic collapse. But what undergirds this statist view? In Scott's (1998) analysis, it depends upon (1) a gross simplification and quantification of nature and society, (2) a high-modernist ideology that favors the imposition of scientifically rational order on diverse peoples and landscapes, (3) a state that is sufficiently authoritarian to enact such plans, and (4) a "prostrate civil society that lacks the capacity to resist these plans" (Scott 1998, 5). Those are not the conditions that will lead us to a pluralist, radically democratic society in which people construct and enjoy conditions of justice, dignity, and minimally exploitative economic activity. In order to see how barter might contribute to *that* type of society, we need to take seriously the idea of prefiguration. Does barter permit less commodified ways of living? A reconceptualization of work? Communities that support the development of alternative philosophies, ethics, practices, and livelihoods? And if so, how do these effects spread—what links them from the experimental present moment to a larger-scale future?

To provoke far-reaching postcapitalist transformations, barterers likely need to establish complementary initiatives that target the specific cultural and structural dynamics of hegemony. In Julio's words, "If it's just about the market, then it doesn't work." These might include efforts to forge deeper solidarities, community and government projects to insulate individuals from material vulnerabilities and build assets for diversified production, efforts to expand institutional engagement with diverse economies, and strategies to permit and encourage traders to dedicate ever-increasing portions of their time to nurturing their barter commons. And yet the market itself does important work. While some of barter's impacts might have come from *any* effort to revive collectives, much of the solidarity and humanization provoked by barter is due specifically to this form of exchange. Barter markets are one of the only times when many people are encouraged to think of themselves as skilled, capable producers, and one of the few spheres in which these producers confront one another face-to-face, through negotiated prices based on use-value and mutual satisfaction, in momentary escape from the stresses of the cash-based bottom line, and, often, in relations of extended commitment.

There is good reason to believe that Medellín—and not just its alternative corners like Santa Elena—might be a "propitious environment" for this type of scaling up. Medellín has nearly three decades of barter experience, a history of support and experimentation even from conventional economic sectors, a large and diverse solidarity economy sector and growing middle-class interest in fair trade, dynamic industrial and agricultural sectors, and a broader culture of pragmatic pluralism that encourages economic diversity. But weaving these together into a broad, deep, and enduring postcapitalist transformation will take tremendous skill. In the next chapters, we study two aspects of activist strategy to date: their ways of cultivating new subjectivities and economic cultures and their efforts to link barter to (and insulate barter from) conventional economies. If my analysis is correct, getting these strategies right will be essential for making barter revolutionary.

# 5

## "A Barter That Runs through Our Veins"

### Culture, Power, and Subjectivity

In August 2010, four barter activists and I gathered in a stark, sterile office to launch the barter training for the Solidarity Economy School (SES). The SES was a city-funded program to support micro-business development by poor households, and to link these via solidarity economy institutions such as associations, cooperatives, and micro-finance organizations. During the school's first year, there was a mention of barter. In the second year this increased to a full class session and barter simulation. This year, we offered a thirty-hour barter diploma program for low-income entrepreneurs and the city's Solidarity Economy Promoters and coordinated twelve barter markets. This was big: imagine if your government dedicated funds to alternative economy trainings for micro-entrepreneurs and economic development officers, encouraging people to integrate barter into their business plans along with loans, production, cooperatives, marketing, and the like.

As five o'clock approached, we frantically reviewed our roles, reorganized the office into two semicircles of plastic chairs, and arranged our poster paper, markers, string, nametags, and attendance list. Each student arrived amid a clamor of buzzing doorbells, clanging metal doors, and screeching locks, followed by greetings that echoed down the ceramic-tiled entryway. They were timid and talkative, some gently easing into chairs in the back of the room, others jumping in to help reorganize the space. All wore their class clearly: some in work clothes, some in the everyday wear of too-busy housewives, and others in the self-consciously cared-for but slightly tired dress clothes of people who are fighting to defy social stigma. Only two arrived wearing the hippieish garb of stereotypical (though not typical) barterers.

As the course began, we unwittingly revealed our mixed emotions about barter in Medellín. What was supposed to be a tightly focused and inspiring introduction to local barter experiences became a challenging mix of soaring expectations and honest self-critique. Two organizers dominated the first hour of the session, presenting one exciting local project after another and then detailing where they went wrong. The style of barter was ill conceived, organizers burned out, campesinos left once subsidies dried up. These improvised presentations revealed how we had all been thinking about barter. Santiago reiterated his firm belief that "barter is not a game. It's an economic alternative that can expand to support household economies across the city." But each hope was quickly eclipsed by stories of grappling with the shortcomings of our markets and our organizing. Santiago continued, "There are beautiful things [in barter] but also downsides, and this is the challenge for this course: to ensure that barter doesn't die in the community. Projects die because of people, and then we have to ask how strong were these projects in the first place? For our part, we're not interested in more fairs. We're interested in processes, and permanent ones. For that we need a team. Right now we might be just five [organizers], but after this course, with you, we might be ten or twenty or twenty-five. But it's difficult. Breaking our paradigms is difficult."

Our transparency may have been admirable, but the timing was less than perfect. The audience responded predictably: they were thrilled by the prospect of a functioning alternative economy and asked why we hadn't launched a citywide campaign to spread these invaluable opportunities, but they also asked with increasing concern for evidence of "successful experiences." Had we had any success working with the elderly? In schools? In Barrio Belén? Why is there no barter system in your own neighborhood? What about the internet? The organizers handled these questions well and perked up a bit. "We've done a lot," they explained. "We've experimented with different systems, learned a lot, and we're hosting this training to find other people who are passionate and creative and would like to advance these great ideas."

After sitting quietly for some time, Gabriela spoke up. Unlike the other students, she had extensive firsthand experience with barter, even helping run the Santa Elena system several years earlier. Although her expanding home business gave her no time to organize, she loved the markets, was dedicated to maintaining their noncapitalist ideals, and had spent a great deal of time considering the challenge of making barter work. "It seems really important," she said, "that the barter processes think about what to do in the face of our context. Our environment is so strong and has filled us with such strong ideas." Pointing to her head, she continued, "We already have this chip. How do we change it? I think our environment plays a huge role in this. It's so strong, it's violent with its information and its perspective that money is the ultimate. . . . It's so strong that even when we have lived other possibilities, other economies, we sometimes forget that they are possible. We need to change this chip. We need to clean out the cucarachas from our minds."

Santiago agreed, using a more organic metaphor. "Barter has to run through our veins," he said, "and to achieve this we need to form a community with other people who have the same thing running through their veins. But," he always says, "the first thing is values." If capitalism creates and depends on a particular set of values regarding competition, accumulation, permissible exploitation, and calculative rationality, then one path toward a different economy and society is to learn and teach new values. Barter organizing thus extends beyond markets and materiality. It is also a struggle to transform the inner lives of barterers—their values, mentalities, consciousness, and knowledge—and ultimately the broader cultural context. This is why activists describe barter as a fight against a depraved capitalist culture, an effort to revive pre-Columbian traditions, and a movement to birth a new culture. Barter thus reflects many "new social movements," which focus on cultural and identity politics rather than policy change, but it also illustrates how cultural politics connect to material concerns (Johnston et al. 1994; Melucci 1989).

By highlighting the cultural processes through which capitalism gains power in everyday life, Gabriela called attention to a central concern of modern politics: subjectivities. Ortner describes subjectivities as "the ensemble of modes of perception, affect, thought, desire, and fear that animate acting subjects . . . [and] the cultural and social formations that shape, organize, and provoke those modes of affect, thought, and so on" (2006, 107). Gabriela didn't use the term "subjectivities," but her vision of "capitalist mentalities" goes beyond consciousness. In her analysis, they are like SIM cards (chips) that Colombians pop in and out of cell phones to switch service providers. They are an operating platform, shaping how we reflect on our experiences, what we can and can't see, the options we consider feasible, and the ways we choose among them in order to act. Subjectivities, then, are particular ways of sensing and thinking the world that inform how we construct our place within it. Consciousness is one facet of subjectivity, but a focus on consciousness distracts from the many other sensory, bodily, and psychological components of subjectivities (Ortner 2006). These are the more subtle forces that lead us to "forget that other economies are possible even when we have lived them."

Because subjectivity describes "the intersection of sociocultural structures and individual experience and agency" (Brotherton 2008, 269), it is extremely useful to studies of activism and Gabriela's question about how to change the chip. However, scholars have paid significantly more attention to the top-down production of subjectivities (to create hegemony and serve power) than their transformation (as projects of counterpower) from the grassroots. Work on the production of hegemonic subjectivities helps us understand how our "chips" are created and how those cucarachas get into our heads. However, to advance scholarship for social change we need to understand people's agency in reinventing subjectivities to alter culture and power. This requires that we more clearly define the complexity of subjectivities and distinguish them from similar terms like subject, subject-position, culture, and hegemony.[1]

That is my project in this chapter. I describe the multiple components of subjectivity and the strategies by which activists seek to cultivate the new selves necessary to enact and maintain their alternative visions. In the preceding chapters, I have hinted at elements of this struggle—developing an anticapitalist ideology, learning a new language for the economy, thinking in terms of use-value and social-value, fostering predispositions toward mutual recognition, and developing a new ethics through barter practice and social pressure—but in this chapter I look more closely at how barterers are re-creating their selves and how these changes might generate broader cultural change.

Barter organizers have a relatively consistent (though not explicitly articulated) theory of cultural change. The spark for broad-scale change, they believe, is lit within individuals. Organizers hope that, through ethical self-work and economic experimentation, individual barterers will learn to think, desire, imagine, and act outside of the cultural frames of the dominant economy. They will become noncapitalist subjects, modeling values and lifeways based on solidarity, reciprocity, mutual respect, and satisfaction. Organizers, then, must offer barterers tools or "technologies of the self" to facilitate this ethical self-work (Foucault 1988). Then, if organizers can project these new values and subjectivities as alluring to a broader public, and at the same time expand opportunities for bartering, they may be able to convert barterers' individual transformations into large-scale cultural change. In short, cultural change depends on a cultural-material double move: they must articulate a broadly shared, noncapitalist worldview and ethos, a descriptive "model of" and a prescriptive "model for" living in solidarity (Geertz 1973), and they must simultaneously create institutions for alternative material practices.

To describe organizers' efforts, I walk through the experience of a barter novitiate, beginning with introductory presentations and workshops to reframe the economy, then examining the lessons learned through initial barter experiences, and finally analyzing the intended and unintended subjective changes experienced by long-term barterers. Like activists elsewhere, Medellín's barter organizers target subjectivities primarily through the conscious realms of language and values.[2] However, the greatest transformations are often provoked by the more subtle, unconscious aspects of barter: its sociality, the emotions it provokes, and the everyday experience of negotiating the market. This presents new opportunities for strategizing around cultural change.

## Activist and Academic Theories of Subjectivity

Although economic anthropologists have only recently begun using the word "subjectivities," a long line of work illustrates how the individual, culture, society, and economy are mutually constituted. Culture, power, and economies come to life and create our worlds through the work of individuals and communities. This is why *subjectivities* are so important. They are characteristics of individuals that refer to both biographical and social histories, and they shape people's social context, decisions, and actions in such a way that economic practices become "relative permanences," systems and institutions that we take for granted as natural (Harvey 1996). Socioeconomic relations and cultural consensus shape individual experiences and subjectivities, and those subjectivities then reverberate back on sociocultural dynamics. Any effort to change the economy or society therefore depends on sustained subjective change.

The importance of subjectivities is also borne out beyond academia, in the work of political and economic activists who insist that self-transformation is essential for radical politics. Much of Gandhi's writing, for example, describes his efforts to transform India through "experiments" to reconstruct himself as a moral being (Gandhi 1960). He used ethical debates, bodily practices, political stances, economic alternatives, and social relations to prepare himself for the India of his dreams, to establish new norms and social pressures, and ultimately to bring a new India into being.[3] Gibson-Graham and the Community Economies Collective have come to similar lessons in their participatory action research, discovering that remaking the economy entails a fight against our worldviews and libidos (Gibson-Graham 2006b). And as noted in the introduction, Argentine factory workers described their efforts to establish collectivist economies after the nation's economic collapse as "a struggle against themselves" (Chatterton 2005); after years of socialization as workers within a hierarchical chain of command, new economic conditions demanded that they assume a new role as comanagers, which in turn permitted them to imagine new economic goals and conditions.

Because the concept of subjectivities prioritizes individual experience and people's negotiation of sociocultural forces, it provides a unique window onto antihegemonic possibilities and practices. Not surprisingly, social movement scholars have taken this agency-oriented view of subjectivity furthest through research on what makes people join movements, what types of cultural or identity work movements perform, and how to forge solidarities among people with diverse identities and life conditions (Alvarez et al. 1998; Della Porta and Diani 2009; Escobar and Alvarez 1992; Keck and Sikkink 1998). This has generated terms that are deceptively similar to the word subjectivities, such as "a subjective sense of solidarity," "subjects of history," or "social subjects." However, scholars have largely failed to distinguish between subjectivities and these (and other) similar concepts and have thus lost the complexity of subjectivities.[4] As a result, the concept remains theoretically and methodologically slippery.

Aiming for greater clarity, I draw from Ortner and others in prioritizing three particularly influential components of subjectivity. The first is embodied social and material practice. Gramsci (1972) and Agrawal (2005) illustrate how changes in social and material practice—even when *imposed* by factory bosses or government foresters—can reshape subjectivities, leading people to adopt new values, motivations, logics, and even imaginations of what types of action are possible. Research on themes ranging from medical treatment to state violence to political demonstrations shows that direct physical experience, bodily practices, and both top-down and peer-to-peer governance are central to the construction of subjectivities, as are the ways people remember and represent these bodily experiences (Biehl et al. 2007; Razsa 2015).

The second central component of subjectivities is language. Language creates and maintains particular subjectivities, largely through its effects on perception, cognition, and commonsense understandings of problems and their solutions (Foucault 1972, 1980). We see these linguistic effects in broad cultural tropes (such as Malthusian narratives that frame socioecological problems as issues of scarcity, Tragedy of the Commons mythology that naturalizes self-interested extractivism, and particular ways of framing the problem of poverty) and in smaller-scale linguistic norms (such as ways of talking about whiteness, race, or climate change) (Escobar 1995; Esteva [1992] 2010; Hill 2008; Mitchell 2002; Norgaard 2011; Schwartz 2006).[5]

Finally, emotions are a critical but hard-to-study third component of subjectivities. Luhrmann goes so far as to define subjectivity as "the emotional life of the political subject" (2006, 345). While this misses the full complexity of the term, her explication reveals what these apparently internal, personal feelings actually involve. Emotions are individual physiological responses, understood within a social context that makes them meaningful, using a limited language for comprehension, and in reference to social norms and systems of evaluation. As "our most basic moral reactions," they teach us about our world in noncognitive ways and sometimes in contradiction to our cognized values (355).

Subjectivities, then, describe particular ways of sensing and thinking the world and one's place in it. Also, as Agrawal says, they strongly affect reasons, motivations, and possibilities for action: subjectivities affect what you conceptualize as real, what you care about, what you act in relation to, and how you situate your actions. And, as Ortner (2006) writes, these ways of sensing, thinking, and orientations become fully formed subjectivities when they become habitual. The shared sets of meanings and values that we call culture are clearly related to subjectivities, but a focus on subjectivities reveals the diverse ways that individuals internalize and transform those shared meanings as they move through their lives. Consciousness is an important aspect of subjectivity, but a focus on consciousness distracts from the many other ways subjectivities are constituted.

A full consideration of subjectivities captures how these personal dynamics are produced through experiences with "social organization, modes of production, knowledge structures, and symbolic forms" (Biehl et al. 2007, 5). But subjectivities are not imposed from above or given by material conditions; they involve choice. People might experience massive political-economic and cultural changes—including changes in property relations, labor, bodily practices, schooling, language, the production of new standards of evaluation or fairness, etc.—but it still remains to be seen if these changes will have the "subjective force" (Brotherton 2008) to alter how individuals think, feel, strategize, imagine, and evaluate their work. As St Martin argues, these sweeping changes make new subjectivities possible, but "there [always] remains the question of the inhabitation of these subject positions by [people] themselves" (2007, 543).

Ultimately, subjectivity differs from culture, hegemony, and ideology in two ways. First, it focuses more on individual experience and variation than collective consensus, and it prioritizes slippages rather than determinism. Second, it integrates material and social practices, language, consciousness, and emotion more explicitly than hegemony and ideology do. Seeing subjectivity as a researcher and targeting it as an activist requires attention to all of these realms and the ways they affect one another; for example, how different languages and practices generate distinct emotional experiences, which then feed back on people's orientation to political action. This can be discerned in part through interviews and written records, but it also requires substantial attention to people's experiences. And it must then be related back to broader cultural, social, and economic systems.

## The Transformation of Subjectivities in Medellín

### Conventional Economic Subjectivities

As a product of culture, power, and personal experience, subjectivities necessarily vary significantly by socioeconomic class and individual biography. However, barterers and barter activists consistently underscored three features of conventional subjectivities that impeded the construction of sustained barter systems: the intellectual centrality of money, a general orientation toward competition, and concerns about status that affected all social classes, though in slightly different ways. Incidentally, these three challenges illustrate the value of focusing on subjectivity rather than ideology or culture: each is a shared cognitive or meaning-based influence on action, but each also works through emotions and experiences that give rise to individual-level interpretation and internalization.

Gabriela's comments provide a good starting point for considering how these work against alternative economies. Many barterers agree that it is difficult to sustain faith in barter and escape the mindset that "money is the ultimate." In fact, the challenge extends beyond faith and consciousness. People often see money not only as the ultimate path toward well-being, but also as the only path. However robust a barter system may be, and however committed the barterer, people continue to need pesos for electric bills, taxes, and other expenses. The necessity of operating in a monetary economy makes it very difficult to think about value without using money as a referent; in other words, money is central to dominant modes of perception and evaluation. This appears to be true across the class spectrum. As barterers say, "We are *metalizado* [metalized: referring to metal coins], always thinking in terms of money." Even in barter markets, it is hard to evaluate trades based on use-value or reciprocal satisfaction rather than "thinking only about 'the zeros' [that you see on every peso or price tag]." We all occasionally find ourselves slipping from use-value to exchange-value, converting from alternative currencies to pesos, calculating and comparing items based on conventional prices.

The metalized mindset is so intractable because assessing value is not simply a conscious, mathematical activity. It is also a deeply engrained disposition that is connected to cultural preferences for accumulation and beliefs about economic competition. People in Medellín often cited the difficulty of teaching solidarity to avaricious and hypercompetitive Paisas. "Our Paisa culture is so strong," explained Gabriela during one interview. "It's all about 'being on top of the other' and wanting to 'get ahead and screw the others if they let you.'" Paisas often explain these cultural traits either through racist genealogies that link their culture to lost Jewish tribes, or to the history of Antioqueño colonization. The lawless frontier created a particular "spirit of capitalism": a rugged individualism and devil-may-care entrepreneurialism without ethical restraints. What is important for my purpose is not whether these historical narratives are true, but that they are broadly adopted as part of people's identities and ways of interpreting others. Much like the American mythology of moving from rags to riches, this regional identity as entrepreneurial movers and shakers is embraced by many wealthy people as an explanation for their success, and by many poor people as a basis for their future plans.

These cultural mythologies endure because they are tied to intimate notions of status, prestige, morality, well-being, and identity, because they are experienced via emotions of fear, hope, disappointment, vulnerability, and pride, and because they are reproduced through everyday practice and language.

Barterers often lament the common perception that only the most destitute people must stoop to trading away their possessions. Though newspapers are littered with ads for wealthy people looking to trade (*vencambiar*) land, homes, and expensive trucks, barter (*trueque*) is conceptually linked to poverty, informality, and questionable morality. Julio described these types of resistance in the early days of the Pajarito local exchange system. His neighbors didn't trust that barter would work, "and they would make jokes like, 'I don't want to buy the clothes of some dead man.' Used clothing seemed dirty, like a marker of poverty." The preoccupation for preserving one's status is probably more acute among the lower and middle classes, but it certainly influences the upper classes as well. Decent people don't wear someone else's clothing. Rent is not just an economic matter, but a question of masculinity, of supporting the family and being a responsible father. Good fathers, valued workers, and clean, decent people all conduct their affairs in the modern, formal, cash economy. Using money marks them as responsible and the ability to make money signifies their worth. People perpetuate these norms—even if they are not particularly liberating—by using them as standards for judging and disciplining themselves and each other. The same dynamic is replicated on the national scale, where a monetized, growth-oriented economy marks Colombia and Colombians as modern, rational, and worthy of international respect. As a result, national economic and development policy is also thoroughly "metalizado," neglecting opportunities to promote well-being through nonmonetary means.

In Pajarito, for example, barter didn't take off at first "because it was new, because the monetary system already has so much power but these alternatives are unknown." The JAC pursued other community-building activities and reintroduced barter a year later, when Julio had built a reputation as a faithful community servant. He managed to convince his neighbors to suspend their disbelief and give barter a chance. "We started small," he told me, "and then after a while when they saw it working, everybody really got into it. The change was incredible. You would meet people on the street and they'd say, 'Oh, I got this shirt at the Bazaar.' And then someone else would say, 'I got these pants at the Bazaar, too,' and they would all laugh about it. People became accustomed to wearing used clothing. . . . And that's great because the use-value is extended for a longer time. But it wasn't just clothing. We also had appliances, books, music, vegetables. . . . Eventually, the bazaars *filled* with people because it was a *spectacle*. In one day at the bazaars we would go and trade the equivalent of 1.5 million pesos." That people began to wear used clothing in public—and openly declared they were doing so—shows a denaturalization of the criteria of social evaluation and a willingness to buck conventions, to take the risk of being different. In Ortner's terms, it shows that the cultural and social formations had shifted enough to enable other modes of fear and desire, and other patterns of action.

A large part of barterers' project is to denaturalize basic assumptions and evaluations, and to make it safe for people to be different. It is not surprising, therefore, that they often celebrate children as exemplary. They are less "metalizado," less "contaminated" by social ideals, and more capable of thinking freely about use-value and enjoyment. In barter fairs, children are often seen as more creative and dynamic than adults. Their ability to quickly identify what they really want, and to trade creatively in order to get it, regardless of its conventional price, is held out as a model for adults. While children are seen as relatively blank slates, the rest of us need to unlearn conventional modes of perception, evaluation, affect, and desire, and relearn others. Let's look at how barterers try to achieve this.

## Reframing the Economy

Much like public health and climate change communicators, barter activists seek to change subjectivities primarily through consciousness. In presentations and workshops, they reframe inequality, suffering, and the very purposes of the economy in order to expand people's belief in alternatives. Luis Alberto had developed this into an art.

One morning, I met him at an all-girls Catholic school where he was facilitating a barter program. The auditorium was a typical high school scene: girls ambled in, spread out across the back rows, and seized upon this break in structure to chat, ignoring their teachers' pleas for attention. Paola, one of the teachers, welcomed everyone to the Fifth Entrepreneurs' Day. Our goal, she said, was not to learn to become businesspeople but to use our imaginations. "That's why we're doing barter this year. . . . These activities are conversation starters. The goal is to provoke dreams and get rid of obstacles that get in the way of our creativity." Paola, clearly more accustomed to high school girls than I, was unfazed by the girls talking through her introduction.

Luis Alberto took the mic and thanked everyone for coming. "Today," he said, "I am going to talk about a very important issue, an issue that determines the lives of the majority of people in the world." He paused, allowing the thought to settle. "I'm going to talk about money." The girls were quiet now, more attentive to the guest than their teacher. "We already know," he continued, "that with money we can get whatever we want, but without money we'll have nothing. We'll have no food, no home, nothing. And for a lot of us, this means that we don't live very happily. But what I want to show you is that it's possible to live happier and with more dignity. How can we do that? By trading."

This tells us a lot about how activists think about conventional and alternative subjectivities. Luis Alberto knows that the goals, language, and objects of the conventional economy have been naturalized, so he must appeal to concepts like money and desire. But he also knows that the conventional economy depends upon simultaneous and contradictory dynamics of desire, exclusion, and exploitation that leave many people deeply dissatisfied. Even as people believe in mainstream goals, many feel that those goals are forever out of reach. Barter introductions expose this contradiction between conventional economic narratives and everyday lived experience, leveraging it to prompt a deeper rethinking of economic goals.

However, it's not enough to dwell on disappointment. To avoid paralysis, organizers must provoke a rethinking that is hopeful and sustained. The rest of Luis Alberto's talk therefore honed that sense of disaffection while offering a vision of an alternative that can actually be practiced without difficulty and a new conceptual vocabulary that would help the girls continue questioning the economy. "Although this is a very small city," he said, "there are so many projects here that people just don't know about, so I'm excited to share one of these projects."

"What types of things can we trade?" he asked. After a short pause, a small voice said, "CDs and DVDs," and others added that they could trade books or tutoring or makeup. "Right," responded Luis Alberto. "And so what does this mean about money?" A girl answered that we can get things without money. "Yes! That's right! Products, services, and knowledge. We say these are the things that are necessary to live happily and with dignity, and to meet all of our needs. And we can *trade* for them."

"How are things in the world today? If we don't have money, we almost don't even leave the house. Isn't that right? Who likes to go out if they don't have money, at least a few hundred pesos in their pocket, enough for bus fare or a cup of coffee or an ice cream?" Students nod. "It's that without money our value is reduced, just because of this little piece of paper. This makes us feel alone and without direction."

"But what's the goal of money? What's the purpose of those little pieces of paper?" A few girls respond that it's to take care of our needs. Luis Alberto agrees but suggests that, in a broader sense, money exists to give us security. "Just thinking about money we start to smile, right? And when you think of an orange?" Several girls laugh and say, "No." "No, not so much. But really it's not the money that we need. It's not that piece of paper. It's what that money allows us to get."

This is a common trope. The idea that we are confusing means and ends is provocative, and it offers one of the central concepts that frequent barterers carry with them: the belief that economies are meant to provide satisfaction and security, so we should ensure they do so. Luis Alberto goes on to explain that money creates a sort of artificial scarcity.

"What do we have to do to get money? We have to work, work, work. But the problem is that there's not always enough work, especially right now. How many of you have family members who are out of work right now?" About a third raise their hands, somewhat tentatively. The discomfort is palpable. "So few? Well, you all are lucky." This is a key point in the barter narrative. People don't have work, so they can't get money. But their needs don't go away, and neither do their skills. By placing money at the center of our economy, we ensure that people's needs go unmet and that their skills benefit no one. "There are about a hundred thousand families right now in Medellín without water or electricity because they don't have the money to pay. And did you hear the story of those three kids who died?" The crowd offers a mix of yeses and nos. "Three little kids died this weekend because they didn't have electricity and their stove fire got out of control while their parents were out looking for work. They were desperate because they had to find money however they could, and so they left the kids at home alone."

This crescendo of suffering brings us to the key transition in the talk, where Luis Alberto sells us on alternatives. Money and the economy are social constructs that we created and that we can re-create. "This thing called money is so important in our lives . . . but it's more and more common for people to get less and less money. So we started to think about how people survive when they don't have money. . . . Money is a new thing. We only have about three hundred years of history with money, and we have, well, we have been in the Americas for thousands of years."

"So how do we satisfy our needs in some other way? Well, the doctor needs a mechanic, right? And the mechanic needs a baker? And the baker needs a teacher? Just like this, by working together, it's possible to find all of the things we need. There's nothing new about this, right? The other thing is that this comes from here. Barter is something that's right here, in our past. A long time ago, some people were nomads and some people were . . . [he pauses to allow the students to fill in the blank, knowing that they've been studying this]." "Sedentary," someone says. "Right, sedentary. And there were people who had gold and people who had salt and people who had other things and the nomads would travel around and trade things from one region to another. This is something from *here*, from *our* ancestors."

Luis Alberto continues like this for a while. He describes barter as a life raft, a way of cutting out the middleman of money, addressing artificial scarcity in the economy, and helping us refocus on our needs. With barter, he says, we don't have to be poor any more, materially or symbolically. Also, barter is simple and natural. Not only is it part of our ancestral heritage, but we do it all the time without knowing it, trading with friends or washing the dishes in exchange for parental love. So it's easy to imagine it growing. And finally, Luis Alberto ties his talk back into conventional values to keep barter from feeling too odd or threatening. It may come from our Indigenous past, he tells the girls, but barter is modern and cosmopolitan. People around the world are bartering, from Colombia to Argentina, from New York to Japan. "There are more than one hundred countries where people are trying to live without money, because it's getting increasingly difficult to live with it, and because every day money gets us less." And with that he introduces a short video that will show the girls "examples of specific projects right here in our little city, and also from other places like Argentina."

Through these types of talks, activists seek to channel people's emotional discomfort and sense of injustice toward a belief in a real, viable alternative. They aim to leverage this "affective resistance" to prompt a deeper rethinking of economic goals and, most importantly, a rethinking that is hopeful, that can actually be *practiced* without difficulty. A new economic language offers extremely important tools to begin tinkering with their economic selves. Satisfaction becomes a key reference point, which helps emphasize use-value as the true measure of economic success. Eventually, activists argue that because we are aiming for a *solidarity* economy, we have to think about this as mutual satisfaction, an economy in which our trade is fair and just for all parties.

The most important new concept is the *prosumer* (producer + consumer).[6] The prosumer is the ideal barter subject: a protagonist, someone who seeks to broaden their role as self-managing producers. Prosumers reject the model of consumption as a passive activity delinked from production, facilitated only by wage labor, and manipulated by the corporate construction of desire. In Medellín, the image of the prosumer is also used to establish an ideal of individuals who are linked in a broader economic community. Unlike the self-interested rational actor, prosumers produce for mutual enrichment. Orienting the economy around a collective referent in this way is actually quite a significant shift. We are accustomed to thinking of economic collectives—that is what we do when we speak of the GDP or the health of the national economy, for example—but these are typically abstract collectives, groups that we do not know and cannot visualize. Outside of our families and, occasionally, a small business, there are few human-scale economic collectives that we interact with. Medellín's barter systems change that by embedding traders in a small, intimate group and putting them face-to-face with their economic interdependence.

Taken together, these barter trainings are "intellectual and moral leadership" highlighting the contradictions of the existing social configuration, mobilizing a constituency for social and economic change, and instilling in that constituency the faith that they have the capacity to create something new and desirable.[7] This alternative language and the identity of the prosumer provide tools to emphasize the barter difference and prevent slippage back into conventional economic mentalities and values. Ultimately, like standards of judgment in the conventional economy, this ideal of the prosumer "works" because it gives people something to measure themselves and each other against. The rules, insults, fear, and shaming that we saw in Santa Elena (chapter 3) are all part of the governing structures and systems of feedback the keep people on the path toward more enduring alternative subjectivities. These interventions in barter *consciousness* open possibilities for change; to realize these possibilities people must be able to claim new identities grounded in their livelihoods, everyday practice, and social relations. They must be able to establish a unity between alternative consciousness and alternative practice, to displace the common sense of the conventional economy, and to enact an alternative to its contradictions.

As Luis Alberto ended his talk, he asked the girls, "Do you think something like this is possible here?" All respond, in the flat drone typical of students in an assembly: "Yeeeeees." But he took it in stride. "That's the proposal for tomorrow. You're going to bring products and you're going to set up your own barter fair with all of the other girls." Some students perk up. "What types of things could you bring?" Bracelets, necklaces, bags, stuffed animals, shirts, makeup. "Do you think you might participate?" They respond positively, with more excitement this time, and they leave thinking of barter as an actual practice in their immediate future rather than just a floating series of abstractions and possibilities.

## Initial Barter Experiences

Most people are guardedly optimistic after barter presentations. The barter story is a good one, connecting with basic values of justice and contentment and detailing concrete practices that have been pilot tested. People want to feel the way organizers say is possible. But it is also a challenging story. Despite efforts to pitch barter as an easy practice that we're constantly engaged in, for many people, trading suggests a society so different from the present, with such different ways of valuing people and things, that they don't know what to make of it. How can they ignore pesos when valuing goods and evaluating trades, thinking instead of use-value and the social value of economic inclusion? How can they match their desires to the limited pool of things produced locally? And why should they hitch their own well-being to that of others? Barter seems antiquated and antimodern, and it inverts notions of wealth and poverty in a way that feels troubling. Worst of all, something so unusual and altruistic raises alarms; people often wonder, "What's the scam here? Who is making money off of this?"

That's why talking about a different economy is only one aspect of the barter project; practice is also critical for opening minds and changing subjectivities. Barter organizers insist that you cannot simply go into a community, advertise, and hold a barter market. You need *previas* (preparatory activities), usually an introductory talk and barter simulation. It took a long time before I understood the need for *previas*. People were clearly intelligent enough to grasp the idea of barter without extensive training, so activists' insistence that we dedicate large amounts of resources to organizing, planning, and conducting these *previas* seemed like self-sabotage. I kept wondering if we wouldn't achieve more by skip-ping the *previas* and using our limited time to organize stronger markets. I am still not sure which strategy would be most efficient, but I now understand that *previas* are less about teaching barter and more about allowing people to feel alternative economies in an embodied, experiential manner.[8]

Returning to the Catholic school, we can see how barter organizers com-bine discourse and practice to shift subjectivities. It was essential that the girls barter, and that they organize their own fair, so they would learn that they had both the power and the responsibility to create their own economy. This also forced them to think through what *they* wanted barter to achieve, and thus to develop their own sense of economic justice. Their market wound through the schoolyard and was organized as a gradient from the lower school to the upper school because they wanted to ensure that each age group would be comfort-able but also facilitate interaction across ages. While jewelry and makeup were ubiquitous, the lower school featured more stuffed animals and dolls and the upper school had more books. Pedagogical materials evoked the least excite-ment, but within an hour, nearly all of the several hundred products had exchanged hands. Only one group of students offered services—a trio of sec-ond graders who offered math and English tutoring, leading to a fun exchange in which they taught me English while I read them a bilingual children's book.

The sheer fun of barter is itself a key lesson of the *previas*. I saw more smiles in that schoolyard than at any other time in Colombia. The fair was packed with girls and loud with laughter. Cliques gave way to conversations across age groups, and teachers jumped in to trade their own products or encourage timid students. When students completed a trade, they ran to friends and teachers to show off their new goods. As the fair wound down, small groups of girls drifted to the corners to play with their dolls or try on new jewelry. The slogan painted on one of their banners—"Barter: a just market where you also find hugs and laughter"—proved accurate.

Fun rarely figures prominently in revolutionary strategy,[9] but it is integral to barter as both a means and an end. As a means, fun is supposed to hold people's attention long enough that they begin to consider economic politics. Fun is more than a way of attracting new barterers. It counters the monotony of the conven-tional economy and offers a sensorial support for the claim that economies can do more, connecting people and providing personal fulfillment. Fun is meant to shake participants out of their habitual economic stance, their wariness of being taken advantage of, and their harried fretting about the bottom line. It creates "fugitive energies" (Connolly 1999), "momentary eruptions that break familiar patterns of feeling and behavior and offer glimmers of possibility" (Gibson-Graham 2006b, 51). Organizers don't always manage to harness liberated emo-tions for political ends, but their goals are clear. Finally, fun helps compensate for some of the material shortcomings of these nascent markets.

Demonstrative barter fairs don't just combat initial resistance and spark a change of affect; they also give participants a chance to learn how it feels to be a barterer, what affective and mental blocks might limit their full participation, and how alternative economies might contribute to their livelihoods. Our SES sessions featured one of the most impressive barter simulations I have seen. The participants, having already watched barter films and discussed the basic goals, strategies, and downfalls of barter systems, fully embraced the challenge of trading. They arrived with a remarkable array of products produced in their own micro-businesses (pens and notebooks by a man who runs a print shop, an all-purpose cleaner made of local agave plants, candied peanuts, bead jewelry, woven hats, homemade toys, chocolates, and marmalades) or harvested from their homes or neighborhoods (citrus fruits and ornamental tree saplings) and with a wide range of quality used goods (tools, clothing, home décor, a printer, and books).

The fair started slowly, but once we organizers began to trade, others followed suit. Some participants whizzed around the market, wheeling and dealing. A woman offering head massages had a steady stream of customers. But not everybody felt so comfortable. One man particularly stood out. The energy of the market seemed unsettling to him, and he was reluctant to strike up conversations, make offers, or negotiate the value of his products. Unfortunately, he didn't have a good day of trading. He decided from the beginning that he wanted the printer but never acquired the mix of products and facilitators necessary to get it.

Evaluating the session, one trader said the simulation was where "theory and practice met." Practicing barter taught things that could not be expressed in words: practical lessons like how to negotiate value and address problems of fairness, and deeper lessons about barter's cultural effects. People were surprised by how capable their group was, how many goods and services they could offer one another even in this small experiment. This is important because a central resistance that new barterers express is a fear of their own incapacity and the inadequacy of their community. Strong markets can instill a sense of capability and wealth in individual producers and economic communities.

The community that formed through exchange also left a lasting impression. One participant said, "I don't know if this is social capital or what, but there was a lot of really nice interaction during the barter." There were good conversations and gifts, and a lot of laughing and smiling. A man who had forgotten to bring items to trade agreed. He felt excluded at first, but used this as a chance to observe the market. That helped him understand "the mutuality of the market" and the difference between price and use-value. Like others, he began to see what it means to take responsibility for the economy by helping others find mutually beneficial trades.

But the collision of theory and practice was not always easy. Students agreed that one of the most important lessons was that barter is not just trading goods, it's "an art that you don't learn on the first time." Difficulties arose because "we bumped up against the culture of barter, which we don't know yet." Another participant elaborated: "You don't just need the products. A lot of this is about the mentality, and there is a very strong capitalist mentality that we have. We struggled to focus on satisfying needs rather than acquiring money for its own sake." In some cases, though, the market nudged people to think beyond their capitalist mentalities. One man said that the creativity really began after he had traded all of his products, which revealed a new aspect of solidaristic thinking: "That's when . . . I saw the possibility of trading for things that I didn't need but that I could retrade for things that I did need. I think I learned that there's not just a use-value and an exchange-value, but also a value in exchanging. The exchange brings people together and even products that I might not use are useful to me, because I can re-exchange them later." He experienced what it means to take on the economy as your own and work through questions of fairness, inclusion, and dynamism.

As these comments show, people's first experiences with barter often generate quite different orientations to the market than they typically have as consumers. Barter urges people to rethink their own capacities, recognize the previously invisible resources within their communities, and consider alternative possibilities for meeting needs and satisfying desires. It also illustrates—as Mauss and Lévi-Strauss argued long ago—that the very act of exchange builds community. Most importantly, the firsthand experience of barter achieves something that presentations cannot: it allows people to feel, however partially or ephemerally, what it must be like to have a community economy, one that they contribute to and are responsible for, and one whose justice outcomes are not given but can be modified. It forces them to debate the plight of our timid new friend who never got his printer, and to consider ways of building care for all into our economy. This is one of the biggest impacts of these *previas*: by changing the rules of the economic game, they make cultural values and habits of thought explicit, temporarily interrupting the unreflective consent and quiescence that is central to hegemony.

Initial barter experiments don't radically transform subjectivities, but they create openness to change, expose people to new social and economic possibilities, and suggest other ways of living and practicing the economy. Barter fairs are imperfect and challenging, and a small number of participants decide that barter simply isn't for them. A much larger group thoroughly enjoy their first market experience and love the idea of barter. The thrill of their first trade lingers for a long time, along with curiosity about whether this could become a viable economic support for their family. But life gets in the way and they never return, or do so only sporadically. We were often disappointed by this outcome, but it is not an unambiguous failure. The idea of barter circulates, the memory of practicing an alternative economy sticks, and the taken-for-grantedness of the conventional economy dissipates a bit.

For a small group of first-time barterers, though, the experience resonates so deeply with their suspicions about the conventional economy and their hopes that economic practice can be different that they return over and over again. The particular points of resonance vary—and this is precisely where the biographical aspect of subjectivities and subjective change comes into play. Some like barter because it rekindles fond memories of their grandparents' era, others are attracted to the promise of new social connections or increased control over their own life and work, and still others hope it can facilitate a more ecologically sustainable economy. Many of these long-term barterers report that they felt strange in conventional society—they were never interested in fancy brand names, they have always liked the pragmatism of reusing clothes, they want to get away from the chemicals in commercial products, or economic competition never sat well with them—and they like barter because it accommodates this strangeness. In short, this group already expressed unconventional subjectivities, and they adopted barter as a "technology of the self" that they could use to express and deepen their difference from the conventional economic subjectivity. It proved especially valuable in this regard because it provided not only new ideals and a social context to reinforce them but also a material economic system to support their transformations.

## Becoming Prosumers and Postmaterialists: The Experiences of Long-Term Barterers

The experience of Medellín's frequent barterers shows how complex subject formation is. In this discussion, I highlight three simultaneous processes: barter attracts people who are willing to deviate from their typical economic subjectivities, it is a tool they use to shape that deviation intentionally, and it structures economic action in a way that affects subjectivities even beyond their intent. Diego was particularly eloquent about the personal changes that have accompanied his barter practice. You may remember him from the introduction to this book. Diego owned and operated a successful restaurant but found the demands and pace of restaurant management oppressive. Searching for a higher quality of life, he made the risky decision to quit and go into the *rebusque*, selling juices on the streets and making money through odd jobs. As he said, "I was asking myself, 'What other way is there to live without being a slave?' . . . and in barter I've found a solution."

Diego had lost his fascination with fast-paced city life and material wealth that comes only at the expense of personal fulfillment and freedom, and he decided to make some radical changes. He and his brother invested in a piece of land in the country, set up a house and cabins there, planted a garden and experimented with homemade products, and began to build a more liberated life. Barter was not a magic bullet that freed him from slavery, but in barter Diego found a social and economic institution that supported the broader transformations he was seeking. By providing him access to food, clothing, and a host of materials for his rental cabins, barter resolved some of the difficulties that would otherwise have constrained his project of self-liberation. In his words, "What people don't see and don't value is that these are the spaces in which micro-businesses are created, and the people themselves are in charge of them and in the future they'll be the really rich ones. Not just rich in economic ways. The most important is to live how you want to without being enslaved."

Furthermore, barter embedded Diego in a community with other people who were also willing and, in some cases, eager to challenge social norms. It therefore resolved some of the social and psychological impediments to his project for transformation. Diego explained how hard it is to embark on something so different and unknown. In his case, his marriage suffered because his wife thought barter was a waste of time and that he was crazy for jumping into it. "I think it's the same as a kid who wants to become independent and is searching for possibilities," he said. "Of course the family starts to attack him, asking 'Why are you spending all of your time with those crazy people? Why do you want to exchange things? You should be working in a business or as a security guard,' or whatever. It can start a really difficult conflict." This makes the camaraderie of barter even more important than simple friendship. As Santiago puts it, "If I am one person doing this on my own, then I'm just a *loco*. But if there are thirty of us, we're not so crazy anymore. Now it's really something to be taken seriously."

The actual practice of barter was also extremely important for changing Diego's modes of perception, evaluation, and action. The Santa Elena market was not his first barter experience, but it was his first time in a formal, organized barter system, and that made him think differently. The idea of the prosumer was especially provocative: for the first time he contemplated not just trading used products but also producing especially for barter. Suddenly, barter seemed like it could form a larger economic system. As I mentioned in the introduction, this led him to reimagine the urban landscape as a treasure trove of goods and services he might use or raw materials that he might reassemble for someone else's benefit. It also changed how he thought about himself, his capacities, and his relationship to other economic actors. As a prosumer, he felt possessed of enormous creativity and capacity, and he quickly learned that these barter systems expanded that creativity and capacity through cooperation. Within months of dedicating himself to the Santa Elena market, other barterers began to share their recipes and production processes with him, essentially helping their competitor develop better products more efficiently. Numerous barterers underscored this point. Unlike conventional markets, where farmers and artists feel the need to compete for customers and protect their intellectual property, barter markets offered a sense of freedom and collaboration that prompted sharing.

What is most interesting, though, is that barter markets make their own demands. Diego echoed many other barterers when he explained that

> in the barter market, you have to be more open, more loose and willing, in the sense that if you go and you receive these facilitators, you have to be willing to keep moving and keep trading. Because you can't find everything you might hope for at the market, you have to be less demanding of specific things and more open. Your eating habits start to change. The things you acquire start to change. If a book comes and it's a book that I don't want, I'm willing to take it, because if I'm closed to that kind of thing then there's not going to be movement through the system. You have to take the risk of learning about and trying new things, and this is a problem . . . because not everybody has this disposition. You have to think, "I'm going to try something new." You can't always be thinking, "I don't want *this*, I want that other thing." It's not like going to the [supermarket]. But that doesn't mean it's not useful. There are also a lot of reused things: clothes, books. All of my clothes come from barter. And my music, books, things for the cabins. Lights, plates, carpets.

In other words, barter's community- and place-based "inefficiencies" demand a different orientation to desire, expectations, and the temporal horizons of economic life. Diego said that "it works for patient people, people who are not in a hurry, who are okay acquiring things little by little. This is for people with a certain austerity, who want to live with calm and not get mixed up in luxuries." On another occasion he said that "barter is like an exercise. It's like trying to figure out how to free ourselves and enjoy. You can't come and think that you're only going to live from this. Many people come and they think that barter is going to solve everything, but it's not. It's only going to help with your spirit. And with things, too, but deep down it's about other types of benefits. When I go there, I'm going to enrich my life. If you go with the expectation that you're going to find everything then it's not going to work. You get rich in other ways: socially, spiritually. And then maybe on the economic level as well, like with the wines that I learned to make."

Among the spiritual changes Diego has experienced, he especially highlighted a general willingness to slow down, to notice and enjoy the world around him, and a change in values. "It takes away the accelerator, and this austerity brings really good things." The limited goods in the market taught him "to enjoy each little thing more instead of acquiring more in order to enjoy it. And so you value things more. And when there is an abundance you know how to use it, and you know how to live responsibly with abundance."

Most of the barterers I interviewed support Diego's claim that the markets demand a different orientation to needs, desires, and consumption. Because you can't get anything you want in a barter market, you have to shed the normal consumer mentality that is predicated on the transcendence of all limitations. You have to gradually cultivate a postscarcity subjectivity—like that which Esteva described (see the introduction)—in which the space and time of desire and consumption become inseparable from the space and time of possibility and production. Long-term barterers thus internalize, through embodied and unconscious practice, many of the lessons that organizers are trying to teach. One significant change they note is not thinking as much about money. This is part of what Carla, a jeweler, had hoped to get out of barter, and it delivered. She sees it as a way "to think that money isn't necessary for everything. To look for alternative ways of having things [so] money isn't always the priority.... The important thing is the use it has for me, not the brand or anything else." Barter converts these aspirations into habits of thought and feeling by giving them a material expression and by inserting Carla into a community with similar interests, a community that is supportive and inspiring but also critical and shaming when necessary.

Gabriela put barter's effects in characteristically metaphysical terms: "It's a shame, but as human beings we still have a long way to go with our inner work. We lack consciousness of how impermanent we are because our culture teaches us that we are eternal, that we can take advantage of each other, of everything. And when we realize that we're not eternal, then suddenly we have to take advantage of the little that we have." This sense of being eternal, of being boundless and unlimited, is replicated in the marketplace, where we increasingly expect the universe of possibilities to be at our fingertips. Big box stores and mega-supermarkets feed the sense that only money limits our opportunities, and even that obstacle is surmountable with easy consumer credit. Local environmental conditions, the capacities and talents of our neighbors, the spatial and temporal characteristics of supply chains, all of these become invisible and intolerable. Post-Fordist production through global supply chains has created a new type of Nietzschean über-consumer bent on demolishing all limitations to consumer power. And this aspiration toward limitlessness exists only in contrast to an equally strong fear of scarcity and insufficiency. Barter counters this.

Gabriela translates this type of change into a more general shift away from capitalism and consumerism. "Barter teaches that not everything has to come with bar codes. We basically have only capitalist referents now, but this shows that every once in a while you can pass above this. It makes you less capitalist over time, slowly." When I asked if she could pinpoint what exactly makes people less capitalist, she had a hard time identifying a single cause. "It's internal," she responded, a less ego-centric perspective, more concern for others, the presumption of trust rather than fear or competition, and a break from the constant search for personal gain. "We inherit this from capitalism, this preoccupation for who earns more. But in barter people learn how to get by without the supermarket. Another big benefit is trust. This group turns into a network of people you can trust, and if someone is part of the network, it might be that I barely even know you, but I know that I can trust you. It's a break from this constant looking to generate an income. We're looking to benefit in other ways."

Because barter demands such a different orientation to consumption, though, it is challenging for many people. Diego, like many barterers, says the biggest difficulty is fear. "The fear of feeling, of feeling new things, of being vulnerable. People want to feel what they're already accustomed to since their childhood. They don't want to feel new things. They're afraid of change. Barter is for those people who are willing to take a little risk in order to do things differently. You have to teach people that the fear is small and they can risk it. But people don't like this. If you're different then you're crazy, you're suspect. You can't feel weird. You always have to be good, fine, happy." Much of the fight against conventional subjectivities is a struggle to make that which is fearful, unknown, or impossible seem otherwise.

This fight against conventional economic subjectivities, however, is not devoid of its own paradoxes. While the alienation and frustration of the conventional economy is a useful foil for articulating a barter-based counterproposal, it can also be a major obstacle to the changes that organizers seek. One of their main failings has been the inability to establish a sense of collective responsibility for maintaining barter systems. A collectivist rhetoric is present, but in practice many people still want to be leaders and followers. This generates a free-rider problem and conflict among leaders with contradictory perspectives and little experience or willingness to develop consensus.

In addition, long into my fieldwork I realized that a large subset of barterers participate not because they want to change the world but because they want to feel good. Barter is one of only a handful of economic activities each month that they know will feel good and they don't want to turn it into yet another responsibility. For many people, experiences of alienation stoke a desire for tranquil recreation and renewal, not struggle and community labor. It would be a mistake to think of these traders as uncommitted to social change, but they are not active movement builders—they're perfectly happy to participate and take advantage of barter while it exists and even to support its more transformative effects, but becoming organizers would make barter into a burden. It would cost more and be less fun. And that was never their goal. This highlights one of the big challenges for organizers. How can they turn the fun and fulfillment into politics? How can they re-create organizing so that it too is fun and fulfilling, so that it has the same exciting, experimental, meaningful quality as market participation, rather than just the self-critical heaviness of so many of our meetings? How can they change this other part of the chip?

## Conclusion

Barterers are wise to identify subjective transformation as a central piece of their activism. As Gibson-Graham write, a counterhegemonic politics requires "dis-identification" with the subjectivities and identities offered by hegemonic sociocultural structures and "identification with alternative and politically enabling positions" ([1996] 2006a: 77). Barter activists therefore seek to amplify disaffection with the conventional economy in order to create alternative economic subjects. Becoming prosumers helps cut out intermediaries in the economic process so that production, consumption, and exchange are all controlled by individuals and communities rather than distant and abstract forces. Activists also recognize that this requires cultural work to decrease competitiveness, increase people's sense of security and capacity, change their basic perspectives on the nature of economies and scarcity, and generate collectives.

We see signs of success in barter activists' cultural work, even at some of the first introductions to barter. While many people who attend barter trainings do not go on to become barterers, introductory sessions and barter simulations help bolster people's belief that there is an alternative to the status quo, and this seems to work to some degree even when they are not convinced that barter is the *right* alternative. Not surprisingly, though, barter's most visible subjective impacts can be seen among people who are already striving for a different life and who commit to frequent bartering. Barter provides an economic practice and a social network that make it easier for these people to deviate from the norm, to live more extensively outside of the conventional economy, and in that way it deepens their nonnormative subjectivities and aspirations. Barter does not revolutionize unwilling subjects, but it does provide a tool for those who strive for a different relationship to the economy. As in the case of others who are teetering between capitalist/neoliberal and collectivist/community subjectivities (St Martin 2007; Brotherton 2008), barterers must adopt the new subjectivities that barter makes available, and they must then work with these new subjectivities, tailor them, and reshape them until they fit well. This is no easy task given the material and sociocultural power of the conventional economy, but barter cultures and barter economies make it increasingly possible.

When we look closely at activists' strategy, consciousness is a big part of their success, as is a new economic language that can anchor people's longing for a different and more just economy. However, these are only part of the picture. Even among organizers, ideology alone does not translate into a lived commitment to barter practice. In the end, barter seems to support and require a more significant subjective transformation, one that transcends thought and language to affect more subtle characteristics like emotional dispositions, habits, systems of evaluation, desires, and especially material practices. To understand

and advance resubjectification, scholars and activists need to grapple more effectively with the full complexity of subjectivities.

Barter activists do this to some extent. They recognize that conventional subjectivities consist of conscious and unconscious elements and that they are forged through explicit cultural values as well as material experiences and social relations. However, when imagining *alternative* subjectivities, they rarely strategize around these complex interconnections. Activists' attempts to teach values and enforce a morally "correct" vision of barter target only the conscious, linguistic aspects of subjectivity—the things that can be addressed in obvious ways at presentations, workshops, and barter simulations—largely ignoring the ways that subjectivities are constructed through material practices, embodied action, and emotions. The experiences of longtime barterers suggest a different logic for cultural activism. Barterers' narratives show that *practice* is critical for generating powerfully subtle changes, and in many cases it is precisely the inefficiencies of barter that encourage the most radical shifts in desire, expectations, and identities. The questions to ask when organizing a barter market or barter system are therefore not only "How can we teach people to be solidaristic barterers?" or "How can we facilitate trade?" but also "How can we facilitate a type of trading that nudges us toward solidarity even when we're not thinking about it?" If conventional economic practice and market organization encourage particular ways of doing, thinking, and feeling the economy, then our alternative economies might fruitfully be planned for these same goals.

However, if the inefficiencies of the barter market truly are the most powerful sparks for subjective change, this presents activists with a serious dilemma. Truly transformative politics—the kind that alters subjectivities and eventually provokes cultural change—might require a certain level of discomfort, of out-of-controlness, because it is through accepting and living our dominant subjectivities that we consistently pull ourselves back into control, back into our comfort zones. As long as we succumb to those desires, we are allowing those dominant modes of perception, thought, evaluation, affect, and action to define who we are and what society we reproduce. This then challenges organizers to strike a delicate balance between fun and discomfort. It requires that they cultivate countersubjectivities that people will choose to embrace even as those subjectivities challenge and push us beyond our own intent. It demands that they create productive inconveniences that prompt us to negotiate the everyday in new ways. In short, if hegemony is coercion and consent, countering hegemony may require coercing ourselves. This is not just self-work; it is also collective governmentality through new rules, new incentive structures to reshape "the conduct of conduct," and new systems of evaluation. Just as conventional subjectivities involve subjection, usually to forces beyond our control, alternative subjectivities require carefully negotiated subjection to alternative forces of our own devising.

These findings inform a strategic debate among barterers and other activists: the debate between scale and depth, whether it is more productive to soften the movement so more people can get on board, or to keep the movement "pure," challenging, and clearly counterhegemonic (see also the discussion in chapter 2 about "thin simplifications" of barter). Among barterers, this debate is framed in terms of how much barter markets should approximate conventional markets, and how much they should counter the conventional consumer ethic. All organizers agree that barter markets must offer more products to sustain themselves and become more useful. Julio, the founder of the Pajarito system, worries that this gradual approximation of the conventional market reduces barter's subject-changing potential. Inspired by ecological economists, he sees small, slow, local-level barter systems as a solution to the ecological contradictions of capitalism and necessary to provoke cultural change. Increasing and accelerating production, trade, and consumption is ultimately unsustainable, violating the second law of thermodynamics. Carlos Alberto, the founder of Altamira's barter system, sees no tension between scale, speed, and barter's counterhegemonic effects. He dreams of a national and international barter system that provides access to virtually all of the goods and services that people currently enjoy, but outside of the circuits of empire and inequality. He is less impressed by austerity and postconsumerism and more interested in barter as a support for socialism and a counter to the corrupting psychosocial influence of money. We hear similar debates within many contemporary movements, most notably environmentalism.

The academic literature and this research show that subjectivities—those deeply internalized habits of thought, feeling, and action—are shaped by collective practice, individual identities, emotions, and morality, and that language, cognition, and regimes of evaluation are especially important as intellectual anchors for people seeking to reshape their subjectivities. Perhaps most importantly, though, much of the subjective change I witnessed in Medellín came from the unanticipated effects of the technologies and institutions that barterers created. This suggests that taking subjectivities seriously requires that activists consider not only how a movement might attract more adherents, and not only how the movement might be used as a "technology of the self," but also how that technology *forces* changes upon the tool user. Subjectivities are both chosen and imposed; they shape political economies and are shaped by them. And as I have noted, they are conscious but simultaneously far more than that. Our activism must therefore approach them in more complex ways, as must our activist scholarship. In the next chapter, I explain *why* barter activists have made the strategic choice to focus primarily on the conscious aspects of subjectivities, and I discuss what this reveals about the challenges and contradictions of organizing for noncapitalism.

# 6

# Strategies for a
# New Economy

## Bridges, Boundaries, Culture,
## and Economy

Throughout August and September 2010, the barter organizers and I returned to that clean, echoey, white-tiled classroom each week to run the Solidarity Economy School barter program. Our nine sessions covered the history of money and trade, international experiences with alternative currencies, how to administer a barter market, and alternative economy project design. Through these, we hoped to equip students with the knowledge and skills to expand alternative economies across the city.

We asked participants, for their homework, to develop alternative economy proposals based on examples we had presented. Then, during class, they shared their ideas and formed working groups around common interests. Each team was charged with developing a detailed plan for a project that they might actually carry out after the course. José, a solidarity economy educator employed by the city, became the center of one of these project teams.

"My project," José explained to his group, "is to develop an internet platform called freebarter.com so people can trade easily. It will be geared mostly to small businesses—helping form a commodity chain so they can access raw materials without cash—but individuals will also be able to trade, so it will also offer a new market for these businesses."

People loved the idea. Using the internet seemed modern and sophisticated, and integrating businesses promised to expand barter across the city and even to wealthier traders. By drawing people together across commodity chains, it would also significantly strengthen barter economies. But not everyone was convinced.

Elisa, also a city-employed solidarity economy promoter, asked how José would ensure that people barter properly. "You can't just let people go barter however they want. Do people have to become members, and do workshops first to teach them how barter works? What rules will you have to regulate bartering and ensure that people don't abuse the system? It's great to have a citywide bartering system, but how do we ensure that people don't take advantage of it?"

José leaned his chair back with a confident, troublemaker's grin. "I won't," he said. "I'll just make the platform and let them trade. It's not my interest to control them. They can do what they want with it. If some people want to barter in solidarity, they can; if others want to barter like capitalists, they can, too."

José's position is anathema to most barterers, even bordering on the absurd. Barter and local currencies are not supposed to provide room for capitalist logics of asocial utility maximization and calculative rationality. In many people's minds, it is impossible to "barter like a capitalist" because barter is, by definition, a "solidarity economy." A totally free barter market is therefore effectively off the table. Yet this is not, technically, impossible. Therein lies the danger of barter: though it may lend itself to certain forms of social connectedness or systems of valuation, it can be deployed in multiple ways according to diverse ideologies.

Barter is a way of exchanging goods and services that could be procured in any number of ways: by family businesses that control their own labor and means of production, by government agencies managing public funds, by private firms that expropriate surplus value from their workers, by worker-owned cooperatives, or by slaves, feudal serfs, or thieves. Barter exchange can involve the types of social-value, use-value, and mutual recognition and satisfaction that Medellín's traders value, but it can also be a platform for selfish competition and one-off trades without enduring commitments. And bartered goods can be used and consumed in a wide range of ethically divergent manners: in ceremonial displays of power, for household survival, to reinvest in capitalist firms without having to spend limited financial resources, to support collective projects, to help paramilitary or drug-trafficking organizations, and so on. In fact, it may do some of these at the same time, for example by providing "free" (money-less) food for households so their members can labor in capitalist firms for less pay and contribute to narco-economies. Put simply, the ethics of barter is nothing more than the ethics that organizers and participants give to barter through their decisions about who is allowed to barter, how they may do so, what types of goods and production processes are recognized as contributing to solidarity, and what role barter should play in people's other economic activities. In Medellín, where barter is largely an effort to reassert personal dignity and collective ethics in the face of violent social division, getting the rules "right" makes quite a difference.

Although José and Elisa were new to barter, their conversation highlights the central dilemmas of barter organizing. They are questioning what it means for barter to be an *alternative* and *noncapitalist* economic project. What type of relationship should barter systems and individual participants have with the conventional, capitalist-monetary economy they seek to challenge? To what extent can concerns for self-interest be carried over into the barter economy? And how can organizers control this, or should they even try? The way barter activists answer these questions fundamentally shapes organizing strategies, market design, participant experiences, and the overall social and economic impacts of their project, but the answers are not obvious.

In this chapter, I discuss how activists' responses to these questions emerge from their particular way of understanding capitalism, power, and their own agency. This anthropological, meaning-centered approach to social movement strategy moves beyond typical sociological questions of political opportunity structures, resource mobilization, the framing of grievances, and ideologies, to explore how power and strategy result from the inner workings of culture. Sociological approaches would provide valuable lessons, but this anthropological approach seems especially valuable for activists engaged in constructive rather than contentious politics because it redirects attention away from strategic choice in response to institutions of power and toward grassroots actors' own feelings and senses of the world. Here I focus primarily on activists' understandings of capitalism because, as Gibson-Graham note, "representations of capitalism are a potent constituent of the anticapitalist imagination, providing images of what is to be resisted and changed as well as ... the strategies, techniques, and possibilities of changing it" (2006b, 3). In Medellín, however, activist strategy is also significantly shaped by the twin dynamics of social fragmentation and centralized leadership that have accompanied violence. My goal, therefore, is to analyze how the history and cultural legacies of capitalism, diverse economies, and violence interact to shape activism.

I begin by examining organizers' views of the economy and revolutionary possibilities alongside Gibson-Graham's theorizing of diverse economies ([1996] 2006a) and postcapitalist politics (2006b). Contrasting these rather similar perspectives illuminates how barterers imagine their project and highlights two particularly influential tensions within barter strategy. The first is a tension between bridges and boundaries, between linking barter with other economies or striving for a pure, alternative, noncapitalist economy. I detail the tendencies toward articulation and isolation present within the barter movement and trace their effects on material practices, subjectivities, and the construction of an alluring, counterhegemonic barter project.

This argument overlaps with, but is distinct from, two other conceptualizations of articulation. The first comes from anthropological and historical work on how capitalist and noncapitalist economies interrelate (articulate).[1] My focus differs from this literature because I do not attempt to describe economic diversity or explore whether noncapitalism can survive capitalist absorption. Rather, I examine whether economic articulation is an effective strategy for grassroots activists. The second use of "articulation" is Laclau and Mouffe's (1985) theory that societies are structured primarily through a discursive politics that consists of linking (articulating) statements, meanings, and ideas into a discourse that is so cohesive that it can absorb potential alternatives (through additional articulation) or make them invisible (by erecting borders to thinking about them), and that "wins the day" by redrawing social alliances to build people power. Examining barter activism through a strict application of their theory would also draw our attention to the bridges and boundaries that activists erect as they represent the economy in different ways and welcome different types of actors into their project. However, I find their perspective too meaning-centered to serve barter activists: it overemphasizes meaning and language at the expense of the material, economic, and social aspects of life that also shape subjectivities and social change.

The leads us to the second tension in barter strategy: the tension between sociocultural activism (including the types of moral trainings that Elisa recommends) and economic activism (the more materially focused market building that José advocates). As I illustrated in the last chapter, these two types of activism are mutually reinforcing, but given their limited time and resources, activists must often choose between them. Ultimately, the way barter organizers navigate these two tensions has a strong bearing on how transformative it becomes, shaping whether barter achieves broad and deep impacts at the individual level and wide-scale and long-lasting impacts at the societal level.

## Rethinking Economy and Revolutionary Strategy

Gibson-Graham argue that contemporary strategies for social change are deeply constrained by an inaccurate and narrow view of the economy, which they refer to as capitalocentrism. Capitalocentrism begins with a fear of capitalism's power as an ever-expanding, self-reproducing system that must be resisted, but it develops into a way of thinking that limits resistance. The fixation with capitalism mirrors ethnocentrism: noncapitalist economic and social activities (capitalism's Others) cannot be understood on their own terms but only in relation to the normal, natural, and largely unquestioned "real" economy of capitalism. Capitalism's Others are not granted coevalness (Fabian 1983);

they do not fully *belong* to contemporary space and time and are therefore of no political relevance. Since the only politics that matter are those centered on capitalism, we cannot develop a more complex postcapitalist politics for the here and now. We cannot mobilize around barter, cooperativism, and other already existing noncapitalist economies. We cannot expect that building noncapitalism into our everyday lives will have anything beyond a marginal, self-serving effect. Real transformation must wait for the revolution—the total overthrow of capitalism and the coming of a new global order.

Medellín's barterers, however, see things quite differently. Like the academic Marxists that Gibson-Graham critique, they are appalled by the exploitation, exclusion, inequality, and suffering they observe around them, and they also blame these conditions on an economic system built on accumulation, manufactured scarcity, commodification, and ruthless self-interest. However, they feel no need to wait for the end of capitalism before creating other economies. Building an alternative economy seems like a more immediate, fruitful, and radical response to their social and economic problems, and something that might be scaled up or replicated to further erode the material and cultural power of capitalism. In the Colombian context, this may also be a safer path, allowing organizers to avoid direct confrontations with powerful armed actors by simply organizing and occupying alternatives. In this sense, the barter project is quite similar to Gibson-Graham's postcapitalist politics, and it follows new social movements that reframe "transformation" to include both state-centric efforts and other strategies to multiply "social relationships that are not primarily relations of domination" (Evers 1985, 64; Escobar 2020).

Gibson-Graham object to a capitalocentric view of the economy on both empirical and political grounds, and they outline an alternative vision that opens the way for more meaningful action in the here and now. Empirically, capitalocentrism overlooks the work of feminist economists, anthropologists, and others who have documented the tremendous amount of economic activity that takes place outside of the familiar triad of formal markets, wage labor, and capitalist firms and that does not involve the appropriation of surplus value by a private owner rather than the worker herself. Numerous studies have demonstrated that the economy is not purely capitalist, that capitalist circuits are not coherent across scales and do not obey an overarching logic, and that capitalism is shaped by local contexts (Castree 1999; Donham 1999; Foster-Carter 1977; Greenberg 1995; Gudeman 2008; Halperin 1994; Ong 2006; Robben 1989). Presumptions of capitalist hegemony therefore hinder thorough analyses of actually existing political and economic landscapes: the full diversity of people's economic activities (including things like household labor, slavery, family firms, theft, the state sector, volunteerism, sharing and gifting, etc.), the social relations and cultural meanings enacted through these noncapitalist economies, and the diverse class positions and identities they create.

In addition, Gibson-Graham argue that capitalocentric discourse raises a political problem. In order to sustain a vision of the economy as essentially capitalist, we must endow capitalism with almost supernatural powers. It becomes all-embracing, ever-expanding, self-reproducing, naturally co-opting, and systemic. It bends other aspects of social, economic, and political life to its will and is homogenous, changing only superficially in order to colonize particularly stubborn Others. Finally, to imagine the economy as essentially capitalist we have to imagine all of the things we call capitalism as sharing one true and autonomous essence. The distinctions between different types of markets, firms, production and exchange practices, systems of valuation, and processes of control and surplus distribution get obscured—ignoring the lessons of a great deal of economic anthropology (Narotzky 1997; Plattner 1989; Wilk and Cliggett 2018)—and the political question of whether these practices present opportunities for decreasing exploitation are lost. Capitalocentrism thus reduces our capacity to imagine and enact anti- and noncapitalist action. It delegitimizes opportunities to construct noncapitalism in the present, at work, at home, and in our communities, in a manner that is meaningful rather than dismissed as merely creating a new site for capitalist colonization.

The dynamics of barter organizing in Medellín dovetail with much of Gibson-Graham's thought. For starters, barterers live in an extremely diverse economy. As I described in chapter 1, most of Medellín's economic activity is noncapitalist and most households depend heavily on noncapitalist practices. Opportunities for paid work include wage labor in capitalist firms as well as high levels of self-employment, work in cooperatives, government agencies, and local and international nonprofits, service work for wealthy households, and contract work for a range of formal and black-market activities. Beyond paid labor, a large segment of the population makes a living through *rebusque*. Each day they visit markets, vacant lots, and dumps in search of whatever can be acquired inexpensively and sold for a profit. For some, the rebusque develops into a small business as a traveling fruit vendor or a scrap metal recycler, but for many it is a precarious, lifelong search. Other important economic processes include self-provisioning, household labor, theft, traditional mutual support systems (*mingas, convites*, and *natilleras*), slavery (especially sex slavery), child labor, and volunteerism. This is just a hint of the diverse productive practices found in Medellín. Exchange often involves money, favors, apolitical barter, politicized barter, combinations of money and barter, and gifting. In short, capitalist production for monetized market exchange is, as Gibson-Graham note, the tip of the economic iceberg; below the water line lie a host of other unexplored and quite distinct economic practices, class processes, and value systems.

Importantly, from the perspective of individuals, households, and even firms, these varied processes of production and exchange rarely constitute discrete modes of production or economic systems. Indeed, it is by articulating these different processes—by interweaving raw materials, labor, products, and social relations from different realms—that households construct livelihoods and firms pursue profits. Creating value by working across this assemblage of diverse economies also has important sociocultural consequences. A vast mythology has arisen to explain, celebrate, and deride the business cunning of *Paisas* and their ability to create profits by constantly and often unreflectively articulating economies through elaborate wheeling and dealing. The unappreciated result of this articulation is that "class" is multivalent. The people of Medellín are wage laborers, self-employed self-managers, home workers, collectivists, and more, often at the same time. Their surplus production is appropriated for private gain, but also flows into their households, government coffers, and collective funds to be redistributed for a variety of collective ends. This was especially evident in microenterprise training programs, where professional business trainers struggled to convince students that they should separate business and household accounts. There is therefore little reason to assume that class identities and economic subjectivities will be based on one's position vis-à-vis capitalist relations of production. Rather, I argue, this constant movement among diverse class processes creates a multiplex economic subjectivity characterized by pragmatic pluralism.

Medellín's barter organizers represent, in many ways, the type of noncapitalocentric thinking that Gibson-Graham encourage, and the norms of pragmatic pluralism would seem conducive to their goals. Barter activists are firmly convinced that the economy is diverse and that capitalism is unstable, incoherent, and impermanent. As we've seen in previous chapters, they regularly draw attention to nonmonetary traditions like gifting, mutual labor, labor exchange, and family based collective savings. World histories of premonetary, precapitalist, and pre-Columbian economies give them faith that major socioeconomic change is possible, perhaps even inevitable. Barterers are firmly convinced that the economy exists not only as a set of overarching institutions and logics but also as informal relationships and practices that are created through our everyday actions, thoughts, and words. Their personal experience as barterers demonstrates that alternatives remain possible in the present, at least on a small scale. Some also find inspiration for large-scale barter in former president Hugo Chávez's proposals for a regional trading bloc organized around barter and a Latin American currency.

Unlike Gibson-Graham, however, barterers' postcapitalist politics is not an intervention within Marxist thought and politics. They are, for the most part, not concerned with specifying the nature and limits of capitalist class processes and opening theoretical spaces for alternatives. The barter project is, therefore, far from uniform. Barterers' ways of imagining the economy show strains of both capitalocentrism and noncapitalocentrism. At the same time that they see diversity, enact alternatives, and believe in change at many scales, barterers are also firmly convinced of capitalism's dominance and fear its expansionary logic. These contradictory representations of capitalism and barter help explain the choice of particular organizing strategies and the outcomes of the barter project. They contribute to the "revolution ... pero" that I described in the introduction and represent the "multiple and contradictory consciousness" that Gramsci attributes to all people.

## Bridges and Boundaries

Barter organizers recognize that it is currently impossible to survive exclusively from Medellín's barter systems. Participants might be able to trade for food and clothing, and perhaps some educational and medical services, but how will they acquire housing? How can they get electricity, water, sewage, and transportation services through barter? Clearly, they have to incorporate substantial amounts of nonbarter activities into their livelihoods, and they often rely on nonbarter goods as raw materials for the things they trade. In many cases, even barter markets themselves depend on conventional currency to rent stalls, space, sound systems, and the like. In Medellín's diverse economy, people are already engaged in a whole range of economic enterprises, and organizers do not expect them to abandon these in order to begin bartering.

In response, organizers have tried to create bridges between barter and nonbarter realms. For example, sales were permitted in Santa Elena so barterers could recuperate their travel costs and other expenses. Similarly, organizers seek financial support from the government, cooperatives, nongovernmental organizations, and even private corporations. Sometimes institutions commonly associated with the conventional economy are very useful for constructing alternatives: government contracts fund markets and workshops, corporate donations of cleaning supplies can be used as "seed capital" to stimulate trading, and in-kind donations of printing services generate barter manuals.

While this reliance on the nonbarter realm could be superseded if barter economies were large and diverse enough, I don't think that these strategies to bridge barter and other economic realms are simply concessions. Rather, I suggest that they grow directly out of the common sense of how one operates in the diverse economy: by trying things out, moving between realms, mixing a little bit of this and a little bit of that. Remember Olga's advice about how to barter: "I put 25 percent of my earnings in barter. My *earnings*, not my capital. . . . You have to think about how to bring your business to the barter market." For barterers who have figured out how to weave barter into their broader economic portfolio, it has proven quite valuable. The winemakers Roberto and Isabel provide the most obvious success story. In some measure they owe their whole livelihood—its barter and nonbarter elements—to the barter market. José's proposal for an amoral online exchange offers a new tool for pragmatic pluralism.

Conventional analyses might look at the stories of Olga and Roberto and Isabel as evidence that noncapitalism is merely serving the interests of capital by covering the start-up and maintenance costs of small firms, but that ignores the actual relations of production, class processes, institutions, and subjectivities that barter supports. In both households, barter permits livelihood systems and identities that are more autonomous of wage labor and capitalist exploitation. They have used barter to increase control over the means of production and their own reproduction. Importantly, this control is tied to their position within an interdependent community of traders and therefore creates a stake in strengthening that collective. This collectivism creates the potential for barter producers to take more of a political role than is conventionally attributed to the petite bourgeoisie. Barter also provides material and social support for these families' goals of developing alternative subjectivities; it helps them build an ethic centered on sufficiency, social relations, community work, and nonmonetized goals rather than accumulation and consumption. In this broader analysis of barter's articulation with the monetary economy and these two small firms, we therefore see a range of noncapitalist and even counterhegemonic economic, social, and subjective processes. Most barterers can tell similar stories about how barter forms part of a *proyecto de vida* (life project, but more akin to livelihood system) that is built around goals of freedom and social interconnection.

Even as they weave together barter and nonbarter realms, organizers and participants also work to insulate barter from the capitalist economy. Although there is no single notion of barter, Medellín's barter organizers are constantly defining and redefining it as they lobby government officials for support, run educational workshops, and participate in other solidarity economy events. Occasionally, they describe barter on its own terms, using relatively neutral, noncapitalocentric language. More often, however, they frame their project primarily in oppositional language, explaining that they are against a monetary and trade system built on scarcity, competition, accumulation, the elevation of profit over social concerns, and the commodification and depersonalization of human relationships. As the Altamira organizers demonstrated, they are trying to say *Adios al vil metal!* (Goodbye, vile metal!), and many of the emails and parables that organizers share have to do with the ways money generates insecurity and inequality.

To many organizers, this antimonetary stance is equivalent to anticapitalism because they see money as the lifeblood of capitalism and capitalism as the central organizing framework of our bankrupt monetary economy. As one barter manual noted, "The capitalist point of view seeks to convert everything into money, appropriating it in the name of progress and civilization, with no respect for the social structures of any given community, only interested in its own dominion and total submission, affecting many peoples of the world, putting at risk all of the world's living systems" (Manual del Trueke [Bello] 2008, 9). Of course, when outsiders ask if it isn't hypocritical for barterers to create their own currencies, these organizers back up and explain that some money is actually not so bad and that their facilitators are not money as it is commonly understood. (Some purists think that no currency should be used because even facilitators are close enough to conventional money to allow people to act with a capitalist, consumer mindset. Most, however, accept money that acts primarily as a medium of exchange and occasionally as a limited store of value.)

As you can see, these self-taught anticapitalists interpret capitalism in a much broader sense than Gibson-Graham. Their capitalist enemy includes more than the private expropriation of surplus value through wage labor; it is also, and perhaps primarily, market society, money, and other social relationships, material practices, and systems of meaning that seem oriented toward asocial or antisocial accumulation. For example, a mother who runs a sewing business out of her house, owns her own equipment, controls her own labor, and receives and manages the business's profits for the benefit of her family could be conceived of as a capitalist if she demonstrates an overly ambitious desire to benefit at the expense of her customers. Capitalism, in their eyes, is greed, ambition, a view of human relationships as pathways to profit, the lack of ethical restraint, and social disembeddedness as much as it is a wage-labor relationship. This is why Elisa was so concerned about José's freebarter web site. If it doesn't force people to act with solidarity, then it seems like another form of capitalist exploitation.

As organizers debate the challenges that barter faces, they often represent capitalism as a total system, a hegemonic, self-reproducing, dominating force that has subsumed the entire economy and the whole of society. We are constantly barraged by messages about money, they say, to the extent that we have become "metalized," made to think in terms of only money and conventional measures of value. In barter organizers' narratives, this broadly defined capitalism, a symbol of all that is evil within the economy, is often contrasted with barter, a pure, natural, money-free, prosocial, and ancestral form of exchange. This is exactly the capitalocentric view that Gibson-Graham argue will steer people away from noncapitalist action, and yet in this case it doesn't. This lends some empirical support to critics of Gibson-Graham who argue that strong, systemic views of capitalocentrism need not be disabling.

The elements of capitalocentrism in barterers' views do, however, affect their strategy in other ways. They see capitalism as having colonized nearly all of social and economic life, even our innermost thoughts and desires, and having banished other practices, motives, and desires to the margins. With barter and capitalism understood in such stark, morally absolutist terms, organizers' task is clear: they need to protect the purity of barter by insulating it from the economy of greed. As one organizer used to say, "On twenty-nine days of every month we do capitalism; for this one day we should just do barter."

Organizers go through significant efforts to erect transactional boundaries that limit the ability to link barter and capitalism, moral boundaries that separate the "solidarity economy" of barter from capitalist avarice, and conceptual boundaries that decrease people's ability to imagine how they might effectively link barter and nonbarter realms. These types of boundaries are not unique to barter; in fact, they are probably universal characteristics of economic embeddedness (Polanyi 1944; Douglas and Isherwood 1996) and the inherent tension between mutuality and competitive trade (Gudeman 2008). These boundaries are more than just pragmatic. Norms about how to negotiate different spheres of exchange are also deliberations about ethics, the commensurability of things and people, and the negotiation and preservation of different systems of value (Douglas and Isherwood 1996; West 2006; Wilk and Cliggett 2018). As we will see, the rules for linking barter to other economies have major significance for the economic utility of barter and the success of barter activism.

*Transactional boundaries* are the most direct means of control; organizers simply determine the general rules of exchange—if and when money is allowed, with whom you can sell and with whom you must barter, how exchanges will be made. Most markets have either fully excluded conventional money or tried to separate money from barter by allowing money only during certain times of day. By regulating how alternative currencies can be used, they introduce their ideologies into the markets. For example, some facilitators expire at the end of the market so there is no possibility for accumulation or gross inequality. When the monies are accumulable across several months, requiring barterers to bring products in order to have their facilitators validated ensures that all participants continue to contribute to the market. This reinforces the sense that everybody must contribute to the economic community in order to benefit from it and that there will be no free riders. Similarly, the highly centralized multi-reciprocal barter system that early organizers adopted (see chapter 2) resolved problems of egalitarianism and transparency, though with the unfortunate side effect of removing personal interaction and reciprocity from the market.

The vast majority of organizers' time and energy is spent erecting *moral boundaries* between barter and capitalism through education and sociocultural activism. As Santiago says, "The first thing is always values." Moral training aims to control markets proactively, by inculcating values that lay the foundation for other economies. That is why it was so important to Elisa that José's online barterers receive the right kind of instruction. In pursuit of these goals, barterers have developed an impressive range of pedagogical materials—manuals and instructional guides, newsletters, videos, a comic strip, stickers, signs and banners, slogans, electronic newsletters. As I described in the previous chapter, Medellín's barter organizers see economic subjectivities as a critical site of political struggle; through moral education, they seek to "change the chip" and "clean out the cucarachas" of their capitalist mentalities in order to "create a new culture of solidarity."

The "solidarity values" of barter are appealing, and traders regularly help maintain a barter ethic. During my fieldwork, barterers from Santa Elena who were incensed by traders who "only wanted to make money" successfully pressured the organizer to change the rules so barterers had to accept trades from fellow barterers even if they chose to sell to tourists. Participants also promote noncapitalist practices and sensibilities through social pressure, insults, and gossip and refusing to trade with people who don't barter properly. Participants' most frequent complaints revolve around various forms of favoritism, like hiding or reserving goods for certain people or offering lower prices to friends. The biggest insult is that a barterer is "just here to sell"; these people violate not only the barter process but also the ethic of barter as a noncommodified, antiaccumulationist practice.

Surprisingly, one of the most effective barriers to articulating barter and nonbarter economies has been a *conceptual boundary*. Barter organizers teach that barter is unique because it is about use-value. Good barterers (in both senses of the term) should not approach goods and services in terms of their relative exchange-values as calculated in the formal market, but rather for their use-value. My interview with Dolores, one of the *campesinas* trading in Santa Elena, demonstrates how this isolates barter. As I recounted in chapter 3, Dolores belongs to a women's association that produces value-added food products like marmalades and cookies. However, she almost never barters these products because they are from the group and it is difficult to find goods in return that the entire group can benefit from. In making these calculations, Dolores is thinking exclusively of the use-value of bartered goods but ignoring their possible exchange-value. If she were to trade the group's marmalades at the barter market, where they are valued highly, she might be able to acquire clothes, books, jewelry, and other items that could be sold at cash markets or bartered elsewhere for a net gain. This type of economic calculation is common: it is the speculative mentality that guides the rebusque and pragmatic pluralism. It is nearly impossible, however, when traded goods are seen as only having a use-value. The result, in Dolores's case, is that barter becomes an impediment to, rather than a support for, a solidarity-based collective production scheme. It is surprising that this conceptual reframing would be so effective among people renowned for their enterprising nature, but I think it has been helped by (and contributed to) the relatively low volume of products in the barter markets.

## Culture and Economy

These moral and conceptual boundaries require significant cultural activism. Barter organizers see economic change and sociocultural change as inextricably linked: each will lead to the other, but each also requires the other. The dilemma that emerges for organizers, then, is where to begin. If you develop new economic systems but do not work on people's habits and values, as José suggests, is there anyone to enact your new economy? Alternatively, if you change people but do not provide a material, economic system through which they can express and enact their new selves, will these cultural changes last?

This tension between sociocultural and economic activities is one of the key differences between activism in crisis and noncrisis contexts. During economic crises in Argentina, Russia, and Greece, activists' strategies were obvious: they had to deal with short-term survival needs by building alternative economies. Sociocultural change could come later. Outside of a crisis, though, activists have the luxury of focusing on sociocultural change. In fact, outside of a crisis organizers *need* to emphasize the social, cultural, and ethical difference of barter in order make a compelling argument for why people should participate in these unorthodox and sometimes less convenient economies. Given limited time and resources, activists have to choose how to intervene based on their best guess about what types of change are possible and which activities will have the greatest multiplier effects. These decisions, often made intuitively, have enormous implications for the outcomes of their project and offer a powerful window onto the sociocultural dynamics that support hegemony.

In Medellín, barter organizers have adopted primarily social and cultural strategies and neglected or at times explicitly downplayed the economic relevance of barter. For example, only Pajarito was initially conceptualized as an economic *system*; most barter experiments have been designed as markets, events, and demonstrative activities intended to open minds and reveal possibilities. Santiago echoes the sentiments of many organizers when he says that "barter is just an excuse. It is not a goal in itself, but just a means for getting people together, having fun, getting to know each other, and teaching values of respect." Of course, as someone who dedicates substantial time to barter and partially depends on it for his livelihood, he clearly sees barter as more than an excuse or a pedagogical game, and yet this perspective continually emerges in his discourse and practice.

By treating capitalism and noncapitalist alternatives as primarily *cultural* phenomena, activists divert attention from the material changes that they seek to create. This has real consequences. For example, when Santiago and Olga created a partnership opportunity with a chain of supermarket cooperatives, they celebrated this as a chance to make inroads into the larger cooperative community, where they could use barter to teach "solidarity economy" values. Until I asked, none of the organizers considered how this relationship might be used to strengthen barter economies, which is especially surprising because bringing these supermarkets into the barter fairs could have provided the basic household products the markets were lacking and thereby sparked renewed interest from *campesinos*. This shows the extent to which organizers sometimes reduce barter to a sociocultural project. Ignoring the *economy* of barter in this way threatens to undermine all of the organizers' goals: social, cultural, and economic.

What explains this contradictory and self-limiting form of action? In part, it matches organizers' goals, which are not purely economic, but there are a number of other important factors at play. To some extent, organizers de-emphasize the economic in response to new participants. When new barterers have difficulties adjusting to barter transactions (as described in chapter 3), organizers tend to emphasize the more easily recognizable social benefits of the markets. They see the fun and the sociality of the market as its main strengths and justify their work by emphasizing those qualities.

Capitalocentrism plays a role here as well. Even as activists try to sustain a belief that change is possible, they imagine the capitalist *economy* as an enormous system that is extremely resistant to change. By contrast, capitalist *culture* seems small, contained within the individual, limited to their values, logics, and behaviors. Even if barterers see culture as constantly being reproduced through the media, schools, and other institutions, it seems more mutable than the capitalist economy. Focusing on cultural activism thus shifts their project from transforming grand social structures to training individuals in new ways of thinking and being, a task that feels far simpler because the scale is more comprehensible and the targets of change more human.

Finally, culturally based activism is extremely common across Medellín, where the local government frequently addresses complex social problems through simplistic cultural "fixes." Addressing the structural (and infrastructural) roots of social problems is difficult, controversial, and costly, so when the city has to reform its image as a war zone they launch a marketing campaign and build fancy modernist libraries in poor neighborhoods, when road congestion and traffic-related deaths peak they encourage people to use their "street smarts" (*inteligencia vial*), and when they want to encourage the solidarity economy they pump money into theatrical presentations and school programs that emphasize a "solidarity culture." Sociocultural activism is cheaper than large-scale structural change, it can be implemented piecemeal, it raises far less controversy, and "success" can be easily measured by the number of events you organize rather than the complex impacts those may or may not have. In this context, theatrics has become a particularly widespread component of governmental and nongovernmental programs and a commonsense form of activism.

## The Consequences of Oppositional Politics
## in a Diverse Economy

How do we make sense of barterers' simultaneous promotion of bridges and boundaries? How do we explain this tension between an everyday economic practice that includes capitalism, a project to promote noncapitalist barter markets within a diverse economy, and an oppositional, anticapitalist politics? And why do activists continue to select cultural over economic strategies? I don't think we can conclude that barterers are uncommitted, disingenuous, hypocritical, or ignorant. Nor are these tensions and strategies a simple result of the resources available to barter organizers, their ideologies, and the political opportunity structure. Such explanations do not account for the full complexity of barterers as dynamic cultural beings. The key to these questions rests in an understanding of the two separate registers through which barterers conceptualize, describe, and enact their alternative economy.[2]

In the formal register of public discourse, political speech, and barter activism, barterers often adopt an oppositional and ideological stance that promotes the isolation of barter from capitalist economies. Here they are largely following the predominant model of political discourse, which is characterized by polemical attacks, unreflective opposition, moralism, and false choices. It is a politics perhaps best characterized by George W. Bush's statement, "You're either with us or against us," transferred into a Colombian context in which entire opposition parties can be massacred. But there is more to it than mimicry. Conflict, fear, and polarization support the types of essentialism and Othering that undergird capitalocentrism. There is a palpable sense, in barter activists' language, that the darker sides of Medellín are a real threat. Capitalism, violence, alienation, and our own human urges toward selfishness and greed are so powerful that even the smallest hole in our defenses might prove overwhelming to the barter project. Importantly, this way of framing good and evil also does important cultural work by unambiguously establishing barterers' moral worth; it contributes to a narrative of wholeness and dignity in the face of Medellín's more turbulent histories.

On the other hand, in the informal and less-cognized registers of private conversation and actual economic practice, barterers take a pragmatic and pluralistic approach that encourages the articulation of barter and nonbarter spheres. These tendencies toward articulation represent a historically constructed economic sensibility, developed and reinforced through everyday practice in a diverse economy. As people strive to make a living in Medellín, they are constantly linking capitalism and noncapitalism, shifting value from one sphere to another without even conceptualizing them as distinct, much less opposed. The resulting economic subjectivity is strongly pluralist and antiessentialist, a sharp contrast to the ideological and oppositional nature of politics. Seeing how these two registers rub against each other—i.e., understanding the contradiction between barterers' political and practical selves—provides a fuller picture of how capitalocentrism works against the construction of viable noncapitalist alternatives.

Barterers' oppositional politics certainly underscores their critique of capitalism and hopes for a different society. However, these same politics—and the strains of capitalocentrism that inform them—also lead to a strategy of isolation that reinforces the material and symbolic power of capitalism and weakens barter in at least four ways. First, capitalocentrism encourages organizers to divert limited human and financial resources away from the construction of a diversified economic system by reinforcing the notion that the capitalist economy is enormous and extremely resistant to change. This may not be true in all cases—people could easily argue the reverse, that economies are easier to change than deeply embedded culture—but it is part of what lies behind the prioritization of sociocultural forms of activism in Medellín. As a result, the barter systems that do exist are not sufficiently diverse and lack reliable supplies of basic necessities. Ultimately, this works against their goals of subject transformation as well. Their attempts to teach values and enforce a morally correct vision of barter target only the conscious, symbolic aspects of subjectivity, ignoring the ways that subjectivities are also constructed through material practices and embodied action.

Second, the boundaries that protect barter's purity also isolate it from tremendous flows of value. Barter is a small economy that depends in part on capitalist and market-oriented production. Any action that limits articulation decreases opportunities to use the resources flowing through other markets or created through other labor processes to strengthen this noncapitalist, solidarity-based alternative. Barterers get stuck in their own small world, or they leave. To be clear, I am not arguing for large barter systems; smallness may be a virtue. North (2005) suggests that the large scale of Argentina's barter networks increased their contribution to household economies but decreased their ability to embody and transmit alternative values. In Medellín, barterers are divided on the question of whether they should aspire to small barter systems or large and ever-expanding ones. Virtually all agree, however, that markets with a larger quantity and diversity of goods would better fulfill their household needs and increase the appeal of barter economies more generally.

Third, and most importantly, is the clash between capitalocentrism and pragmatic pluralism. When organizers try to put capitalocentrism into practice, they violate people's basic common sense for economic action, the "pragmatic pluralism" that has developed through decades of practice in a diverse economy. If their basic assumption about the twenty-nine days of pure capitalism were correct, then one day of pure barter might work nicely as an opportunity to experiment with noncapitalist possibilities. However, because none of their days is purely capitalist, switching to a purely barter economy doesn't just have the intended effect of countering capitalist mindsets. It also violates people's entire embodied understanding of what it means to do the economy, to pursue well-being, and to create value. The anticapitalist element of barter becomes antipragmatic as well, and noncapitalism comes to seem naïve and uneconomic. The main problem with capitalocentrism in Medellín is not (as Gibson-Graham would have it) that it narrows political imaginations; rather, the main problem is that capitalocentrism suggests isolationist strategies that contradict dominant economic subjectivities in ways that are not counterhegemonic.[3]

Through their boundary making, organizers create barter not only as different or alternative, but as a separate and almost totally incommensurable economic realm. Markets are designed so that value cannot flow from one economic system to the other and barterers are encouraged to reject commonsense notions of how to pursue well-being. The result is that well-being and pragmatism are ceded to capitalism, tied to notions of profit, competition, finding the best deal, and so on. A firmly bounded barter seems either noneconomic or antieconomic, and therefore unrealistic. It may provide a social and economic space within which committed participants can develop alternative subjectivities and counterhegemonic imaginaries, but this isolated sphere of exchange merely reinforces hegemonic beliefs of many casual observers.

This results in the fourth problem: a public relations issue. Many solidarity economy activists who would otherwise be interested in barter are turned off. They complain that barterers are so radical that they "aren't serious." They are overly romantic and don't realize that "a return to the old days when people only bartered" is not enough for people who need to eat today. Mirroring Smith and Stenning's (2006) important questions about how noncapitalist practices alter power relations, these local observers interpret barter's cultural focus, small scale, and nonpragmatic appearance as evidence that it is ineffective as a means of challenging material injustices. What would make barter more "serious"? According to a number of critics and barterers, the only solution is the very type of diversified economic development that organizers would like to achieve but are afraid of pursuing, lest capitalist values creep in to taint their project.

## Conclusion

At the beginning of my fieldwork, Luis Alberto complained that there are no barter systems, only demonstration projects and educational activities. Elisa's response to José took up the opposite problem: a citywide barter system would be great, she said, but where are the rules, norms, and trainings to ensure that people behave as barterers should? The work of sociocultural and economic transformation takes place in the space defined by these two critiques. Throughout my fieldwork, barter organizers continually asked for my opinions and evaluations of their work. They very reasonably wanted to ensure that my analysis would be useful to them and not just another academic exercise. I was always eager to dialogue but hesitant to present conclusions prematurely. These last three chapters are, in many ways, my attempt to answer their queries.

Barter activists already knew that their project could go only so far through demonstrative activities and efforts to change values, inculcate new beliefs, and liberate imaginations, but they seemed trapped in these types of activities. In my opinion, it is organizers' contradictory postures toward economic change—a capitalocentric schizophrenia in which they simultaneously think that economic change is possible and impossible—that lead them to prioritize sociocultural activism and at times neglect or ignore the economic aspects of these alternative economies. Many of the stories that I told in chapters 4 and 5, however, demonstrate that alternative economic *experiences* are necessary for generating and sustaining the sociocultural changes that barterers seek. This points the way toward more effective organizing.

My analysis goes beyond the question of why there are no economic systems to highlight *how* alternative economic systems might need to be designed and promoted to match the pragmatic pluralism of Medellín's economies. Conceptualizing capitalism as powerfully systemic, self-reproducing, and ever-expanding, barter organizers have sought to erect boundaries that will protect barter as a pure, alternative, noncapitalist economy. Contrary to Gibson-Graham's concerns, this capitalocentric perspective does not produce political nihilism, but it does shape activist strategies in a way that hinders the creation of an alluring and broadly transformative noncapitalism. Activists' boundary building and anticapitalist opposition contradict conventional subjectivities oriented around economic diversity and pragmatic pluralism.

If my analysis is correct, the remedy seems clear. A *politics of articulation*—not of boundary making—can help generate a noncapitalist politics that builds on people's intuitive pragmatic pluralism. The goals of such a politics would be to strategically connect barter with nonbarter economies in order to (1) strengthen barter economies by drawing on material and human resources from other economic spheres, (2) make barter seem more practical, economic, and alluring by allowing people to barter in a way that is consistent with the pragmatic pluralism of their other economic action, and (3) simultaneously infuse this pragmatic pluralism with barter's ethical concerns in order to nurture increasingly noncapitalist and noncapitalocentric subjectivities. I imagine organizers and participants forging more intentional links to businesses of various types, but developing their strategy on the basis of ethico-political considerations.

These suggestions will not sit well with many organizers, who fear that articulation with capitalism and other economies raises the threat of co-optation and deradicalization. I agree. However, designing barter around commonsense notions of how to pursue and create value may be necessary to create the alternative economic *systems* that so many activists long for and, by extension, to create the alternative solidarity culture of their dreams.[4] In this case, perhaps we cannot allow the perfect to be the enemy of the good.

Fortunately, we can learn from how this strategy has been applied elsewhere. North (2014) details a similar shift globally among alternative exchange systems, from LETS-style systems that were challenging to businesses, to Time Banks and paper-based local currencies meant to invite broader participation. While businesses have managed to use alternative currencies fairly extensively, this has rarely sparked a significant transformation of commodity chains. Businesses dependent on global inputs are often unable to use all of the local currency they acquire, and many are reluctant to urge their suppliers to consider accepting alternative currencies. The result, as in Medellín, has been a lack of "economic systems" that are diverse and integrated enough to support most of economic life. Where large numbers of local suppliers are in place, however, alternative currencies have functioned well to sustain local and ethical economies. North therefore concludes that activists should dedicate significantly more time to identifying "what we want to produce and consume locally," "deepening the range of what is produced locally in ethical ways," and "exposing exploitative local businesses" that might draw consumers away from the ethical ones (2014, 263). The barter-supported businesses that I have profiled in this book illustrate some of the ways local producers articulate barter and nonbarter realms to support local, ethical production. If activists pool resources to support similar businesses, they may be able to produce the economic systems they so desire.

# Conclusion

## "Para que Cambiemos"

Neoliberal policies, global economic instability, environmental change, rapid urbanization, and violence have exacerbated livelihood vulnerabilities for poor and middle-class Latin Americans in both rural and urban areas. As government social programs give way to export-oriented "economic stimulus" policies, nongovernmental organizations struggle to fill the social service provision gap. In Colombia, as elsewhere in the Western Hemisphere, general social vulnerability is exacerbated by ongoing urban and rural violence, which has created more than four million internally displaced people (CODHES 2008). Traditionally marginalized groups such as Indigenous people and Afro-Colombians face social exclusion and discrimination, despite significant advances in the 1991 national constitution, and "the poorest of the poor" are often maintained at the level of bare survival rather than supported through sustained development. Research from other parts of Latin America suggests that the "survival strategies" of the poor are increasingly inadequate (González de la Rocha 2007) and that even the middle classes are severely affected when neoliberal policies change their working conditions and challenge their social position and associated cultural understandings (Lomnitz and Melnick 1991).

The neoliberal wave has generated numerous alternatives and resistances from Latin American states like Venezuela, Bolivia, and Brazil, and from grassroots groups. State-led reforms in socialist and center-left countries initially seemed favorable, dramatically lowering poverty rates, increasing social spending, and establishing new channels for grassroots political participation. Over time, however, country after country has succumbed to economic stagnation, economically unsustainable natural resource policies, and corruption and the weakening of democratic institutions (Acosta 2013; Beasley-Murray et al. 2009; Friederic and Burke 2019; Villalba-Eguiluz and Etxano 2017). The past decade of political experimentation suggests that Latin American states are so deeply entangled in capital accumulation and rentier politics that even workers' parties and socialist governments cannot, on their own, achieve structural transformation in favor of marginalized populations (see, for example, Vergara-Camus and Kay 2017). As Escobar (2008, 21) argues, "Modernity's ability to provide solutions to modern problems has been increasingly compromised." Nonstate and nonmarket grassroots alternatives thus seem increasingly important.

Medellín's barter experiments are especially interesting in this regard because they respond to structural violence, social breakdown, and war not through conventional movement activities but rather through alternative economic practices. These types of alternative economies are increasingly important for addressing socioeconomic vulnerability throughout Latin America and have been promoted in the Global North as starting points for more sustainable and just economies (North 2010, 2016; Hornborg 2016). Numerous researchers have examined the emergence and organization of alternative economies in the North and South (Chatterton 2005; Iriart and Waitzkin 2006; Leyshon et al. 2003; Pearson 2002; Powell 2002; North 1999, 2005; Papavasiliou 2008; Santana 2008), but important questions remain.

In this book, I have focused on three questions in particular: What are the actual social and economic effects of Medellín's barter systems? To what extent and in what ways do they constitute alternatives to capitalism, neoliberalism, violence, and development? And what organizing strategies show promise as ways of creating the material practices, institutions, and subjectivities necessary to enact and sustain alternative economies that are more just and ecologically sustainable? I have typically conceptualized my research as a conversation with alternative economies organizers and interested academics in Medellín and abroad. In this conclusion, I bring these concerns together in a final examination of barter's revolutionary potential and a series of suggestions for how—in my opinion—Medellín's barter organizers might more effectively advance their project.

## The Effects of Barter

Studies of alternative economies frequently highlight significant economic and social benefits among a select group of participants and use these to paint compelling pictures of these economies' broader potential (North 2007; Pacione 1997; Williams et al. 2001; Gibson-Graham 2006b; Leyshon et al. 2003). Aldridge and Patterson (2002) suggest that scholars "get real" about these alternatives, highlighting the difficulties, within the current sociocultural context, of creating alternative economies that achieve conventional economic goals. Potential, they argue, is insufficient. While their critique is valuable, a thorough analysis of alternative markets shows real prefigurative possibility—that is, it shows that barter and local currencies are changing both the material and cultural foundations undergirding capitalist exploitation. Particularly influential is barter's tendency to shift the mode of production toward household autonomy and collective satisfaction, to shift value regimes toward use-value and social-value, and to combat the cultural construction of scarcity.

Barter allows the most active traders to access some basic needs and raw materials, to make long-term investments in products like books and educational materials that they would not otherwise acquire, to achieve a higher level of consumption without recourse to credit, and to start and expand family-owned businesses. Socially, although barter markets have not led to the types of strong and materially important social ties that some anthropologists might expect, they have encouraged people to come together across class, generational, and lifestyle divides, to interact with and learn to appreciate people who are quite different, and to form relations based on mutual respect. These types of fun, collaborative, noncompetitive markets are important contributions to a city searching for *convivencia* and *solidaridad*.

Barterers think of these social benefits as a form of peacefare (Wolf 1987); I think that barter can also contribute in small ways to the *economics* of peacefare by allowing people to access goods and services without contributing to the extortion rackets and money-laundering schemes that undergird the war system (Richani 2002) and that have so thoroughly permeated the city, and by establishing interdependencies that reinforce a sense of moral solidarity. Admittedly, this economic peacefare is limited. Armed actors would stamp it out if it significantly threatened their businesses. However, just as war seeps into everyday life through a million small acts, perhaps we can expect the same from peace. This is especially important in Colombia today, after the 2016 peace accord between the government and the Fuerzas Armadas Revolucionarias de Colombia (FARC), when people must invent forms of peacefare to bring the promises of this accord into reality.

As I noted, barter organizers have especially dedicated themselves to sociocultural activism, moral education, and the transformation of subjectivities. At a minimum, their work introduces doubts about hegemonic subjectivities and highlights the possibility of other ways of being in the world. For a small group of people who are genuinely interested in pursuing these other ways, barter offers important material and social support. The economic benefits of barter liberate them from some of the material demands of the conventional economy and help them escape ongoing socialization into a culture of consumerism, commodification, and surrender to exploitation. In this way, barter reverses the process of commodification. To reverse West's (2006) logic, the decommodification of goods *in some instances* affects how goods and labor are valued *in all instances*. Although other goods and labor are not always decommodified, there is now always the potential for them to be produced and valued for solidarity and mutual satisfaction rather than private gain.

Barter-supported opportunities to run their own businesses and produce goods that are visibly beneficial to others are especially important in this regard; they allow people to partially establish control over the means of production, processes of social reproduction, and the appropriation and distribution of surplus, and they counter the alienation and learned uselessness of the conventional economy. Importantly, the ethics, economics, and inefficiencies of barter *force* some of these changes on traders, requiring them to engage economies as practices of collective interdependence and to develop different standards regarding the temporality and scope of consumption. Most notably, they begin to approximate Esteva's commoners, who see desires and productive capacity as inseparable and therefore create sufficiency-based systems for satisfaction rather than scarcity-based systems for accumulation and exploitation. This is what Diego was referring to, in our opening vignette, as freedom. It was freedom from the economization of everyday life, from the logic of scarcity.

It is through this combination of material and sociocultural impacts that barter can become counterhegemonic (if activists seek to establish a single new hegemony based on solidarity) or nonhegemonic (the more likely possibility given that so many activists see barter as one current of a diverse economy). While advocates of nonhegemonic politics often celebrate small autonomist projects, I think we should engage questions about barter's scale. Jara (2014, 242) argues, for example, that "the solidarity economy alternative must be a mass-driven transformative project" if it is to disrupt capitalist exploitation, create "new conditions and possibilities for human development," and spark new logics of production, distribution, and consumption. I would not argue that Medellín's barter systems *must* do this in order to be significant, but my research provides clear evidence that scaling up and diversifying barter systems can deepen their counterhegemonic or nonhegemonic effects as long as increased size and diversity do not compromise barter's alternativity. This is where it helps to see the four dimensions of revolution that I have emphasized—individual depth and co-revolutionary breadth as well as societal scale and temporal endurance—rather than becoming fixated just on questions of scale.

Although my narrative mimics the optimism of previous alternative economies scholars, my goal has been to be "real" about the many impediments to change. Barterers and barter organizers face significant material and sociocultural challenges. However, I want to actively work against representations of these challenges as stable, coherent, and necessarily hegemonic. Both the barter movement and resistance to it are marked by deep contradictions that cannot be reduced to a noncapitalist/capitalist binary. Complicating economic activism in this way does away with easy solutions, but introduces a new, empowered dynamic. Activists have many tools to draw from and no coherent and all-powerful enemy. Their process is necessarily one of deliberation and ethical experimentation in the midst of significant internal and external resistance. Another part of "getting real" involves taking prefiguration seriously and recognizing that sociocultural and political-economic changes take time to achieve all four dimensions of transformation.

## Mere Reformism or Viable Noncapitalism?

Many of the stories in this book show that barter stimulates businesses that then engage in conventional markets and that it permits a higher quality of life than the conventional economy allows. We should seriously question, then, if barter is helping to counter capitalist exploitation, creating an alternative, or forestalling the mass discontent and protest necessary to overthrow capitalism. In many ways, barter could be seen as functioning similarly to microcredit, facilitating popular participation in pseudo-capitalism as preparation for incorporation into the "real" capitalist economy. However, we also need to account for the ideological, political, and subjective aspects of barter. For barter to function as an alternative, and for barter businesses to do something other than reproduce docile workers for capitalist firms, it should help people rethink the economy and develop social relations, practices, and lifestyles based on alternative ethics. In Medellín, we see clear signs that barter is achieving this.

North (2007) asks similar questions about alternative currencies and LETS, examining them as forms of micropolitical resistance against the disciplines of conventional money and the commoditization and capitalization of everyday life. Comparing experiences in the United Kingdom, Hungary, Argentina, and New Zealand, he examines whether they are "precursors to a new twenty-first-century economy . . . focused on need rather than profit [or] Luddite throwbacks to a precapitalist economy that emerges in periods of crisis" (North 2007, xiv). North points out that the long list of failed alternative exchange systems appears to reinforce Marx and Engels's concern that cooperatives and alternative trade are often coping mechanisms rather than initiatives with revolutionary potential. I think we need to contextualize these "failures" adequately and compare them with the perceived success of market, state, and class-solidarity-based solutions. Is the vision of a collectively managed alternative trading system really more naïvely utopian than dreams of a self-regulating free market in which the pursuit of individual self-interest results in socially beneficial outcomes? Given historical experiences, is it more realistic to hope for an enlightened state that will effectively represent the political and economic interests of all citizens in a consensual and nonoppressive manner? And have international workers' politics fared better, giving rise to enduring noncapitalist and nonexploitative solutions, or have they more often than not fought for industrial capitalism with fringe benefits, often along racist, sexist, and xenophobic lines of exclusion?

My goal here is not to tear down these union, statist, and market approaches—my research doesn't provide a basis for such a critique—but simply to point out that they offer weak platforms for critiquing alternative exchange. A better solution might be to think about how multiple strategies can be linked to deepen their radical potential and decrease the likelihood that they will degenerate into co-opted reformism. Marx and Engels, in fact, anticipated these strategic synergies: they objected to alternative economies when they were presented "as a panacea to be implemented through persuasion" but welcomed them when they were linked to trade unions and other forms of mass politics (North 2007, 181). Class politics might go further when integrated with progressive, collectively regulated, noncapitalist markets whose scale and speed promote localism and resist capitalist expansion. And these alternative markets and grassroots-owned production systems might give political actors the additional economic autonomy they need to advance their cause.

Not coincidently, given that they are rooted in the same systems of exploitation, antiracist politics and climate change activism might benefit from similar synergies between political action and the construction of community economies. The Black Panther Party's embrace of free breakfast and health care programs illustrated how direct action to meet community needs can support consciousness raising and free up time for formal politics. Cooperation Jackson is pursuing a similar "build and fight" strategy today, "democratically transform[ing] the economy" through cooperative production and alternative exchange while using electoral politics to create additional openings for people's power (Akuno 2017). Research suggests that meaningful climate action might require transcending conventional political strategies as well. For example, reorganizing the political economy of the energy sector—by shifting utilities from private and state ownership to community ownership—may be essential for overcoming the barriers to reasonable climate and energy policies (Becker and Naumann 2017; Bozuwa 2019; Next System Project 2018).

The diverse cases that North studied show that alternative exchange systems can function at a very large scale and over a long time period, that they can provide significant economic benefits outside of conventional state-capitalist economies, and that they can effectively politicize the economy. These results depended, however, on effective local-level organizing and a welcoming political environment. By carefully documenting the material, social, and cultural changes provoked by barter, my work builds on North's, providing a broader theoretical basis for contemplating social change strategies. The regnant position in the social sciences is that, since the economy is fundamentally capitalist, "successful economic activism must accommodate itself to that 'reality' rather than pursuing the utopian chimera of noncapitalist invention" (Gibson-Graham [1996] 2006a: 172). Gibson-Graham's theoretical and political contribution is to call attention to alternative points of intervention and strategies for change. An example that is particularly relevant for this book is that of self-employment. Many scholars have described the increase of self-employed laborers (including "freelancing" contract workers and temporary laborers) as part of a post-Fordist casualization or flexibilization of labor. Capitalist firms can rationalize their workforce by shifting employees from regular workers to self-employed contractors. These workers then lose their job security and benefits, representation in employees' associations and unions, and the capacity to make claims on firms or states for a share of the surplus value that they produce. Flexibilization of labor, therefore, seems to perfectly fit the logic of capitalism and the neoliberal state, and liberation from capitalist relations of production seems to bring only misery.

An alternative perspective on the casualization of labor, though, might ask about the actual or potential consequences of moving so many people into alternative, noncapitalist employment. Such a perspective can recognize the negative effects of informalization and ask, "What comes next? What responses exist beyond mobilizing for more favorable inclusion in business as usual?" The self-employed generate and control their own surplus using their own resources; they are noncapitalist, strictly speaking, though their working conditions are not always just. We've seen that alternative markets like barter create networks and flows that solidify worker-owned businesses and expand their surpluses. Can the left use the fact that capitalist firms are creating noncapitalist workers to push for more human-centered, democratic, and nonexploitative economic relations?

In an answer to this question, Gibson-Graham imagine how labor unions might "set themselves the goal of bringing increased security, compensation and opportunity to the . . . self-employed" in ways that do not simply reproduce the role of "the capitalist firm or government bureaucracy as the only providers of secure and well-compensated employment" ([1996] 2006a: 169). Unions might, for example, extend representation to the self-employed, push for universal health coverage as a human right rather than a right of (capitalist) workers, establish portable pension plans, and pursue other political possibilities that extend beyond the capitalist firm such as universal basic income (see also Ferguson 2015). Other strategies for noncapitalist class politics might help the self-employed make and keep larger profits, and "thereby make self-employment a more viable alternative to employment (and exploitation) within a capitalist firm" (Gibson-Graham [1996] 2006a: 169). This could be done by providing child care and public transportation at reasonable costs and by supporting the business ventures of the self-employed through training programs, access to community-controlled credit, and the creation of purchasing, production, and marketing cooperatives. In other words, the challenge is to take advantage of capitalist firms' creation of noncapitalist workers, to convert this into an opportunity to strengthen a *desirable* and *just* noncapitalism, rather than simply repeating labor movement ideologies for reincorporation into capitalism. Achieving this, Gibson-Graham argue, requires the construction of new subjectivities and new institutional supports for noncapitalist subjects.

Wainwright (2012) offers a historically informed vision for this new labor politics. She argues that the current economic-ecological crisis is a crisis of capital but not of labor. Workers still have the capacity to care, create, design, teach, meet people's needs, and benefit society. Today's challenge, then, is to reactivate labor without resorting to capital. Barter systems are a promising manner of organizing and unleashing workers' creative potential. They also meet basic material needs, thus freeing people for other types of activity, political or nonpolitical. They might therefore serve as a pivot for a broader politics that supports the construction of other noncapitalist practices, institutions, and values. A closer examination of the concept of hegemony will sharpen our analysis of how alternative exchange can be leveraged to support this broader politics.

## Hegemony, Counterhegemony, and Nonhegemonic Movements

Historians and anthropologists increasingly view the state not as a "thing" that already exists and can be expected to endure, but rather as a "claim" for the necessity, naturalness, and coherence of a particular set of ruling practices and institutions (Brown 2006; Corrigan 1994; Gupta 2006; Mitchell 2009; Roseberry 1994; Sayer 1994). From this perspective, the state is less a set of institutions than a confluence of processes for constructing and naturalizing a particular configuration of power. According to these authors, the formation of the state and its citizens depends in large part on their continual performance of state functions; people make real and legitimize the state's claims by participating in seemingly mundane practices such as using the postal service, applying for driver's licenses, filling out birth registries, and using the official currency.

This view of power makes contradiction and dynamism central to hegemony, reconstituting it not as a state of domination—or a dominating state—but rather as a "field of contestation" (Roseberry 1994). Because the state, and hegemony more generally, requires the participation of a broad segment of society, it must internalize a series of contradictory understandings of and expectations for power and identity. The ruling elite (who are themselves diverse) often must hide or gloss over differences and incorporate counterhegemonies into their governing project. As Sayer notes, "The hegemony of the state is also exactly what is most fragile about the state, precisely because it does depend on people living much of what they know to be a lie" (1994, 375). Barterers call out some of these lies: that the economy is an unchangeable, official realm of experts; that regular people must simply follow preestablished roles; that the economy functions best when governed by "rational" efficiency and profit motives rather than ethics; that pursuing profit-oriented exchange-value is the surest path to individual and collective well-being.

Following Gibson-Graham, I argue that we can see "capitalism" and "capitalist hegemony" in similar terms. Capitalism is not as much of a "thing" as we think, and capitalist hegemony is created when we perform a capitalist economy, frame our actions and selves in relation to it, and accept a delimitation of the possible preached by the emissaries of capital. Capitalism is not wholly discursive or performative—it is also very powerfully concretized in supporting institutions—but its hegemony is fragmented, contested, and vulnerable. This fragmentation is evident in the rhetoric, values, and initiatives of government agencies and private firms, as well as in the pragmatic pluralism forged in Medellín's diverse economy. The critical question for activists is how capitalist hegemony can be further eroded by challenging the material and sociocultural processes, political alliances, and consent that uphold it.

Gramsci's analysis of "relations of force" suggests two arenas of action. The first is the construction of alliances among the dominated that are increasingly broad and deep, shifting from mutual obligation to mutual self-interest to a firm belief that their interests are fundamentally the same. This, he writes, creates "not only a unison of economic and political aims, but also intellectual and moral unity" (1972, 181). It is achieved in part by shifting attention from "conjunctural" conflicts directed at narrow group interests and reforms to "organic movements" directed at the very functioning and organization of society. In the case of barter, natural allies include solidarity economy and workers' organizations. Barter organizers have pursued inroads to the powerful *cajas de compensación* in Medellín, but they will need to do more. A number of NGOs and large cooperatives might be willing to convert their isolated barter events into ongoing barter projects if they were presented proposals for well-designed exchange systems with reliable economic and social benefits.

Per Gramsci, however, these networks will need to spark solidarity grounded in increasingly radical critiques of political and economic exploitation rather than just be marriages of convenience. Barterers, cooperatives, and NGOs might push each other to see how their struggles are all linked to the violation of basic human rights and a development model that results in the maldistribution of assets, productive power, and market influence. A solidarity economy worker who promotes women's economic autonomy in Medellín offered one of the most strident critiques of barter systems that I had heard, and then went on to explain how they could become great tools for addressing violence and poverty. The alternative currencies, she said, need to provide access to enough of people's basic needs. They need to be articulated not in terms of romantic tradition but in terms of a biting critique of the conventional economy, including the economic power of paramilitaries and loan sharks, and of the corporate banks. They should build popular knowledge to "debunk accumulation." And then barterers should really develop the theory of use-value in practice. "We need barter promotors," she said. "In the same way that we have human rights defenders, we need barter defenders." She then described a project to bring truckloads of vegetables from small farmers in a paramilitary-controlled region to the low-income neighborhood in which she works, saying that they have discussed paying half in pesos and half in barter, but they need stronger barter allies to make this work. Similar solidarity-generating, critically informed partnerships are possible across the city and would explicitly link barter to the critique and transcendence of the current, unjust configuration of power.

The second arena of action is within and against the state. Although "the state is seen as the organ of [the dominant] group," according to Gramsci, it constantly shifts to balance diverse class interests (1972, 205–206). One way the modern state has secured this equilibrium is by offering programs of "development" that are broadly appealing but carefully avoid challenging the structures that reproduce inequality. If barterers can continue to exploit sympathetic pockets within the state, they can take advantage of its resources while simultaneously pushing government officials to pursue social and economic policies that support noncapitalist investments in people and communities. We have seen similar proposals and actions in Argentina (Ranis 2010), Brazil (da Costa 2017), South Africa (Bennie 2014), and Venezuela (Dittmer 2011). In the United Kingdom, organizers of the Brixton pound are exploring links with the state taxation system, as well as with banking and digital purchasing systems, to expand the functionality of their alternative currencies, invite broader participation, and thereby affect large-scale financial and political systems. The extent to which these effects are reformist versus revolutionary will depend on how other social movements and economic forces drive the state. For example, Dittmer (2011) explained that a flood of oil money and social welfare programs competed with state-sponsored barter systems in Venezuela, but promises of state support for economic diversification through collective production might have ultimately given barter a more important role as a means of exchange if the Venezuelan polity and economy had not collapsed.

Hornborg (2016) offers the most ambitious vision of state-based barter. Through a masterful analysis of money, magic, modernity, economic globalization, ecological imperialism, and conventional and heterodox economics, he suggests that the most promising way to curb "the destructive consequences of economic globalization" might be to bifurcate the economy so that "local values (such as those concerned with food, shelter, energy, place, community, and face-to-face relations)" are coordinated exclusively through government-issued local currencies, while global currencies are restricted to products that can generate the greatest public good only through global coordination, such as information and communication technologies and pharmaceutical research. He argues for a local currency distributed by national or municipal authorities as a universal basic income, useful only for local goods, coordinated with special banks to promote interest-free saving and borrowing, and with a system permitting businesses to convert local currencies to global ones. Such a system would likely overcome many of the shortcomings of previous alternative market experiments by inviting a diversity of participants and products, guaranteeing a larger scale, and directly and immediately affecting production and consumption as well as exchange.

Ultimately, as Gordon Nembhard notes, these strategies of alliance building and state engagement contribute to a third aspect of change that was also important to Gramsci: resubjectivation and the construction of a new common sense. "The theory of change behind this model," she writes, "is that the more people practice economic democracy, collective ownership, and economic transparency, the more they will come to expect . . . these practices in the rest of their lives. People will work to make the changes necessary to enact this system" (2016, 11). This is the essence of co-revolutionary contagion (Harvey 2010b): that decommodifying and collectivizing our barter lives will lead to a revolution of values and actions in other spheres of life.

Medellín's barter experiments already challenge state claims to control over the economy, and they stretch predominant visions of the possible. Barterers' work with the state also amplifies contradictions within the dominant hegemony—contradictions that were already present in the state's support for the solidarity economy and the influx of former NGO workers into government offices in recent years. Because barterers are deeply uncomfortable about their work with the state, and because the very nature of the barter project challenges the legitimacy and effectiveness of the state's exclusive control over the economy, their work continually raises challenging questions about the goals, strategies, and exclusions of the conventional political economy. Like many of Latin America's social movements (Stahler-Sholk et al. 2008), barter ultimately asks who has the power to decide. In so doing, it challenges authoritarian politics, authoritarian economics, and authoritarian violence.

However, the barter experiments straddle the distinction between counterhegemonic and nonhegemonic movements (Day 2005). In some ways and at some times organizers seek to marshal state-sponsored barter to impose a new dominant ideology and a new configuration of society, a counterhegemony. But at other times, they aim to create a parallel, alternative economic system that people can adopt freely, absent coercion, as a nonhegemonic or pluriversal opportunity. Many scholars and activists view only the directly counterhegemonic as potentially revolutionary, but Sayer and Corrigan's view of state formation demonstrates how "opting out" can be a radical, direct challenge to hegemony. No longer participating, no longer legitimating, no longer accepting the dominant framing of possibility or the vision of development that shores up state-capitalist legitimacy, no longer accepting processes of rule and identities of leadership and followership: these *also* constitute radical and direct rejections of power. Moreover, the apparent increase in anarchist thought on political mobilization—evident in the Zapatista, global justice, and Occupy movements—suggests that it will be increasingly important to understand the potential of these strategies to challenge and reconstruct power (Day 2005; Escobar 2020; Juris 2008; Khasnabish 2008; Razsa 2015).

## Deepening Barter's Impact

It should come as no surprise by now that I concur with traders, organizers, and other solidarity economy workers who believe that Medellín's barter experiments should be made more "serious" and systematic. Given high levels of need, the massive proliferation of small businesses, the scarcity of money and commercial opportunities, and the interest in local development solutions led by the solidarity economy, there are ample opportunities to expand barter so it offers more and more diverse products. Also, the need for social healing to complement formal peace accords increases the urgency for economic reorganizations that enforce material and social solidarity.

Increased dedication to economic activism, however, should not distract organizers from their sociocultural goals. Barter organizers—like activists more generally—often imagine individual action and political practice as an outgrowth of consciousness, and therefore adopt moral and political education as their key tactics. Their "intellectual and moral leadership" seeks to expand economic imaginaries and exploit discontent with the conventional economy. Their decision to prioritize education and conscientization is shaped by power and hegemony—particularly the belief that activists can do little to change institutions and the economy—but it has important impacts. Unfortunately, organizers have not adequately analyzed how political subjectivities are constructed through nonconscious practices and experiences. I have illuminated ways that barter practice and market characteristics shape subjectivities. In further developing and systematizing barter, activists might consider how to achieve sociocultural change through economic practice, not just conscious education. As we saw in chapter 2, early barter organizers promoted a style of barter that could be quickly spread and easily adopted, but in doing so they compromised their broader goals. Scaling up may be as much a sign of *failure* as success. Today's organizers need not repeat this mistake. Instead, they might choose to design into barter systems some of the productive inconveniences that I have identified, particularly slowness, the realignment of desires with the productive possibilities of one's community, and the difficulty of calculating value without evaluating mutuality.

In chapter 6, I suggested that barter organizers might adopt a politics of articulation that links barter and nonbarter economies in ways that reemphasize the economic value of barter and rob capitalism of its (apparent) monopoly on economic common sense. This requires a delicate balance because it means increasing barter's economic impacts without eliminating the productive inconveniences that help generate counterhegemonic subjectivities. To manage articulation as a form of counterhegemonic or nonhegemonic politics, organizers would need to sharpen their guiding ethico-political principles. Gibson-Graham suggest four ethical referents for postcapitalist politics—necessity, surplus, consumption, and commons. To date, barterers have paid relatively little attention to the management of surplus and the production process more generally, and doing so might deepen their politics by enabling them to focus more precisely on what types of production they hope to promote and how profits might be reinvested for personal and collective goals. At the same time, my interpretation of barterers' words and actions reveals an emerging ethics based around inclusion, satisfaction, reciprocity, capability, and pragmatic pluralism. These might form an emic basis for an ethico-political project that is proposive without necessarily imposing boundaries.

When considering market rules, educational programs, alliances with supporting organizations, and outreach to potential new traders, barterers should consider, first, which strategies will amplify the economic and sociocultural changes that are already being provoked by barter. My research shows that these are rooted in four features of barter in Medellín: a focus on use-value and social-value; acceptance of productive inconveniences, like slower trading and decreased availability, because these changes promote social-value, localism, and an alternative sense of well-being; a local common sense of pragmatic pluralism, which makes people willing to accept barter whenever it proves useful; and a simultaneous shift in barterers' sense of their productive capacity and their desires, which weakens the culture of scarcity by bringing desires and their fulfillment together into the present moment and into their own hands as prosumers. The greatest impacts of barter have often resulted from people using barter to force themselves to make changes that violate economic norms; to deepen barter's impact, organizers should design markets for this type of self-compulsion.

Second, barterers might ask how new strategies, alliances, and educational programs will build traders' individual and collective capacity for production and autonomous organization, how they strengthen and broaden networks of reciprocity and bonds of mutual respect, and how they foster more useful, satisfying, inclusive, and alluring barter economies. As Smith and Stenning note, articulations lend "a sociality to economic life which requires mutual, reciprocal, and embedded forms of economic action" (2006, 192). The guiding questions behind a politics of articulation should therefore direct us toward the reciprocal and embedded relations that support our ethics. And an important aspect of this reciprocal support is material. It is a question of what we need and want and how we can build local productive capacity for that. If Olga's bakery, Roberto and Isabela's winery, and Diego's cabins are strong examples of barter-involved businesses, how can activists simultaneously strengthen them and use them to broaden and deepen barter? Could they work collectively to introduce these businesses to new markets (even conventional capitalist markets) while also using them as sites for generating surplus that can be invested in new barter-based businesses, as well as training grounds for new barter entrepreneurs? Could we work together to produce local raw materials that can support these businesses? Should we invest collectively in Diego's new project to grow food on the edges of the city and similar efforts among barter-involved farmers? Might some of Medellín's cooperative banks be willing to experiment with barter and alternative currencies, as credit unions have in parts of the United States and United Kingdom (North 2010)? The possibilities exist for stitching together more cohesive economic systems, but this requires a new type of activism.

Ultimately, the best anticapitalist strategies may be whichever strategies undermine hegemonic imaginaries of capitalist power, strengthen alternative ethics and subjectivities, and increase people's direct control over the means of production and the distribution of surplus by creating viable and alluring noncapitalist social relations. In some cases, success may require using capitalism rather than avoiding it for the sake of "purity" or out of fears of co-optation; perhaps the most pernicious and intractable aspects of capitalism are not private firms, market institutions, and profit motives but rather the capitalocentric insistence on singularity and the presumed impossibility of an ethical pluralism. In Medellín, I think barterers may be able to erode the sociocultural power of capitalism by creating material and conceptual bridges between barter and other forms of exchange and production (including capitalist ones) and developing a more explicit *barter* theory of value, economy, and well-being that draws from the local, historically developed, economic subjectivities of pragmatic pluralism. This would capture not only the old concept of use-value, but also the concepts of good-use-value and social-value that barterers expressed in Santa Elena (see chapter 3).

Such a project would dovetail nicely with a growing interest in *desarrollo integral* (holistic development) among local academics and NGOs, and it would present opportunities for new alliances and more "seriousness" in the eyes of potential participants and others in the solidarity economy. There is a danger here, however. Part of what makes barter so appealing and what contributes to its transformative and alternative effects is that it *feels* less economic. Barterers report feeling less pressure, less seriousness, lower stakes, and less competitiveness in the market. They are not as worried about the risks of miscalculating costs and benefits, and this freer mindset is part of what enables them to forge different social relationships and subjectivities. If barter is to become more serious, it must also remain free and fun.

These recommendations require increased dedication to barter organizing and better collaboration. These have been constant challenges in Medellín, where participants have often succumbed to traditions of passive followership and leaders have often burned out or become embroiled in egoistic battles to defend "their" projects and their reputations. My time in Medellín began and ended with conflicts among barter organizers. These revolved around different visions for barter, but more importantly they were about how to divide and manage two different surpluses: an economic surplus generated by grant money and government contracts, and a prestige surplus based on who gets recognized as the most genuine and authoritative barter promoter. On several occasions, passionate and committed barter organizers explained apologetically that they simply could not avoid these types of conflicts. "We have no models for collaboration," one said, "and our cultural processes are slow." A protagonist of another particularly ugly conflict told me, in an ambivalent self-critique, "Now you understand how much of a pain in the ass we *Paisas* are. Deep down, we can't trust each other because you never know what the other person's agenda is or where they are coming from." Making barter into a serious, revolutionary, noncapitalist project will not be possible *hasta que se cambien*—until barterers find the trust, the solidarity, and the confidence to set a new standard for leadership and followership; until organizers craft a new vision of protagonism as collective empowerment rather than individual recognition. But it is precisely through the practices of bartering and barter activism, and through increased internalization of the values of satisfaction, solidarity, capacity, and mutual recognition, that I believe they can create these new models.

## The Neverending Search for Freedom

Given Colombia's history of violence and the degree of inequality in the country today, we might expect to find a ubiquitous cynicism or nihilism there. It is true that I spoke with many Colombians who expressed something approximating hopelessness, a sense not that change is impossible but that any meaningful change is significantly constrained by the power of the oligarchy and the possibility of violence, by the absence of the state and the lack of an open democratic sphere. That the armed left has swallowed up any meaningful space for a nonviolent political left does not help. But alongside this pessimism, I have been continually inspired by the large number of utopian experiments in Colombia. Through barter systems, alternative currencies, eco-villages, innovative forms of urban planning, youth political cooperatives, fair trade stores, poetry festivals, eco-neighborhoods, and other initiatives, people have tried to rescale change in order to not surrender their agency. They have sought to create change at smaller scales and in less overtly political ways, with the hopes that myriad small projects will eventually spark broader social transformation. This is the face of Colombia that I have tried to show.

Through this research, I have sought to study experiments with transformation. A great deal of anthropological literature examines phenomena with significant historical or political economic heft, things like traditional practices, race and gender, colonialism, development, capitalism, and religion. This study differs by focusing on the emergent: the small, tentative projects of grassroots actors; the often-contradictory experiences, feelings, and deliberations of people as they work through these experiments; and the ways people use experiments as springboards for personal and societal transformation. In writing this book, I debated what to call these grassroots activities. The activities in Medellín do not quite constitute a movement, though many barter organizers aspire to a project whose level of participation and consolidation is worthy of the term. To refer to barter as a project also suggests more consistency and solidity than I found. There are certainly barter projects in Medellín, but they don't quite come together as a (single) barter project, and some flirtations with barter are too tentative to be considered projects at all. I settled on the word "experiment" because, in its colloquial sense at least, it conveys the type of open and indeterminate activity that I found in Medellín. And yet I remain convinced that these experiments can have deeply transformative—even revolutionary—consequences as they upset the dominant order, expand political imaginations, build institutions and cultures of collective self-governance, and permit people to mobilize their own resources and engage in production in a freer and less alienated way. Some barter experiments have involved more explicit trial and error, while others have been more informal, but all carry a sense of trying things out, seeing how they work, and adapting as they go. This is the "revolution . . . pero" that lies at the heart of sociocultural change.

I would like to close with one barterer's reflections on these experiments. One evening Julio and I rode home together from Santa Elena. Throughout the journey he told me about his personal trajectory—his experiences as a hydrologist, working with citizen science projects, studying ethics in school, and his passion for experimental theater. These diverse elements of his life were woven into his barter politics as well. As we were getting off of the bus, Julio started to talk about Kafka. "Have you ever read *A Report to an Academy*?" he asked. I confessed that I hadn't. He explained that this particular story is about a monkey who was placed in captivity but refused to be bound by his cage. In his struggle to find freedom, he learned to emulate the humans around him. He began to study and learned to read, write, and think advanced thoughts.

According to Julio, the monkey knew that no matter how much he learned and no matter how hard he worked, he could never become free. Yet he kept working. He kept working and learning and searching for a path to freedom because he knew that even if there was no way out, the only way to live was through continually searching for and trying to create that revolution, that moment of freedom. And that's what our experiments with barter are about, Julio told me. Even if they don't work, that's okay, because part of the value is the searching.

Julio interprets this story differently than many commentators, but this difference of interpretation is important and typical of him, and of other barter organizers. They are not bound by common interpretations and do not seek to follow conventions. They are seeking a different analytic on the world, one that sustains the possibility of freedom even while acknowledging the barriers thrown up by power and culture. Their insistence to see the world differently and to inhabit the world differently in order to make the world different is, perhaps, the most important legacy that barter will have as one current in a broader movement to remake economy and society.

# Acknowledgments

This book has only my name on the cover, but it would have been impossible without an immense web of partners, supporters, and influencers, from Bob Burke and Lynda Laliberte, who raised me with trust and passion, to María Chona Cruz, who turned my world right side up when she introduced me to environmental anthropology, to Karin Friederic and Nico Burke, who fill my days with questions, insights, meaning, and the best distractions.

My most important partners of course are Medellín's barter activists, barterers, solidarity economy workers, and intellectuals (whether by title or deed). This includes people not mentioned in this book, several people who might be surprised that I even remember our brief connections, and Cecilia Luca Escobar Vekeman, Santiago, and both Julios and Claras (the real and the pseudonymic). You are some of the most generous people I have known, and I will always value our work together, through all of its ups and downs. In many ways, I feel like a simple chronicler of your experiments, innovations, and insights. I am still learning from the ways you all create a vibrant and humanizing city. I hope there is use-value, social-value, and mutual satisfaction in this project.

The intellectual and political foundations for this work were built through conversations with mentors and colleagues at Williams College, the International Honors Program, the University of Arizona, the University of Georgia, the School for Advanced Research, and Appalachian State University. Michael Brown, Peter Just, Kai Lee, Corrine Glesne, Diane Austin, Marcela Vásquez-León, Jim Greenberg, Linda Green, Tom Sheridan, Tim Finan, Norma Mendoza-Denton, Ana Alonso, Brian Silverstein, and Jen Roth-Gordon: you all taught and modeled approaches to anthropological thinking, doing, and being that have shaped me in important ways. My commitment to grassroots power and social change was stoked by Gustavo Esteva, Smitu Kothari, Peter Bunyard, Peter Horsley, Joan Tiffany, Eric Holt-Gimenez, and Rachel Brock.

Katie Meehan introduced me to J. K. Gibson-Graham at a crucial juncture in my search for empowering scholarship, and Boone Shear helped me articulate, grapple with, and adapt their perspective. Many people have helped me remember that, amid the soul-sucking, anti-intellectual, and dehumanizing wreckage of neoliberal universities, there are still pockets of humanity, community, and power. Chief among them are the habaneros and the treehouse collective, Nick Rattray, Wendy Vogt, Paola Canova, Micah Boyer, Tara Deubel, Karin Friederic, Andrew Gardner, Karyn Fox, Nik Heynen, Meredith Welch-Devine, Dave Porinchu, Jenn Rice, Susan McKinnon, Karen Hébert, Maylei Blackwell, Dinesh Paudel, Jen Westerman, Rick Rheingans, and Laura England.

On a more practical level, I received funding from the Inter-American Foundation, the University of Arizona, and the Bureau of Applied Research in Anthropology, and additional editorial and conceptual input from Stephanie Friede, Sydney Blume, Jacqui Ignatova, Anatoli Ignatov, Michael Brown, Nicole Taylor, Anitra Grisales, Gisela Fosada, Peter North, and Jeffrey Juris. Finally, I apologize to anybody I've ever accused of shameless name-dropping in acknowledgments; this is actually a lovely moment to recognize our partners and teachers.

# Notes

## Introduction

1   All participants in this research have been given pseudonyms.
2   Readers familiar with Colombia may find this term awkward, as people from Medellín typically refer to themselves as *Paisas*. I use *Paisas* when speaking about the broader identity of people from Antioquia and the coffee-growing region of Colombia's Western Andes but prefer *Medellinenses* when discussing my research subjects in and around the Metropolitan Area of Medellín.
3   North (2007, 4) summarizes theories about money as an economic and political problem. While barterers' beliefs seem logical, "the relationship between money and the economy is unresolved," with significant disagreement about whether economic change causes monetary and sociocultural change, vice versa, or both.
4   "Working with" hints at Lévi-Strauss's notion that totemic animals are powerful because they are "good to think [with]." However, I take this a step further by treating local knowledge not as an object for expert analysis but as an equally legitimate form of knowledge with which I engage in cothinking. See, for example, Taussig (1980) and Marcus and Fischer (1986) on anthropology as cultural critique, West (2006) and Crapanzano (1992) on "shadow dialogues," Maurer (2005) on "lateral reasoning," and Rappaport (2005) on indigenous organic intellectuals.
5   Most sociological studies imagine social movements as "contentious politics" to influence the powerful (McAdam et al. 2001) and are therefore ill suited to movements to build autonomous institutions rather than achieve reform. Furthermore, they often assume that strategy is determined by more or less rational choice in response to the political environment, so they fail to capture the internal, personal characteristics that shape strategy.
6   Of course, ethics and calculation are not necessarily separate. Hirschmann (1977) reveals that capitalist practices of amoral calculation arose through efforts to make economies and governance more ethical. Seventeenth- and eighteenth-century scholars believed that full-fledged "civilization" required a shift from governance based on passions and moral sentiments to enlightened, rational social organization. Thus, carefully calculated self-interest was regarded as dignified, prosocial, rational thinking.

7  I am not arguing that the notion of scarcity originates with capitalism. Cultures of scarcity likely preceded capitalism and continue to exist beyond capitalism. However, this notion of scarcity is useful to capitalism and is reproduced when capitalist practices create material deprivation and reinforce scarcity-based notions of efficiency, fairness, and success as referents for individual actions and public policies.

8  Esteva's argument about the *prevention* of scarcity merits more attention because it is so easy to misunderstand. These commoners do not aim to produce more and distribute it more effectively, as an economist, planner, or entrepreneur might. They do not learn to limit their wants to fit their means or Earth's resources, as environmentalists and advocates of voluntary simplicity might. They are not simply cultivating a new self-image so they can appreciate their different forms of wealth rather than seeing themselves as poor or lacking, a solution often attributed to postdevelopment scholars. And they do not prevent scarcity by ensuring that all people can meet their own needs because they have the means of production at their disposal, as a Marxist might. Those responses all preserve the notion of scarcity, taking it as a real condition and seeking to manage it or work around it. Instead, according to Esteva, these commoners hold a radically different world-view in which desires and the means for their fulfillment simply *cannot be conceptualized or felt separately*.

9  Scholars have critiqued participatory research for placing an undue labor burden on research participants, idealizing communities, and ignoring heterogeneity (Cooke and Kothari 2001), but my dilemma deserves more attention from engaged researchers: in Medellín, there was not a cohesive set of organizers with whom to collaborate.

10  Lurking behind this discussion is Castree's (1999) sympathetic critique of Gibson-Graham ([1996] 2006a). Contrary to Gibson-Graham's constructivism and pluralism, Castree seeks to identify "the 'essential' characteristics of capitalism . . . even though, in practice, they do not exist in a 'pure' state" (145) because these theoretical essences highlight targets for political action *on a global scale*. My efforts to ground Medellín's diverse economy in the cultural and economic history of the region are motivated by precisely the converse. I believe that effective politics must engage the actual characteristics of capitalism (and noncapitalism) as they exist in practice and in place.

## Chapter 1   Diverse Economies in the War System

1  As one anonymous reviewer noted, this raises important ethical concerns about anthropological research. While scholars have discussed the perils of accidental and intentional complicity with perpetrators of violence (Hale 1991; Price 2011; Sider 2009), I am not aware of any literature on strategies to mitigate involvement in the everyday *economies* of violence.

2  See chapter 6 for further discussion of articulation and chapter 6 endnote 1 for a brief overview of the concept.

3  This builds on Roseberry's (1994) and Gledhill's (1996, 2002) work on hegemony, which illustrates that analyses of hegemonic contestation must go beyond simple models of elite-subaltern conflict to account for multiple and competing elites.

4  Overemphasizing the democratic ideal of government is one example of how Gibson-Graham and the Community Economies Collective have occasionally

misrepresented the justness of noncapitalist alternatives. More attention to the historical and contemporary power relations through which governments operate will help scholars specify the precise blend of potential and actual democratization achieved through states.

## Chapter 2   The Birth of Barter

1   Again, the parallel with Guatemala is striking. As Green writes, "The political violence was aimed at destroying community, the very fabric out of which Mayas have constructed their relations to each other" (1999, 171). Green details how the perpetrators of violence achieved this through bodily harm, social disruption, memorializing trauma and violence in the geographical landscape, and exacerbating centuries of socioeconomic exploitation.

2   As described in chapter 1, the *cajas de compensación* are private, industry-affiliated worker compensation funds that provide an impressive range of services to members and their families. A portion of the national payroll tax is distributed directly to these institutions to fund member health, education, and recreational services. *Cajas de compensación* such as Comfenalco and Comfama are well-respected social institutions in Medellín.

3   A translation of the flyer appears here:

1. Barter is a form of solidarity economy, in which nothing is lost and nothing is gifted: everything is recycled, everything is valued. 2. Participation is free, open, and diverse. Whoever wants to participate should be willing to renew themselves in values like reciprocity, empathy, mutual aid, collective well-being, solidarity, respect, trust, responsibility, and equity. 3. We barter keeping in mind our own and others' interests, needs, and likes. Therefore it is an exercise that requires permanent dialogue and negotiation. 4. Barter is a life experience: we live it in events like markets and gatherings. The idea is that it becomes an increasingly common part of our everyday lives. 5. We believe that it is possible to replace fruitless competition, profit, and speculation with reciprocity among people. 6. The goods and products that we bring to this space should be high quality and in good condition. If they are food products, they should be agroecological and healthy, have real utility, and not reinforce consumerism. 7. Expand the benefits and importance of this practice in our communities and organizations. 8. Emphasize the use-vale and benefits of the products and services that you get through barter. That way there will be an exchange of knowledge as well. For example . . . the use of a seed. 9. With barter we do NOT seek to promote goods and services, but rather to help ourselves collectively to realize a more meaningful life through work, empathy, and just trade. 10. Live this experience of exchange like a possibility for REINVENTING LIFE at the same time that we reinvent the market, via the construction of new social ties within our small groups.

4   Gaviria's term was cut short when he was kidnapped by the FARC during a march for peace and reconciliation and killed during an attempted rescue. He was committed to peace building through the elimination of structural violence. A letter written shortly before his death echoes barterers' vision of advancing peace through economic activism: "Our task, if we hope for a new Antioquia, is to open the doors to all the possibilities that nonviolence offers and to incorporate them in the different segments of community life—family, education, relationships among

people, communities, and nations—overcoming poverty and inequalities to build a new nation based on human principles."

## Chapter 3   A Day at the Market

1   Plattner (1989) offers a useful model for comparing personal/long-term and impersonal/short-term exchanges, focusing on how people choose their preferred form of exchange based on transaction costs/risks, multiple value systems, and types of social relations, market institutions, and information/communication systems. The stories of Dolores, Beatriz, and other barterers in this chapter illustrate his point that *relationships* built through repeated, long-term, or credit-based trading are especially important ways of reducing personal risk when economic conditions and market institutions are unpredictable.

2   Barterers differentiate exchange from payment. Historically, many monies simply facilitated exchange. Those monies that facilitated exchange *and* acted as stores of value and means of payment in themselves were generally created through "pressures exerted by a … centralised institution with the aim of transferring wealth upward, through tribute or taxation" (Narotzky 1997, 60). By celebrating "facilitators," barterers are rejecting accumulation and hierarchy, though this works in practice only when facilitators are governed accordingly.

3   Robben (1989), Taussig (1980), and Greenberg (1995) also find that everyday economic practices and negotiations form grassroots knowledge and morality.

4   The barter notion of capacities differs from the neoliberal one. Per neoliberalism, people have the potential to develop valuable capacities if they invest in self-improvement and enter the market effectively. Among barterers, people are seen as *already* possessing useful and valuable goods and services; the only real impediment is the lack of public spaces to encounter others in solidarity.

## Chapter 4   What Barter Stimulates

1   Import substitution industrialization (ISI) is an economic policy to spur autonomous development by limiting imports and subsidizing nascent domestic industries. Promoted by dependency theorists and anticolonial movements from the 1950s to the 1980s, ISI sought to offer agricultural and industrial sectors in the Global South the same benefits that had permitted their development in the Global North. ISI is often dismissed as a failed historical experiment, though it may be an important tool in the future (Franko 2007; Rist 2002).

2   However, accurate comparisons are difficult. Because my figures include only regular traders (those who have booths in the market) and North's and Williams's include all members (many of whom are wholly inactive), it is likely that theirs approximate or exceed my estimate.

3   This phrase, and indeed much of this chapter, may call to mind Bourdieu's ideas about habitus (our engrained and embodied dispositions) and doxa (taken-for-granted or self-evident truths, or all that we can imagine as being possible). Barterers are certainly socialized to fit well into the games of capitalism and pragmatic pluralism. However, they show far more flexibility, imaginative capacity, and agency than Bourdieu's theorization would predict. See also note 1 to chapter 5.

## Chapter 5   "A Barter That Runs through Our Veins"

1  My use of subjectivities is very similar to Bourdieu's notion of "habitus." In particular, we both think of subjectivities as dispositions and ways of thinking and feeling that extend beyond conscious thought. These dispositions are inculcated through language, bodies, and emotions, our experience of which is ultimately a product of our position in society. However, I use the Gramscian language of subjectivity/hegemony rather than Bourdieu's habitus/doxa because I believe hegemony better reflects the fissures and internal contradictions of power and subalterns' room for maneuver. That room for maneuver is reflected in barterers' own words and actions throughout this chapter. In my opinion, Bourdieu overemphasizes misrecognition, or people's unconsciousness of their own social position, which creates a model of domination that is too seamlessly controlled by elites based on their interests. See Burawoy's (2019) fine-grained comparison of the two for more details.

2  Many movements today adopt this focus, prompted by the recognition that policy gains cannot address the cultural foundations of socioecological exploitation, and by the general shift toward individualized and private sphere politics. Antiracist and antisexist work, for example, increasingly calls attention to "microaggressions," linguistic exclusions, and habits of interpersonal interaction through which bigotry is reproduced even in the context of progressive laws. This current of antidiscrimination activism uses educational interventions targeting individuals' knowledge and consciousness (offering new concepts and languages to describe discrimination and privilege), as well as their emotions (tapping into deeply held notions of fairness, responsibility, guilt, rage, and hope), in the hopes that this will help people see, evaluate, and pattern social interactions in a way that challenges the taken-for-grantedness of bigoted complicity and impunity. The most significant examples of individually centered cultural politics, however, are public health and environmental campaigns that target "knowledge, attitudes, and behaviors" regarding "dangerous" activities like smoking, alcohol consumption, or climate-damaging lifestyles. Projects that target knowledge and attitudes often fall short because they ignore the complexity of mindsets, attitudes, and behaviors, especially the ways that individuals are produced in dialectical relationships with cultural and material contexts, and because they lack a theory for how individual change leads to cultural change.

3  In this sense, Gandhi can be read as a grassroots anticipation of Foucault, describing how technologies (of production, sign systems, power, and the self) articulate in a practical counterpolitics.

4  Even very good anthropologists of social movements have fallen into a vague use of the term "subjectivities." For example, Stahler-Sholk (2010) examines Zapatista identities and "the construction of new social subjectivities" without ever defining subjectivities. As a result, his otherwise rich discussion reduces subjectivities to debates over the definition of indigeneity. Khasnabish (2008a) provides sophisticated analyses of subjectivities without thoroughly defining them; Kuecker (2008) neglects the emotional and linguistic dimensions; and Di Chiro (2008) highlights social reproduction but neglects emotional experiences and cultural frameworks. Juris (2008) and Khasnabish (2008b) more effectively integrate diverse components of subjectivity in their analyses of how activist practice, affect, and social relations shape new political imaginations and norms.

5   This is why Gibson-Graham (2006b) argue that alternative economies require a politics of language that can generate new ways of imagining, representing, and describing economies, ethics, possibilities, and constraints. Drawing on Laclau and Mouffe (1985), they see politics as a ceaseless struggle to control meaning; to achieve hegemony is to cement a particular discourse in place (always temporarily) so shared values, norms, and perceptions appear natural or unchangeable. Gibson-Graham's language politics seeks to create alternative subjects whose perceptions, practices, and relations might spark cultural change.

6   The term "prosumer" came to Medellín from U.S.-based futurist Alvin Toffler by way of the Argentine barter networks. Toffler saw prosumers as harbingers of "an awesome change . . . that will transform even the role of the market itself in our lives and in the world system" (1989, 267). He believed the boundary between production and consumption was being blurred by people's embrace of noncommodified do-it-yourself work and corporations' adoption of production-on-demand and "mass customization" by active consumers. Toffler expected these to create a more liberating society. Medellín's barterers—who I suspect have never read Toffler directly—are more attracted to the do-it-yourselfers than the "active consumers" creatively networked with capitalist firms. Where Toffler's do-it-yourselfers were prosuming at an individual level, barter gives prosumerism a wider social context as production for a community.

7   For Gramsci, intellectual and moral leadership is essential for creating a "national-popular collective will" or "mass counterhegemonic culture" (Gramsci 1972, 249–260; see also Crehan 2002, 155). While this leadership may emerge spontaneously if economic conditions create a unified working class, it may require the strategic construction of new ideas and a new culture by movement leaders.

8   Scholars have examined emotions as a spur to social movement participation and the emotional impacts of different tactics (Goodwin et al. 2001; Jasper 2011). Perhaps more important is a newer literature on the emotions necessary to weave and sustain activist networks (Juris 2008; Brown and Pickerill 2009). My analysis is somewhat different: the emotions provoked in barter demonstrations are not meant to provoke or sustain activism for the long-term construction of a better world; instead, they are meant to provide a feeling for what it would be like to practice the ideal future of solidarity barter economies right now.

9   However, see Juris (2008) on "tactical frivolity" and "affective solidarity" via Carnivalesque global justice protests.

## Chapter 6   Strategies for a New Economy

1   Previous discussions of articulation took two forms. In the first, ethnographic analyses explored how people moved across multiple economic realms, including via social, cultural, and mental processes similar to what I call pragmatic pluralism (García Canclini 1993; Greenberg 1995; Robben 1989; Taussig 1980; Yanagisako 2002). This literature illustrates how "global" capital and apparently neutral abstractions like money are localized to produce unexpected opportunities and consequences. It also shows that capitalism and noncapitalism are deeply intertwined, shaping each other as they are constructed and maintained through some of the same social relations and cultural dynamics. By contrast, the second stream of literature on articulation offered philosophical and political meditations on if, how, and when capitalism would finally replace precapitalist economies, or

why capitalism failed to develop in "underdeveloped" countries (Foster-Carter 1977). This literature assumed that capitalism has an internal logic and true nature that is everywhere the same, and interpreted discrepancies in economic development as signs either that a full capitalist transition had not yet occurred or that local precapitalist modes of production and social formations modified capitalism. Authors debated whether different modes of production could coexist or, instead, if limited forms of precapitalism survived as holdovers in a capitalist era. Most often, they assumed that capitalism was the inevitable endpoint of economic change and that noncapitalist modes of production would exist only if they served capitalism (by maintaining a reserve labor pool or providing subsistence support that could justify low wages, for example) or were nonthreatening to capitalism. Carrier (1992), Foster-Carter (1977), and Donham (1999, 2001) offer nuanced critiques of this model of articulation, emphasizing especially how it ignores local reality and the "almost infinitely multiplex and variable relations" of production and exploitation that characterize "the complex social formations of the Third World" (Foster-Carter 1977, 75). For them, analysis needed to focus not on the logics and needs of capitalism but on the relations of real social actors living in geographically and historically specific processes that are never inevitable.

2  The term "registers" refers to situationally specific forms of speech and styles of communication. I refer to barter activists' different ways of speaking about capitalism and alternatives as registers—rather than through the other obvious choices of "public" versus "hidden transcripts" (Scott 1990) or "front stage" and "back stage" performances (Goffman 1959)—because these latter concepts suggest that activists are primarily seeking openings within power structures or presenting a polished (and thus less true) self to different audiences. I think these explanations are misleading because barterers base their communicative strategy on other factors, such as their own shifting and contradictory subjectivities, and because the selves and languages expressed in these two different moments of activism are equally genuine, and both are framed for their audiences.

3  This reveals how important it is for scholars to ground (and test) Gibson-Graham's ideas in concrete historical and cultural locales, something that Gibson-Graham did well in their discussions of economic change in Australia and Massachusetts, but that not all followers have achieved. After all, Gibson-Graham's theories of capitalocentrism and postcapitalist politics are just that: theories. They were constructed from careful observation of concrete local case studies. The theories (and the politics they support) will serve us best not if we impose them on new case studies, but rather if we use them to engage dialogically with other experiences.

4  This is one place where materialist and idealist views of articulation coalesce: the economic articulations explored by historians and anthropologists provide a practical space in which to experience, refine, and practice the alternative discursive articulations that Laclau and Mouffe (1985) imagine; and conversely, the alternative discursive articulations (e.g., connecting ideas and languages of profit-oriented commodity exchange with those of solidarity-oriented barter exchange) help actors infuse their practice with counterhegemonic values and assumptions.

# References

Abu-Lughod, Lila. 1990. "The Romance of Resistance: Tracing Transformations of Power Through Bedouin Women." *American Ethnologist* 17(1):41–55.

Acosta, Alberto. 2013. "Extractivism and Neoextractivism: Two Sides of the Same Curse." In *Beyond Development: Alternative Visions from Latin America*, edited by Miriam Lang and Dunia Mokrani, 61–86. Quito: Fundación Rosa Luxemburg.

Agrawal, Arun. 2005. *Environmentality: Technologies of Government and the Making of Subjects*. Durham, NC: Duke University Press.

Akuno, Kali. 2017. "Build and Fight: The Program and Strategy of Cooperation Jackson." In *Jackson Rising: The Struggle for Economic Democracy and Black Self-Determination in Jackson, Mississippi*, edited by Cooperation Jackson (Kali Akuno, Sacajawea Hall, and Brandon King) and Ajamu Nangwaya, 3–42. Jackson: Daraja Press.

Aldridge, Theresa J., and Alan Patterson. 2002. "LETS Get Real: Constraints on the Development of Local Exchange Trading Schemes." *Area* 34(4):370–381.

Alvarez, Sonia E., Evelina Dagnino, and Arturo Escobar, eds. 1998. *Cultures of Politics / Politics of Cultures: Revisioning Latin American Social Movements*. Boulder, CO: Westview Press.

Anderlini, Luca, and Hamid Sabourian. 1992. "Some Notes on the Economics of Barter, Money and Credit." In *Barter, Exchange and Value: An Anthropological Approach*, edited by Caroline Humphrey and Stephen Hugh-Jones, 75–106. Cambridge: Cambridge University Press.

Appadurai, Arjun, ed. 2001. *Globalization*. Durham, NC: Duke University Press.

Asad, Talal. 1991. "From the History of Colonial Anthropology to the Anthropology of Western Hegemony." In *Colonial Situations: Essays on the Contextualization of Ethnographic Knowledge*, edited by George W. Stocking Jr., 314–324. Madison: University of Wisconsin Press.

Asher, Kiran. 2009. *Black and Green: Afro-Colombians, Development, and Nature in the Pacific Lowlands*. Durham, NC: Duke University Press.

Asociación Antioqueña de Cooperativas (Confecoop-Antioquia). 2010. *Estado del Sector Solidario del Departamento de Antioquia. Informe Estadístico General Cierre 2009*. Medellín: Confecoop-Antioquia.

Attanasio, Orazio, Adriana Kugler, and Costas Meghir. 2008. "Training Disadvantaged Youth in Latin America: Evidence from a Randomized Trial." NBER Working Paper No. 13931. Cambridge, MA: National Bureau of Economic Research. http://www.nber.org/papers/w13931.

Bateman, Milford, Juan Pablo Duran Ortíz, and Kate Maclean. 2011. "A Post–Washington Consensus Approach to Local Economic Development in Latin America? An Example from Medellín, Colombia." ODI Background Note, April. London: Overseas Development Institute.

Beasley-Murray, Jon, Maxwell A. Cameron, and Eric Hershberg. 2009. "Latin America's Left Turn: An Introduction." *Third World Quarterly* 30(2):319–330.

Becker, Sören, and Matthias Naumann. 2017. "Energy Democracy: Mapping the Debate on Energy Alternatives." *Geography Compass* 11(8):E12321.

Bennie, Andrew. 2014. "Linking Food Sovereignty and the Solidarity Economy in South African Townships." In *The Solidarity Economy Alternative: Emerging Theory and Practice,* edited by Vishwas Satgar, 249–278. Scottsville, South Africa: University of Kwazulu-Natal Press.

Bernal, Raquel, and Mauricio Cardenas. 2003. "Determinants of Labor Demand in Colombia: 1976–1996." NBER Working Paper No. 10077. Cambridge, MA: National Bureau of Economic Research.

Biehl, João, Byron Good, and Arthur Kleinman. 2007. *Subjectivity: Ethnographic Investigations.* Berkeley: University of California Press.

Blanc, Jérôme. 2010. "Complementary and Community Currencies." In *The Human Economy: A Citizen's Guide,* edited by Keith Hart, Jean-Louis Laville, and Antonio David Cattani, 303–312. Cambridge: Polity.

Bloch, Maurice, and Jonathan Parry. 1989. "Introduction: Money and the Morality of Exchange." In *Money and the Morality of Exchange,* edited by Jonathan Parry and Maurice Bloch, 1–32. Cambridge: Cambridge University Press.

Blume, Sydney. 2018. "Creative Resistance and Utopian Subjectivities: Zapatista Autonomy as Discourse, Power, and Practice." Undergraduate thesis, Sustainable Development Department, Appalachian State University.

Bohannon, Paul. 1959. "The Impact of Money on an African Subsistence Economy." *Journal of Economic History* 19:491–503.

Boserup, Ester. 1970. *Woman's Role in Economic Development.* London: George Allen and Unwin.

Bourdieu, Pierre. 1977. *Outline of a Theory of Practice.* New York: Cambridge University Press.

———. 2005. *The Social Structures of the Economy.* Cambridge: Polity.

Bozuwa, Jennifer. 2019. "Energy Democracy: Taking Back Power." Next System Project.

Broad, Robin, ed. 2002. *Global Backlash: Citizen Initiatives for a Just World Economy.* Lanham, MD: Rowman & Littlefield.

Brotherton, P. Sean. 2008. "'We Have to Think Like Capitalists but Continue Being Socialists': Medicalized Subjectivities, Emergent Capital, and Socialist Entrepreneurs in Post-Soviet Cuba." *American Ethnologist* 35(2):259–274.

Brown, Gavin, and Jenny Pickerill. 2009. "Space for Emotion in the Spaces of Activism." *Emotion, Space and Society* 2(1):24–35.

Brown, Wendy. 2006. "Finding the Man in the State." In *The Anthropology of the State: A Reader,* edited by Aradhana Sharma and Akhil Gupta, 187–210. London: Blackwell.

Burawoy, Michael. 2019. *Symbolic Violence: Conversations with Bourdieu*. Durham, NC: Duke University Press.

Burke, Brian J., and Beatriz Arjona. 2013. "Experiments with Alternative Political Ecologies: Examining the Construction of Ecovillages and Ecovillagers in Colombia." In *Environmental Anthropology Engaging Ecotopian Possibilities: Bioregionalism, Permaculture, and Ecovillage Design for a Sustainable Future*, edited by Josh Lockyer and Jim Veteto, 235–250. New York: Berghahn.

Bushnell, David. 1993. *The Making of Modern Colombia: A Nation in Spite of Itself*. Berkeley: University of California Press.

Cardona, Marleny, Héctor Iván García, Carlos Alberto Giraldo, María Victoria López, Clara Mercedes Suárez, Diana Carolina Corcho, Carlos Hernán Posada, and María Nubia Flórez. 2005. "Homicidios En Medellín, Colombia, Entre 1990 y 2002: Actores, Móviles y Circunstancias." *Cadernos de Saúde Pública* 21(3):840–851.

Carlsson, Chris. 2008. *Nowtopia: How Pirate Programmers, Outlaw Bicyclists, and Vacant-Lot Gardeners Are Inventing the Future Today*. Oakland, CA: AK Press.

Carrier, James G. 1992. "Approaches to Articulation." In *History and Tradition in Melanesian Anthropology*, edited by James G. Carrier, 116–174. Berkeley: University of California Press.

Carroll, Leah Anne. 2011. *Violent Democratization: Social Movements, Elites, and Politics in Colombia's Rural War Zones, 1984–2008*. Notre Dame, IN: University of Notre Dame Press.

Casas-Cortés, Maribel, Michal Osterweil, and Dana E. Powell. 2013. "Transformations in Engaged Ethnography: Knowledge, Networks, and Social Movements." In *Insurgent Encounters: Transnational Activism, Ethnography, and the Political*, edited by Jeffrey Juris and Alex Khasnabish, 199–228. Durham, NC: Duke University Press.

Castellanos Obregón, Juan Manuel. 2009. *Formas Actuales de la Movilización Armada*. PhD dissertation, Centro de Estudios Avanzados en Niñez y Juventud, Universidad de Manizales-CINDE, Manizales, Colombia.

Castree, Noel. 1999. "Envisioning Capitalism: Geography and the Renewal of Marxian Political Economy." *Transactions of the Institute of British Geographers* 24(2):137–158.

Chandler, William. 1994. "The Value of Household Work in Canada, 1992." *Canadian Economic Observer* 3.1–3.9.

Chatterton, Paul. 2005. "Making Autonomous Geographies: Argentina's Popular Uprising and the 'Movimiento de Trabajadores Desocupado' (Unemployed Workers Movement)." *Geoforum* 36:545–561.

Chica Agudelo, Ana María. 2010. "La Educación Necesita Lápiz y Papel." *El Colombiano*, January 12. http://www.elcolombiano.com/bancoconocimiento/l/la_educacion_necesita_lapiz_y_papel/la_educacion_necesita_lapiz_y_papel.asp.

Chomsky, Noam. 2000. "Marginalizing the Masses." Interview by Robert A. Schupp and Richard L. Ohlemacher. *Journal of International Affairs* 53(2):723–737.

Collins, Daryl, Jonathan Morduch, Stuart Rutherford, and Orlanda Ruthven. 2009. *Portfolios of the Poor: How the World's Poor Live on $2 a Day*. Princeton, NJ: Princeton University Press.

Community Economies Collective. 2001. "Imagining and Enacting Noncapitalist Futures." *Socialist Review* 28(3–4):93–135.

Confederación de Cooperativas de Colombia (Confecoop). 2010. "Información Departamental 2009. Información Estadística 2009." http://www.confecoop.coop /images/estadistica/09/departamental%202009.xls.

Connolly, William E. 1999. *Why I Am Not a Secularist*. Minneapolis: University of Minnesota Press.

Consultoría para los Derechos Humanos y el Desplazamiento (CODHES). 2008. *Codhes Informa: Boletín Informativo de la Consultoría para los Derechos Humanos y el Desplazamiento*. No 74. Bogota: CODHES.

Cooke, Bill, and Uma Kothari, eds. 2001. *Participation: The New Tyranny?* London: Zed Books.

Corrigan, Philip. 1994. "State Formation." In *Everyday Forms of State Formation: Revolution and the Negotiation of Rule in Modern Mexico*, edited by Gilbert M. Joseph and Daniel Nugent, xvii–xix. Durham, NC: Duke University Press.

Crapanzano, Vincent. 1992. *Hermes' Dilemma and Hamlet's Desire: On the Epistemology of Interpretation*. Cambridge, MA: Harvard University Press.

Crehan, Kate. 2002. *Gramsci, Culture, and Anthropology*. Berkeley: University of California Press.

da Costa, Reinaldo Pacheco. 2017. "Brazil's Social Economic Incubators." In *Towards Just and Sustainable Economies: The Social and Solidarity Economy North and South*, edited by Peter North and M. S. Cato, 117–134. Bristol: Policy Press.

Das, Veena, and Arthur Kleinman. 2000. "Introduction." In *Violence and Subjectivity*, edited by Veena Das, 1–18. Berkeley: University of California Press.

Day, Richard J. F. 2005. *Gramsci Is Dead: Anarchist Currents in the Newest Social Movements*. London: Pluto Press.

Della Porta, Donatella, Missimiliano Andretta, Lorenzo Mosca, and Herbert Reiter, eds. 2006. *Globalization from Below: Transnational Activists and Protest*. Minneapolis: University of Minnesota Press.

Della Porta, Donatella, and Mario Diani. 2009. *Social Movements: An Introduction*. Oxford: Wiley.

Departamento Nacional de Estadísticas (DANE). 2009. *Encuesta Nacional de Ingresos y Gastos 2006/2007*. Bogotá: DANE.

———. 2010. "Boletin de Prensa: Medición del Empleo Informal. Trimestre Móvil Diciembre 2009–Febrero De 2010." April 13. Bogotá: DANE.

Di Chiro, Giovanna. 2008. "Living Environmentalism: Coalition Politics, Social Reproduction, and Environmental Justice." *Environmental Politics* 17(2): 276–298.

Díaz Tafur, Juana Inés. 2005. "'Ni Un Menos' una Campaña contra el Abandono Escolar." *Economía Colombiana* 311:8–13.

*Dinero*. 2011. "La Bancarización en Colombia Llegó al 62%." May 11. http://www.dinero .com/actualidad/economia/articulo/la-bancarizacion-colombia-llego-62/119116.

Dittmer, Kristofer. 2011. "Communal Currencies in Venezuela." *International Journal of Community Currencies Research* 15:78–83.

Dixon, Chris. 2014. *Another Politics: Talking Across Today's Transformative Movements*. Berkeley: University of California Press.

Donham, Donald L. 1999. *History, Power, Ideology: Central Issues in Marxism and Anthropology*. Berkeley: University of California Press.

———. 2001. "Thinking Temporally or Modernizing Anthropology." *American Anthropologist* 103(1):134–149.

Douglas, Mary, and Baron C. Isherwood. 1996. *The World of Goods: Towards an Anthropology of Consumption*. New York: Routledge.

Echavarría, Juan Guillermo. n.d. "Barrio Unidad Residencial Altamira." Unpublished paper.

*Economist*. 2011. "Income Equality." April 20. http://www.economist.com/node /18587127.

*El Tiempo*. 2011. "En el 2010 Hubo 7.200 Muertes por Sicarios." January 26. http:// www.eltiempo.com/archivo/documento/cms-8800429.

Escobar, Arturo. 1992. "Imagining A Post-Development Era? Critical Thought, Development and Social Movements." *Social Text* 31/32:20–56.

———. 1995. *Encountering Development: The Making and Unmaking of the Third World*. Princeton, NJ: Princeton University Press.

———. 2008. *Territories of Difference: Place, Movements, Life, Redes*. Durham, NC: Duke University Press.

———. 2020. *Pluriversal Politics: The Real and the Possible*. Durham, NC: Duke University Press.

Escobar, Arturo, and Sonia Alvarez, eds. 1992. *The Making of Social Movements in Latin America: Identity, Strategy and Democracy*. Boulder, CO: Westview Press.

Escobar Vekeman, Cecilia-Luca. 2009. "Approche Anthropologique de la Présence du Don Contemporain dans Deux Expériences Locales d'échange Alternatif: Les Foires de Multi-Troc Colombiennes et les Systèmes d'Echange Local Français." PhD dissertation, Département des Sciences Sociales, Université Libre de Bruxelles, Brussels, Belgium.

Escobar Villegas, Juan Camilo. 2009. *Progresar y Civilizar: Imaginarios de Identidad y Élites Intelectuales De Antioquia En Euroamérica, 1830–1920*. Medellín: Universidad EAFIT.

Escuela Nacional Sindical. n.d. [ca. 2009]. "Hacía un Trabajo Decente en Medellín y el Valle De Aburrá." Unpublished paper, Área de Investigaciones de la Escuela Nacional Sindical.

Esteva, Gustavo. (1992) 2010. "Development." In *The Development Dictionary: A Guide to Knowledge As Power*, edited by Wolfgang Sachs, 6–25. London: Zed Books.

Evers, Tilman. 1985. "Identity: The Hidden Side of New Social Movements in Latin America." In *New Social Movements and the State in Latin America*, edited by David Slater, 43–72. Amsterdam: CEDLA.

Fabian, Johannes. 1983. *Time and the Other: How Anthropology Makes Its Object*. New York: Columbia University Press.

Farnsworth-Alvear, Ann. 2002. *Dulcinea In the Factory: Myths, Morals, Men, and Women in Colombia's Industrial Experiment, 1905–1960*. Durham, NC: Duke University Press.

Ferguson, James. 2010. "The Uses of Neoliberalism." *Antipode* 41(1):166–184.

———. 2015. *Give a Man a Fish: Reflections on the New Politics of Distribution*. Durham, NC: Duke University Press.

Fleming, Matthew H., John Roman, and Graham Farrell. 2000. "The Shadow Economy." *Journal of International Affairs* 53(2):387–409.

Foster-Carter, Aidan. 1977. "The Modes of Production Controversy." *New Left Review* 107:47–77.

Foucault, Michel. 1972. *The Archaeology of Knowledge*. New York: Harper Colophon.

———. 1980. *Power/Knowledge: Selected Interviews and Other Writings, 1972–1977*. Edited by Colin Gordon. Translated by Colin Gordon, Leo Marshall, John Mepham, and Kate Soper. New York: Pantheon Books.

———. 1988. "Technologies of the Self." In *Technologies of the Self*, edited by Luther H. Martin, Huck Gutman, and Patrick H. Hutton, 16–49. Amherst: University of Massachusetts Press.

Fox, Richard G. 1995. "Cultural Dis-integration and the Invention of New Peace-Fares." In *Articulating Hidden Histories: Exploring the Influence of Eric R. Wolf*, edited by Jane Schneider and Rayna Rapp, 275–288. Berkeley: University of California Press.

Franko, Patrice M. 2007. *The Puzzle of Latin American Economic Development*. Lanham, MD: Rowman & Littlefield Publishers.

Freeman, Carla. 2014. *Entrepreneurial Selves: Neoliberal Respectability and the Making of a Caribbean Middle Class*. Durham, NC: Duke University Press.

Frideric, Karin, and Brian J. Burke. 2019. "La Revolución Ciudadana and Social Medicine: Undermining Community in the State Provision of Health Care in Ecuador." *Global Public Health* 14(6–7):884–898.

Galeano, Eduardo. 1971. *Las Venas Abiertas De América Latina*. México: Siglo XXI Editores.

Gandhi, Mohandes K. 1960. *All Men Are Brothers*. Ahmedabad: Navajivan.

García Canclini, Néstor. 1993. *Transforming Modernity: Popular Culture in Mexico*. Austin: University of Texas Press.

Geertz, Clifford. 1973. *The Interpretation of Cultures*. New York: Basic Books.

Gershon, Ilana. 2011. "Neoliberal Agency." *Current Anthropology* 52(4):537–555.

Gibson-Graham, J. K. 2002. "Beyond Global vs. Local: Economic Politics Outside the Binary Frame." In *Geographies of Power: Placing Scale*, edited by Andrew Herod and Melissa W. Wright, 25–60. Oxford: Blackwell.

———. (1996) 2006a. *The End of Capitalism (as We Knew It): A Feminist Critique of Political Economy*. Minneapolis: University of Minnesota Press.

———. 2006b. *A Postcapitalist Politics*. Minneapolis: University of Minnesota Press.

Gibson-Graham, J. K., Jenny Cameron, and Stephen Healy. 2013. *Take Back the Economy: An Ethical Guide for Transforming Our Communities*. Minneapolis: University of Minnesota Press.

Gill, Lesley. 2016. *A Century of Violence in a Red City: Popular Struggle, Counterinsurgency, and Human Rights in Colombia*. Durham, NC: Duke University Press.

Gledhill, John. 1996. "Putting the State Back in Without Leaving the Dialectics Out." Unpublished paper, Department of Social Anthropology, University of Manchester. http://les.man.ac.uk/sa/jg/jgepubs.htm.

———. 2002. "The Powers Behind the Masks: Mexico's Political Class and Social Elites at the End of the Millennium." In *Elite Cultures: Anthropological Perspectives*, edited by Cris Shore and Stephen Nugent, 39–60. New York: Routledge.

Goerner, Sally J., Bernard Lietaer, and Robert E. Ulanowicz. 2009. "Quantifying Economic Sustainability: Implications for Free-Enterprise Theory, Policy and Practice." *Ecological Economics* 69(1):76–81.

Goffman, Erving. 1959. *The Presentation of Self in Everyday Life*. New York: Doubleday.

Goldstein, Donna M. 2003. *Laughter Out of Place: Race, Class, Violence, and Sexuality in a Rio Shantytown*. Berkeley: University of California Press.

Gómez-Suárez, Andrei. 2014. *Genocide, Geopolitics and Transnational Networks: Contextualising the Destruction of the Unión Patriótica in Colombia*. London: Routledge.

González De La Rocha, Mercedes. 2007. "The Construction of the Myth of Survival." *Development and Change* 38(1):45–66.

Goodale, Mark, and Nancy Postero. 2013. "Revolution and Retrenchment: Illuminating the Present in Latin America." In *Neoliberalism, Interrupted: Social Change and Contested Governance in Contemporary Latin America*, edited by Mark Goodale and Nancy Postero, 1–22. Stanford, CA: Stanford University Press.

Goodwin, Jeff, James M. Jasper, and Francesca Polletta, eds. 2001. *Passionate Politics: Emotions and Social Movements*. Chicago: University of Chicago Press.

Gordon Nembhard, Jessica. 2016. *Building a Cooperative Solidarity Commonwealth*. Next System Project.

Gow, David. 2008. *Countering Development: Indigenous Modernity and the Moral Imagination*. Durham, NC: Duke University Press.

Graeber, David. 2001. *Toward an Anthropological Theory of Value: The False Coin of Our Own Dreams*. New York: Palgrave.

———. 2011. *Debt: The First 5,000 Years*. New York: Melville House.

Gramsci, Antonio. 1972. *Selections from the Prison Notebooks of Antonio Gramsci*. Edited and translated by Quentin Hoare and Geoffrey Nowell-Smith. New York: International.

Granovetter, Mark. 1973. "The Strength of Weak Ties." *American Journal of Sociology* 78:1360–1380.

Greco, Thomas H., Jr. 2009. *The End of Money and the Future of Civilization*. White River Junction, VT: Chelsea Green.

Green, Linda B. 1999. *Fear as a Way of Life: Mayan Widows in Rural Guatemala*. New York: Columbia University Press.

Greenberg, James B. 1995. "Capital, Ritual, and Boundaries of the Closed Corporate Community." In *Articulating Hidden Histories: Exploring the Influence of Eric R. Wolf*, edited by Jane Schneider and Rayna Rapp, 67–81. Berkeley: University of California Press.

Greenberg, James B., and Josiah McC. Heyman. 2012. "Neoliberal Capital and the Mobility Approach in Anthropology." In *Neoliberalism and Commodity Production in Mexico*, edited by Thomas Weaver, James B. Greenberg, William L. Alexander, and Anne Browning-Aiken, 243–271. Boulder: University of Colorado Press.

Gregory, Christopher A. 1982. *Gifts and Commodities*. London: Academic Press.

Gudeman, Stephen. 2001. *The Anthropology of Economy: Community, Market, and Culture*. Malden, MA: Blackwell.

———. 2008. *Economy's Tension: The Dialectics of Market and Economy*. New York: Berghahn.

Gupta, Akhil. 2006. "Blurred Boundaries: The Discourse of Corruption, the Culture of Politics, and the Imagined State." In *The Anthropology of the State: A Reader*, edited by Aradhana Sharma and Akhil Gupta, 211–242. London: Blackwell.

Gutiérrez L., José Fernando, ed. 2007. "La Generación de Ingresos, Empleo y Equidad. Un Tema Prioritario para la Ciudad." Report of the Mesa de Generación de Ingresos y Empleo, Cuarto Congreso de Ciudad, Medellín. September 2007.

Hale, Charles H. 1991. "'They Exploited Us But We Didn't Feel It': Hegemony, Ethnic Militancy, and the Miskitu-Sandinista Conflict." In *Decolonizing Anthropology: Moving Further Toward an Anthropology of Liberation*, edited by Faye V. Harrison, 128–149. Arlington, VA: American Anthropological Association.

Halperin, Rhoda H. 1994. *Cultural Economies Past and Present*. Austin: University of Texas Press.

Harvey, David. 1996. *Justice, Nature and the Geography of Difference*. Cambridge, MA: Blackwell.

———. 2003. *The New Imperialism*. Oxford: Oxford University Press.

———. 2010a. "The Crises of Capitalism." Lecture, Royal Society for the Encouragement of Arts, Manufactures, and Commerce (RSA), London, April 26.

———. 2010b. "Organizing for the Anti-capitalist Transition." Paper presented at the World Social Forum, Porto Alegre, Brazil. http://Davidharvey.Org/2009/12/Organizing-For-the-Anti-Capitalist-Transition/#More-376.

Hill, Jane H. 2008. *The Everyday Language of White Racism*. Malden, MA: Wiley-Blackwell.

Hirschman, Albert O. 1977. *The Passions and the Interests: Political Arguments for Capitalism Before Its Triumph*. Princeton, NJ: Princeton University Press.

Ho, Karen. 2009. *Liquidated: An Ethnography of Wall Street*. Durham, NC: Duke University Press.

Holmes, Jennifer S., Sheila Amin Gutiérrez De Piñeres, and Kevin M. Curtin. 2008. *Guns, Drugs, and Development in Colombia*. Austin: University of Texas Press.

Honeyman, Catherine A. 2016. *The Orderly Entrepreneur: Youth, Education, and Governance in Rwanda*. Stanford, CA: Stanford University Press.

Hornborg, Alf. 2016. *Global Magic: Technologies of Appropriation from Ancient Rome to Wall Street*. London: Palgrave Macmillan.

Humphrey, Caroline. 1992. "Fair Dealing, Just Rewards: The Ethics of Barter in North-East Nepal." In *Barter, Exchange and Value: An Anthropological Approach*, edited by Caroline Humphrey and Stephen Hugh-Jones. 107–141. Cambridge: Cambridge University Press.

Humphrey, Caroline, and Stephen Hugh-Jones, eds. 1992. *Barter, Exchange and Value: An Anthropological Approach*. Cambridge: Cambridge University Press.

IDEA (Instituto Para el Desarrollo de Antioquia). 2004. "Programa Truequeando Por Antioquia." Press release, February. http://www.Periodicoamigo.Com/376_Educacion_Truequeando.html.

Iriart, Celia, and Howard Waitzkin. 2006. "Argentina: No Lessons Learned." *International Journal of Health Services* 36(1):177–196.

Ironmonger, Duncan. 1996. "Counting Outputs, Capital Inputs and Caring Labour: Estimating Gross Household Product." *Feminist Economics* 2(3):37–64.

Jara, Mazibuko K. 2014. "The Solidarity Economy Response to the Agrarian Crisis in South Africa." In *The Solidarity Economy Alternative: Emerging Theory and Practice*, edited by Vishwas Satgar and Michelle Williams, 227–248. Pietermaritzburg, South Africa: University of Kwazulu-Natal Press.

Jasper, James M. 2011. "Emotions and Social Movements: Twenty Years of Theory and Research." *Annual Review of Sociology* 37:285–303.

Jiménez Morales, Germán. 2010. "La Plata del Míster es Sagrada en los Estratos Bajos." *El Colombiano*, June 27. http://www.elcolombiano.com/bancoconocimiento/l/la_plata_del_mister_es_sagrada_en_los_estratos_bajos/la_plata_del_mister_es_sagrada_en_los_estratos_bajos.asp.

Johnston, Hank, Enrique Laraña, and Joseph R. Gusfield. 1994. "Identities, Grievances, and New Social Movements." In *New Social Movements: From Ideology to Identity*, edited by Enrique Laraña, Hank Johnston, and Joseph R. Gusfeld, 3–35. Philadelphia: Temple University Press.

Juris, Jeffrey S. 2008. *Networking Futures: The Movements Against Corporate Globalization*. Durham, NC: Duke University Press.

Juris, Jeffrey S., and Alex Khasnabish. 2013. "Ethnography and Activism within Networked Spaces of Transnational Encounter." In *Insurgent Encounters:*

*Transnational Activism, Ethnography, and the Political*, edited by Jeffrey Juris and Alex Khasnabish, 3–36. Durham, NC: Duke University Press.

Keck, Margaret E., and Kathryn Sikkink. 1998. *Activists Beyond Borders: Advocacy Networks in International Politics*. Ithaca, NY: Cornell University Press

Khasnabish, Alex. 2008. *Zapatismo Beyond Borders: New Imaginations of Political Possibility*. Toronto: University of Toronto Press.

———. 2013. "Tracing the Zapatista Rhizome, or, the Ethnography of a Transnationalized Political Imagination." In *Insurgent Encounters: Transnational Activism, Ethnography, and the Political*, edited by Jeffrey Juris and Alex Khasnabish, 66–88. Durham, NC: Duke University Press.

Kleinman, Arthur, Veena Das, and Margaret Lock. 1997. "Introduction." In *Social Suffering*, edited by Arthur Kleinman, Veena Das, and Margaret Lock, ix–xxvii. Berkeley: University of California Press.

Kuecker, Glen David. 2008. "Fighting for the Forests Revisited: Grassroots Resistance to Mining in Northern Ecuador." In *Latin American Social Movements in the Twenty-first Century: Resistance, Power, and Democracy*, edited by Richard Stahler-Sholk, Glen David Kuecker, and Harry Vanden, 97–112. Lanham, MD: Rowman and Littlefield.

Laclau, Ernesto, and Chantal Mouffe. 1985. *Hegemony and Socialist Strategy*. London: Verso.

Lancaster, Roger N. 1992. *Life Is Hard: Machismo, Danger and the Intimacy of Power in Nicaragua*. Berkeley: University of California Press.

Leyshon, Andrew, Roger Lee, and Colin C. Williams, eds. 2003. *Alternative Economic Spaces*. London: Routledge.

Li, Tania M. 2007. *The Will to Improve: Governmentality, Development, and the Practice of Politics*. Durham, NC: Duke University Press.

Lietaer, Bernard A. 2001. *The Future of Money: A New Way to Create Wealth, Work and a Wiser World*. London: Century.

Little, Peter D., and Michael Painter. 1995. "Discourse, Politics, and the Development Process: Reflections on Escobar's 'Anthropology and the Development Encounter.'" *American Ethnologist* 22:602–609.

Loaiza Orozco, María Olga, Gloria Inés Sánchez Vinasco, and Guillermo Villegas Arenas. 2004. *Valoracion Económica del Trabajo Domestico: Un Abordaje desde el Valor Agregado en Preparación de Alimentos, en el Aseo de la Ropa y de la Casa*. Manizales: Universidad De Caldas, Facultad De Ciencias Jurídicas Y Sociales, Departamento De Estudios De Familia. http://www.eumed.net/cursecon/libreria/2004/lsv-dom.pdf.

Lomnitz, Larissa, and Ana Melnick. 1991. *Chile's Middle Class: A Struggle for Survival in the Face of Neoliberalism*. Translated by Jeanne Grant. Boulder, CO: Lynne Rienner.

López López, Nestor. 1999. "Cambio Televisor por Clases de Karate." *El Tiempo*, September 5. http://www.eltiempo.com/archivo/documento/mam-903335.

López Montaño, Cecilia. 2011. "La Mujer Latinoamericana, su Nivel de Autonomía y la Economía del Cuidado." Presentation, Primer Foro Nacional: Uso del Tiempo y Trabajo No-Remunerado, Bogotá, Colombia, September 13, http://www.dane.gov.co/files/noticias/uso_tiempo_cecilia_lopez.pdf.

Luhrmann, Tanya M. 2006. "Subjectivity." *Anthropological Theory* 6(3):345–361.

Lutz, Catherine, and Donald Nonini. 1999. "The Economies of Violence and the Violence of Economies." In *Anthropological Theory Today*, edited by Henrietta L. Moore, 73–113. London: Polity.

Malinowski, Bronislaw. 1922. *Argonauts of the Western Pacific: An Account of Native Enterprise and Adventure in the Archipelagos of Melanesian New Guinea*. London: Routledge.

Manual Del Trueke [Bello]. 2008. *Manual del Trueke: Para Que Kmbiemos!!!* Corporación Buena!Dea, Proyektotrueke, and Makondo—Red Global De Trueke. Medellín: Materiales Pedagógicos Mapavira.

Marcus, George E., and Michael M. J. Fischer. 1986. *Anthropology as Cultural Critique: An Experimental Moment in the Human Sciences*. Chicago: University of Chicago Press.

Marx, Karl. (1852) 1999. *The Eighteenth Brumaire of Louis Bonaparte*. Marx/Engels Internet Archive. http://www.marxists.org/archive/marx/works/1852/18th-brumaire/index.htm.

———. (1867) 1999. *Capital: A Critique of Political Economy*. Vol. 1. Marx/Engels Internet Archive. http://www.marxists.org/archive/marx/works/1867-c1.

Maurer, Bill. 2005. *Mutual Life, Limited: Islamic Banking, Alternative Currencies, Lateral Reason*. Princeton, NJ: Princeton University Press.

Mauss, Marcel. (1925) 2000. *The Gift: The Form and Reason for Exchange in Archaic Societies*. New York: Norton.

McAdam, Doug, Sidney Tarrow, and Charles Tilly. 2001. *The Dynamics of Contention*. London: Cambridge University Press.

McIlwaine, Cathy, and Caroline Moser. 2003. "Poverty, Violence and Livelihood Security in Urban Colombia and Guatemala." *Progress in Development Studies* 3(2):113–130.

Melucci, Alberto. 1989. *Nomads of the Present*. London: Century Hutchinson.

Merrifield, Andy. 2011. *Magical Marxism: Subversive Politics and the Imagination*. London: Pluto.

Mies, Maria, and Veronika Bennholdt-Thomsen. 1999. *The Subsistence Perspective: Beyond the Globalised Economy*. London: Zed Books.

Miller, Daniel. 1997. *Capitalism: An Ethnographic Approach*. Oxford: Berg.

Mitchell, Timothy. 2002. *Rule of Experts: Egypt, Techno-Politics, Modernity*. Berkeley: University of California Press.

———. 2009. "Society, Economy, and the State Effect." In *The Anthropology of the State: A Reader*, edited by Aradhana Sharma and Akhil Gupta, 169–186. London: Blackwell.

Moodie, Ellen. 2010. *El Salvador in the Aftermath of Peace*. Philadelphia: University of Pennsylvania Press.

Múnera, Adriana Giraldo, Giovanni Bedoya Bermudez, and Carlos Mario Vargas Restrepo. 2009. "Principales Limitaciones del Empresarismo que Afectan el Desarrollo Económico y Social del País." *Revista EAN* 66:99–112.

Narotzky, Susana. 1997. *New Directions in Economic Anthropology*. London: Pluto Press.

Next System Project. 2018. "The Systemic Roadblocks to Climate Action." September 5. https://thenextsystem.org/learn/stories/systemic-roadblocks-climate-action.

Nordstrom, Carolyn. 1997. *A Different Kind of War Story*. Philadelphia: University of Pennsylvania Press.

Norgaard, Kari Marie. 2011. *Living in Denial: Climate Change, Emotions, and Everyday Life*. Cambridge, MA: MIT Press.

North, Peter. 1999. "Explorations in Heterotopia: LETS and the Micropolitics of Money and Livelihood." *Environment and Planning D: Society and Space* 17:69–86.

———. 2002. "LETS in a Cold Climate: Green Dollars, Self-Help and Neoliberal Welfare in New Zealand." *Policy and Politics* 30(4):483–499.

———. 2005. "Scaling Alternative Economic Practices? Some Lessons from Alternative Currencies." *Transactions of the Institute of British Geographers* 30(2):221–233.

———. 2007. *Money and Liberation: The Micropolitics of Alternative Currency Movements*. Minneapolis: University of Minnesota Press.

———. 2010. *Local Money: How to Make It Happen in Your Community*. Totnes, UK: Transition Books / Green Books.

———. 2014. "Ten Square Miles Surrounded by Reality: Materialising Alternative Economies Using Local Currencies." *Antipode* 46(1):246–265.

North, Peter, and Noel Longhurst. 2013: "Grassroots Localisation: The Scalar Potential of and Limits of the 'Transition' Approach to Climate Change and Resource Constraint." *Urban Studies* 50(7):1421–1436.

Ochoa Valencia, David, and Aura Ordóñez. 2004. "Informalidad en Colombia. Causas, Efectos y Características de la Economía del Rebusque." *Estudios Gerenciales* 90:105–116.

Ong, Aihwa. 2006. *Neoliberalism as Exception: Mutations in Citizenship and Sovereignty*. Durham, NC: Duke University Press.

Ortner, Sherry. 2006. *Anthropology and Social Theory: Culture, Power, and the Acting Subject*. Durham, NC: Duke University Press.

Pacione, Michael. 1997. "Local Exchange Trading Systems as a Response to the Globalisation of Capitalism." *Urban Studies* 34(8):1179–1199.

Palacios, Marcos. 2006. *Between Legitimacy and Violence: A History of Colombia, 1875–2002*. Durham, NC: Duke University Press.

Papavasiliou, Faidra. 2008. "The Political Economy of Local Currency: Alternative Money, Alternative Development and Collective Action in the Age of Globalization." PhD dissertation, Department of Anthropology, Emory University.

Parsons, James Jerome. 1968. *Antioqueño Colonization in Western Colombia*. Berkeley: University of California Press.

Patterson, Thomas C. 2001. *A Social History of Anthropology in the United States*. Oxford: Berg.

Pearson, Ruth. 2002. "Argentina's Barter Network: New Currency for New Times." *Bulletin of Latin American Research* 20:214–230.

Penglase, R. Ben. 2014. *Living with Insecurity in a Brazilian Favela: Urban Violence and Daily Life*. New Brunswick, NJ: Rutgers University Press.

Perelman, Michael. 2000. *The Invention of Capitalism: Classical Political Economy and the Secret History of Primitive Accumulation*. Durham, NC: Duke University Press.

Plattner, Stuart, ed. 1989. *Economic Anthropology*. Stanford, CA: Stanford University Press.

Polanyi, Karl. 1944. *The Great Transformation*. Boston: Beacon.

Powell, Dana E., and Andrew Curley. 2008. "K'e, Hozhó, and Non-governmental Politics on the Navajo Nation: Ontologies of Difference Manifest in Environmental Activism." *Anthropological Quarterly* 81:17–58.

Powell, Jeff. 2002. "Petty Capitalism, Perfecting Capitalism, or Post-capitalism? Lessons from the Argentinean Barter Experiments." *Review of International Political Economy* 9(4):619–649.

Price, David. 2011. *Weaponizing Anthropology: Social Science in the Service of the National Security State*. Petrolia, CA: Counterpunch.

Primavera, Heloisa. 2002. "Riqueza, Dinero y Poder: El Efímero 'Milagro Argentino' de las Redes de Trueque." Red Latinoamericana de Socioeconomía Solidaria (REDLASES). http://redlases.wordpress.com/archivos/.

———. 2009. "Monedas Sociales y Economía Solidaria: Un Matrimonio Indisoluble, con Comunión de Bienes." Red Latinoamericana De Socioeconomía Solidaria (REDLASES). http://redlases.wordpress.com/archivos/.

Rahnema, Majid. 1997. "Towards Post-Development: Searching for Signposts, a New Language and New Paradigms." In *The Post-Development Reader*, edited by Majid Rahnema and Victoria Bawtree, 377–403. New York: Zed Books.

Ranis, Peter. 2010. "Worker-Run U.S. Factories and Enterprises: The Example of Argentine Cooperatives." In *Solidarity Economy I: Building Alternatives for People and Planet. Papers and Reports from the 2009 U.S. Forum on the Solidarity Economy*, edited by Emily Kawano, Thomas Neal Masterson, and Jonathan Teller-Elsberg. 115–124. Amherst, MA: Center for Popular Economics.

Rappaport, Joanna. 2005. *Intercultural Utopias: Public Intellectuals, Cultural Experimentation, and Ethnic Pluralism in Colombia*. Durham, NC: Duke University Press.

Raynolds, Laura T. 2002. "Wages for Wives: Renegotiating Gender and Production Relations in Contract Farming in the Dominican Republic." *World Development* 30(5):783–798.

Razeto, Luis M. 2000. "El Trueque y los Dineros Alternativos." Presentation, Seminario Trueque Y Monedas Alternativas, IEP, Santiago, Chile. http://www.luisrazeto.net/content/el-trueque-y-los-dineros-alternativos.

Razsa, Maple. 2015. *Bastards of Utopia: Living Radical Politics after Socialism*. Bloomington: Indiana University Press.

Razsa, Maple, and Andrej Kurnik. 2012. "The Occupy Movement in Žižek's Hometown." *American Ethnologist* 39(2):238–258.

Reimers, Fernando. 2000. "Educación, Desigualdad y Opciones de Política en América Latina en el Siglo XXI." *Revista Latinoamericana De Estudios Educativos* 30(2):11–42.

Restrepo, Luis Antonio. 1988. "El Pensamiento Social en Antioquia." In *Historia De Antioquia*, edited by Jorge Orlando Melo, 373–386. Medellín: Suramericana.

Restrepo Mesa, Clara Inés. 2000. *Pobreza Urbana en Medellín: Mediciones y Percepciones*. Medellín: Corporación Región.

Reyes Posadas, Alejandro. 2009. *Guerreros y Campesinos. El Despojo de la Tierra en Colombia*. Bogotá: Editorial Norma.

Richani, Nazih. 2002. *Systems of Violence: The Political Economy of War and Peace in Colombia*. Albany: State University of New York Press.

Rist, Gilbert. 2002. *The History of Development: From Western Origins to Global Faith*. London: Zed Books.

Robben, Antonius C. G. M. 1989. *Sons of the Sea Goddess: Economic Practice and Discursive Conflict in Brazil*. New York: Columbia University Press.

Rodríguez, Pedro Gerardo, and Nora Guadalupe Valenzuela. 1998. "Acceso a los Libros de Texto de Secundaria: Escenarios para la Definición de una Política de Largo Plazo." *Revista Latinoamericana De Estudios Educativos* 28(2):9–49.

Roelvink, Gerda, Kevin St Martin, and J. K. Gibson-Graham. 2015. *Making Other Worlds Possible: Performing Diverse Economies*. Minneapolis: University of Minnesota Press.

Roldán, Mary. 2002. *Blood and Fire: La Violencia in Antioquia, Colombia, 1946–1953*. Durham, NC: Duke University Press.

Roseberry, William. 1994. "Hegemony and the Language of Contention." In *Everyday Forms of State Formation: Revolution and the Negotiation of Rule in Rural Mexico*, edited by Gilbert M. Joseph and Daniel Nugent, 355–366. Durham, NC: Duke University Press.

Rosenbloom, Al, and Juan Alejandro Cortes. 2008. "Piercing the Bubble: How Management Students Can Confront Poverty in Colombia." *Journal of Management Education* 32:716–730.

Ross, Eric B. 2003. *Modernisation, Clearance and the Continuum of Violence in Colombia*. Institute for Social Studies Working Papers 383. The Hague: Institute for Social Studies.

Routledge, Paul. 2003. "Convergence Space: Process Geographies of Grassroots Globalization Networks." *Transactions of the Institute of British Geographers* 28:333–349.

Safford, Frank, and Marco Palacios. 2002. *Colombia: Fragmented Land, Divided Society*. Oxford: Oxford University Press.

Salazar J, Alonso. 1990. *No Nacimos Pa' Semilla: La Cultura de las Bandas Juveniles de Medellín*. Bogotá: Corporación Región, CINEP.

Samers, Michael. 2005. "The Mypoia of 'Diverse Economies,' or, A Critique of the Informal Economy." *Antipode* 37:875–886.

Santana Echeagaray, María Eugenia. 2008. "Reinventando El Dinero: Experiencias Con Monedas Comunitarias." PhD dissertation, Centro de Investigaciones y Estudios Superiores en Antropología Social, Guadalara, Jalisco, Mexico.

Satgar, Vishwas. 2014. "The Crises of Global Capitalism and the Solidarity Economy Alternative." In *The Solidarity Economy Alternative: Emerging Theory and Practice*, edited by Vishwas Satgar and Michelle Williams, 1–34. Pietermaritzburg, South Africa: University of Kwazulu-Natal Press.

Sayer, Derek. 1994. "Everyday Forms of State Formation: Some Dissident Remarks on 'Hegemony.'" In *Everyday Forms of State Formation: Revolution and the Negotiation of Rule in Rural Mexico*, edited by Gilbert M. Joseph and Daniel Nugent, 367–378. Durham, NC: Duke University Press.

Scheper-Hughes, Nancy. 1992. *Death without Weeping: The Violence of Everyday Life in Brazil*. Berkeley: University of California Press.

Scheper-Hughes, Nancy, and Philippe Bourgois. 2004. "Introduction: Making Sense of Violence." In *Violence in War and Peace*, edited by Nancy Scheper-Hughes and Philippe Bourgois, 1–32. Malden, MA: Blackwell.

Schwartz, Adam. 2006. "The Teaching and Culture of Household Spanish: Understanding Racist Reproduction in 'Domestic' Discourse." *Critical Discourse Studies* 3(2):107–121.

Scott, James C. 1990. *Domination and the Arts of Resistance: Hidden Transcripts*. New Haven, CT: Yale University Press.

———. 1998. *Seeing Like a State: How Certain Schemes to Improve the Human Condition Have Failed*. New Haven, CT: Yale University Press.

*Semana*. 1999. "Unas por Otras." November 11. https://www.semana.com/economia /articulo/unas-por-otras/52468-3/

———. 2011. "Los Riesgos del Crédito Barato en América Latina." October 3. http://www.semana.com/economia/riesgos-del-credito-barato-america-latina /165181-3.aspx.

Sider, Gerald M. 2009. "Can Anthropology Ever Be Innocent?" *Anthropology Now* 1(1):43–50.

Simon, David. 1997. "Development Reconsidered: New Directions in Development Thinking." *Geografiska Annaler. Series B, Human Geography* 79:183–201.

Smith, Adrian, and Alison C. Stenning. 2006. "Beyond Household Economies: Articulations and Spaces of Economic Practice in Postsocialism." *Progress in Human Geography* 30(2):190–213.

Stahler-Sholk, Richard, Harry E. Vanden, and Glen David Kuecker. 2008. "Introduction." In *Latin American Social Movements in the Twenty-First Century: Resistance, Power, and Democracy*, edited by Richard Stahler-Sholk, Harry E. Vanden, and Glen David Kuecker, 1–15. Lanham, MD: Rowman & Littlefield.

Stahler-Sholk, Richard. 2010. "The Zapatista Social Movement: Innovation and Sustainability." *Alternatives* 35(3): 369–390.

St Martin, Kevin. 2007. "The Difference That Class Makes: Neoliberalization and Non-capitalism in the Fishing Industry of New England." *Antipode* 39(3):527–549.

Stone, Hannah. 2016. "Colombia Elites and Organized Crime: An Introduction." *Insight Crime*. https://insightcrime.org/investigations/colombia-elites-and -organized-crime-introduction/.

Swyngedouw, Erik. 1997. "Neither Global nor Local: 'Glocalization' and the Politics of Scale." In *Spaces of Globalization: Reasserting the Power of the Local*, edited by Kevin R. Cox, 137–166. New York: Guilford.

Tate, Winifred. 2007. *Counting the Dead: The Culture and Politics of Human Rights Activism in Colombia*. Berkeley: University of California Press.

Taussig, Michael. 1980. *The Devil and Commodity Fetishism in South America*. Chapel Hill: University of North Carolina Press.

———. 1987. *Shamanism, Colonialism, and the Wild Man: A Study in Terror and Healing*. Chicago: University of Chicago Press.

Thoumi, Francisco E. 1995. *Political Economy and Illegal Drugs in Colombia*. London: Lynne Rienner.

———. 2005. "The Numbers Game: Let's All Guess the Size of the Illegal Drug Industry!" *Journal of Drug Issues* 35(1):185–200.

Toffler, Alvin. 1989. *The Third Wave*. New York: Bantam Books.

United Nations Development Programme (UNDP). 2011. *Human Development Report 2011. Sustainability and Equity: A Better Future for All*. New York: UNDP.

Uran, Omar. 2010. "Medellín: Participatory Creativity in a Conflictive City." In *Participation and Democracy in the Twenty-First Century City*, edited by Jenny Pearce, 127–153. New York: Palgrave Macmillan.

Uribe, José Ignacio, and Carlos Alberto Ortiz. 2006. *Informalidad Laboral en Colombia 1988–2000: Evolución, Teorías y Modelos*. Cali: Editorial Universidad Del Valle.

Uvin, Peter. 1998. *Aiding Violence: The Development Enterprise in Rwanda*. West Hartford, CT: Kumarian Press.

Vásquez-León, Marcela, Brian J. Burke, and Timothy J. Finan. 2017. "Introduction: Smallholder Cooperativism as a Development Strategy." In *Cooperatives, Grassroots Development, and Social Change: Experiences from Rural Latin America*, edited by Marcela Vásquez-León, Brian J. Burke, and Timothy J. Finan, 3–18. Tucson: University of Arizona Press.

Vásquez Montoya, Dora Marleny. 2005. "El Trueque: Herramienta para Vivir con Dignidad." Undergraduate thesis, Departamento De Sociología, Universidad De Antioquia, Medellín, Colombia.

Vergara-Camus, Leandro, and Cristóbal Kay. 2017. "The Agrarian Political Economy of Left-Wing Governments in Latin America: Agribusiness, Peasants, and the Limits of Neo-Developmentalism." *Journal of Agrarian Change* 17(2):415–437.

Villalba-Eguiluz, C. Unai, and Iker Etxano. 2017. "Buen Vivir vs. Development (II): The Limits of (Neo-)Extractivism." *Ecological Economics* 138:1–11.

Wainwright, Hilary. 2012. "An 'Excess of Democracy': What Two Generations of Radicals Can Learn from One Another." *Red Pepper*, February 11. https://www.redpepper.org.uk/an-excess-of-democracy/.

Weiner, Annette B. 1992. *Inalienable Possessions: The Paradox of Keeping-While-Giving*. Berkeley: University of California Press.

Werner, Karen. 2015. "Performing Economies of Care in a New England Time Bank and Buddhist Community." In *Making Other Worlds Possible: Performing Diverse Economies*, edited by Gerda Roelvink, Kevin St Martin, and J. K. Gibson-Graham, 72–97. Minneapolis: University of Minnesota Press.

West, Paige. 2006. *Conservation Is Our Government Now: The Politics of Ecology in Papua New Guinea*. Durham, NC: Duke University Press.

Whyte, Kyle Powys. 2017. "Indigenous Climate Change Studies: Indigenizing Futures, Decolonizing the Anthropocene." *English Language Notes* 55(1–2):153–162.

Wilk, Richard R., and Lisa C. Cliggett. 2018. *Economies and Cultures: Foundations of Economic Anthropology*. New York: Routledge.

Williams, Colin C., Theresa Aldridge, Roger Lee, Andrew Leyshon, Nigel Thrift, and Janet Tooke. 2001. *Bridges into Work? An Evaluation of Local Exchange Trading Schemes (LETS)*. Bristol: Policy Press.

Wolf, Eric R. 1972. "Ownership and Political Ecology." *Anthropological Quarterly* 45(3):201–205.

———. 1987. "Cycles of Violence: The Anthropology of War and Peace." In *Waymarks: The Notre Dame Inaugural Lectures in Anthropology*, edited by Kenneth Moore, 127–150. Notre Dame: University of Notre Dame Press.

World Bank. 2012. "Colombia Country Profile." The World Bank Databank. http://data.worldbank.org/country/colombia.

Wright, Erik Olin. 2010. *Envisioning Real Utopias*. London: Verso Books.

Yanagisako, Sylvia Junko. 2002. *Producing Culture and Capital: Family Firms in Italy*. Princeton, NJ: Princeton University Press.

Zabala Salazar, Hernando. n.d. "Circuitos Económicos Solidarios." Unpublished paper.

Zaloom, Caitlin. 2006. *Out of the Pits: Traders and Technology from Chicago to London*. Chicago: University of Chicago Press.

Zibechi, Raúl. 2012. *Territories in Resistance: A Cartography of Latin American Social Movements*. Oakland, CA: AK Press.

# Index

## About the Author

BRIAN J. BURKE is associate professor of sustainable development at Appalachian State University. His research examines how communities pursue economic and environmental justice through solidarity economy initiatives and engagement with environmental science and governance. He is coeditor of *Cooperatives, Grassroots Development, and Social Change* and *Changing Climate, Changing Worlds*.